GW01186239

A SHORT HIS
GREEK LITE___

A Short History of Greek Literature provides a concise yet comprehensive survey of Greek literature – including Christian authors – over twelve centuries, from Homer's epics to the rich range of authors surviving from the imperial period up to Justinian. The book is divided into three parts. The first part is devoted to the extraordinary creativity of the archaic and classical age, when the major literary genres – epic, lyric, tragedy, comedy, history, oratory and philosophy – were invented and flourished. The second part covers the Hellenistic period, and the third covers the High Empire and Late Antiquity. At that time the masters of the previous age were elevated to the rank of 'classics'. The works of the imperial period are replete with literary allusions, yet full of references to contemporary reality.

Suzanne Saïd is Professor of Greek Literature at Columbia University, New York. She is the author of *La Faute tragique* (1978), *Sophiste et Tyran ou le problème du Prométhée* (1985), *Approches de la mythologie grecque* (1993) and *Homère et l'Odyssée* (1998).
Monique Trédé is Professor of Greek Literature and Director of Research and Literary Studies at the École Normale Supérieure, Paris. Her publications include *Platon: le banquet* (Introduction and notes, 1991), *Le Monde du roman grec* (1992), *Kairos, l'à propos et l'occasion* (1992), and *Le Rire des anciens* (1998).
Suzanne Saïd and Monique Trédé, together with Alain Le Boulluec, are also the authors of the more extensive *Histoire de la littérature grecque* (1997).

A SHORT HISTORY OF GREEK LITERATURE

Suzanne Saïd and Monique Trédé
Translated by Trista Selous
and others

London and New York

First published in French in two volumes (*La Littérature grecque d'Homère à Aristote* and *La Littérature grecque d'Alexandre à Justinien*) in 1990 by Presses Universitaires de France

First published in English 1999
by Routledge
11 New Fetter Lane, London EC4P 4EE

Simultaneously published in the USA and Canada
by Routledge
29 West 35th Street, New York, NY 10001

Routledge is an imprint of the Taylor & Francis Group

Typeset in Garamond by The Florence Group, Stoodleigh, Devon
Printed and bound in Great Britain by
T.J. International, Padstow, Cornwall.

British Library Cataloguing in Publication Data
A catalogue record for this book is available from the British Library

Library of Congress Cataloging in Publication Data
Saïd Suzanne.
A short history of Greek literature / Suzanne Saïd and Monique Trédé; translated by Trista Selous and others.
p. cm.
'First published in French in two volumes (*La littérature grecque d'Homère à Aristote* and *La littérature grecque d'Alexandre à Justinien*) in 1990 by Presses Universitaires de France' — T.p. verso.
Includes bibliographical references and index.

1. Greek literature—History and criticism. I. Trédé, Monique. II, Saïd, Suzanne, Littérature grecque d'Homère à Aristote. III Saïd Suzanne. Littérature grecque d'Alexandre à Justinien). IV. Title.

PA3055.S25 1999
880.9'001—dc21

99-19803
CIP

ISBN 0–415–12271–6 (hbk)
ISBN 0–415–12272–4 (pbk)

CONTENTS

CONTENTS

INTRODUCTION

Why do we need another history of Ancient Greek literature? First, to introduce a contemporary audience to old texts in a concise and lively manner; secondly, to bring our knowledge up to date, since papyrological discoveries are constantly revealing new fragments of poetry or prose, to present the latest trends in scholarship and propose from time to time our own interpretations. Finally, to turn the spotlight on the works written after the death of Alexander and to give them a place they have long been denied in systematic surveys of Greek literature. After presenting the major works of archaic and classical literature, we intend to follow the development of Greek culture in the Hellenistic world and under the Roman Empire. Our survey, short as it is, covers a domain which is immense in terms of both time (more than twelve centuries, from 'Homer', traditionally located in the eighth century BC, to the closure of the school of Athens by Justinian in AD 529[1]) and of space. Of course, from the time of Homer to the end of the fourth century, Greek authors, who throve first in Ionia, gravitated more and more towards Athens, which became the uncontested centre of intellectual life. But during the Hellenistic and Roman periods Greek authors were living not only in Greece, but also in the vast territories of the Hellenistic kingdoms and the Roman Empire. Moreover, we have decided to include in our literary history a large portion of Christian literature, that is to say the works produced for a learned readership by authors who, though they were imbued with Greek culture, preferred to underline what separated them from the 'Greeks' (that is, the Pagans) rather than what they had in common.

Our survey is divided into four parts and distinguishes, as usual, archaic, classical, Hellenistic and Imperial literature. Yet one may oppose two periods, from Homer to Aristotle and from the death of Alexander to the closure of the School of Athens.

During the first period – from the eighth to the fourth century BC – the great works which are still at the core of Western culture were produced. It was during this period that most of the great genres – epic, lyric, tragedy, comedy, history, oratory and philosophy – were created and reached their peak. It was at this point that the canons of ancient literature were established, canons which were the major spiritual and cultural foundations of the Western world until the end of the nineteenth century.

The literary production of this period shows three main characteristics:

1   It was intended for performance and oral 'consumption' and was not dependent on 'books' and readers. Although the alphabet arrived in Greece in around 800 BC, 'yet ancient Greece was in many ways a society in which the written word took second place to the spoken word'[2] and there is no trace of a book trade before the late fifth century. This primacy of oral communication may explain the importance of verbal echoes and the repetition of terms as well as many other aspects of composition – characteristic of archaic and classical literature.

2   Because most of the literary production was meant to be heard communally, it was always connected to group gatherings, whether private, such as feasts or symposia, or public, such as religious festivals, political meetings or sessions of the lawcourts.

3   Because of this agonistic context, poets and prose writers always vied with one another and with their predecessors. Poetic creation (*poiesis*) was, from the very outset, inseparable from imitation (*mimesis*).

It is for this reason that we have placed authors within the history of the genre which they practised. It is thus easier to evaluate their debt to tradition and, conversely, their innovations. The Greeks themselves had developed a theory according to which their literature, education and civilisation all had their source in the work of Homer. This view, which has the merit of emphasising Homer's tremendous influence on those who followed him, should not lead us to assume that there was a linear development and a continuous progress from Homer to the Classical age. Such a simplistic assumption is belied by a history rich in contrasts and oppositions. Some of the literary output of archaic Greece – be it lyric poetry or philosophical treatises – deliberately places itself in opposition to epic poetry. The victory of the Greek city states over the Persians in 480 in turn opens the way to a new era, in which critical attitudes and open debate replaces the unquestioning acceptance of aristocratic values. Our picture of classical literature emphasises these shifts and contrasts as much as the spiritual filiations and continuities.

The death of Alexander is a watershed in the history of Greek culture. Of course, it would be a serious oversimplification to posit a radical discontinuity between Hellenistic and earlier Greek culture, and there is abundant evidence that poets continued to perform their work publicly. Yet it remains true that the Hellenistic period, when the famous library of Alexandria was established, is a 'bookish age'.[3] Under the patronage of the Hellenistic kings, beginning with Ptolemy, the unprecedented enterprise of collecting together 'the writings of all men, in so far, that is, as they were worthy of serious attention', took place.[4] Alexandrian scholars established a standard text for 'classical' authors, improved their appearance by transliterating them into the Ionic alphabet, invented punctuation and added some accents. Consequently, reading became easier and authors wrote more and more for readers (even though reading was still mostly performed aloud and writing continued to be strongly influenced by earlier oral habits). Their works addressed an elite which, though geographically dispersed – at first throughout an expanded Greek world and then throughout the Roman Empire – was culturally homogeneous.

Written in the shadow of Homer and other great predecessors, the works produced at that time are replete with literary allusions, which explains why they have been discredited in the past and why they now attract scholars familiar with H. R. Jauss' *Rezeption-sästhetik*,[5] G. Genette's *Palimpsestes*[6] and G. B. Conte's *Rhetoric of Imitation*.[7] This literature is indeed a prime example of 'littérature au second degré'. For its authors chose 'the way of imitation and emulation of great writers of the past' to achieve sublimity and agree with 'Longinus' that 'the genius of the Ancients acts as a kind of oracular cavern and effluences flow from it into the minds of their imitators'.[8] Their works, where innovation must take the guise of restoration, and originality is obtained primarily by transforming the context, playing simultaneously upon many passages or creating new combinations of already existing elements, can at first seem repetitive and devoid of reference to contemporary reality. However, this is only a façade. For the perceptive reader, these texts constantly reflect the present by borrowing terms and traditions from the past.

Apart from scholarly trends, contemporary interest in this period also focuses on the relation it bears to its (literary) past. After it, there is a feeling of rupture and an acute sense of discontinuity; it is this sense which gave birth to the mirage of a 'classical' literature.

The great grammarians of the Hellenistic period imparted a sense of order to the literature of the past and became 'the judges of poets'[9] as well as prose-writers. By comparing various copies, 'they determined what the texts should be . . . and succeeded in imposing this text as standard'.[10] Among the writers of the past, they selected and registered in a list – the 'canon' (as it happened to be called in the eighteenth century) – those who were deemed worthy of becoming the 'first class' citizens of the republic of letters – the nine lyric poets, the three tragedians, the ten orators, etc.

During the Imperial and Byzantine periods this process of selection continued, and led to more restricted lists, generally connected with the requirements of schools. As a result, we can only read seven complete tragedies of Sophocles, who is said to have written at least 123 plays.

This is the reason why it is impossible to present a complete picture of the literature of this period, for only a tiny portion of the works have come down to us. Moreover, of all the works which were composed at the time, not one original copy remains. Each poem, each treatise, had to be copied many times on papyrus rolls for centuries. Between the second and fourth century the roll was gradually replaced by the parchment codex, which was easier to consult, more capacious (each codex could hold the contents of several rolls) and, last but not least, more durable. But the codex also contributed to the trimming of the classical heritage by eliminating texts from what was already considered as the best of an author's work in order to put it all under one cover.

The creation of these selective lists of authors and works had not only material but also intellectual consequences. It established a set of paradigms. A system of genres was defined. Certain authors became favoured over others. Homer had for a long time been regarded as 'the poet'. Demosthenes, 'the orator', joined him in the pantheon. Some mythological examples were selected as references: Orestes and Pylades became – and still are – synonymous with the concept of friendship. A repertoire of formulas, similes, 'figures' and 'tropes' which enjoyed remarkable stability throughout the classical millennium became part of a programme of rhetorical teaching that was to remain influential until the end of the nineteenth century. In other words, the very concept of literature and literary culture was then born, from a constant and conscious reference to the great models of the past. Through the centuries the writers and their readers regarded themselves as tributaries of a heritage to which we are still indebted today.

Translations have been taken from the *Loeb* series, with the exception of the Lyric poets which were taken from M.L. West, *Greek Lyric Poetry* (Oxford 1994).

Part 1

HOMER AND THE ARCHAIC PERIOD (EIGHTH TO FIFTH CENTURIES BC)
The Primacy of Ionia

1

HOMER AND THE EPIC AGE (EIGHTH AND SEVENTH CENTURIES BC)

Homeric poetry

Homer

The Greeks attributed the origins of poetry to two mythical poets endowed with magical powers, Musaeus and Orpheus; for us however, Greek literature, and with it Western literature as a whole, begins with the *Iliad* and the *Odyssey*. The name of Homer, under which these poems have come down to us, has symbolised poetry for more than twenty-five centuries. All of Antiquity, from Xenophanes (sixth century BC) to Lucian (second century AD) believed that Homer was a real person who recounted real events: the great deeds of the Trojan War, traditionally dated at around 1200 BC.

Yet we know nothing of Homer himself. In the second century AD Lucian of Samosata included an interview with the poet in his *True Stories*. He asks Homer the questions which modern scholars are still asking today. Where was he born: in Chios, Smyrna, Cyme or Colophon? What does the name 'Homer' mean? Is it an allusion to the poet's blindness (as has been suggested by those who see in it the etymology *ho mè horon*: 'who does not see')? The many works entitled *Life of Homer* written in Antiquity leave these questions unanswered. Thus both the *Iliad* and the *Odyssey* share with a number of other major works of world literature the privilege of having an author about whom almost nothing is known.

Indeed, doubt has even been cast on his existence. In the eighteenth century the so-called 'Homeric question' was posed by Abbé Aubignac in his *Academic Conjectures* of 1715, by Robert Wood in England, by Vico in Italy and, even more clearly at the end of the century, by F.A. Wolf in Germany in his *Prolegomena ad Homerum* of 1795. According to these writers, the *Iliad* and the *Odyssey* date from a time when writing was unknown and the artistic unity that we admire so much in these poems is that of a later editor. Throughout the nineteenth century scholars were split into 'Unitarians' and 'Analysts' holding opposing views on the artistic integrity of the poems and the unicity of their author. The 'Analysts', aware of the existence of doublets and contradictions within the epic narrative, sought to separate the primitive poem, thought to be the work of Homer, from later additions (or inter-polations) and to reconstruct a history of the text giving rise to the standard form we know today. By contrast, the 'Unitarians' stressed the integrity of composition that can be sensed throughout the poems and explained most of the doublets and narrative detours in terms of deliberate artistry. For them, Homer was the poetic genius who produced the harmonious ensembles that have been handed down to us, by combining elements of different origins and ages. The question of Homer's identity thus merged with that of the genesis of the Homeric poems.

Given our lack of certain knowledge about the poet, it is neces-sary to follow the precept attributed to Aristarchus and to use Homer to illuminate Homer.

The *Odyssey* presents two bards, Phemius in Ithaca and Demodocus among the Phaecians. Accompanying themselves on the lyre, they recite and improvise epic poems for the pleasure of aris-tocrats gathered at a banquet. They seem to have a repertoire from which they pick elements at will, selecting a theme and changing it if they are asked to do so, which suggests that both singer and audience had an idea of the whole repertoire and that, at the time of the *Iliad* and the *Odyssey*, there was an already codified epic tradi-tion, symbolised by the Muse whom the poet merely echoed. Homer's poems are rooted in this poetic tradition, which was oral in nature. This alone enables us to explain the particularities of the Homeric style.

Oral poetry

Proof that the style of *Iliad* and *Odyssey* reflects their oral nature has been provided by Milman Parry. In his thesis on *the traditional epithet in Homer*[1] Parry examines verbal formulas consisting of name plus epithet designating gods or heroes, showing that in any given case, at a given point in the line, and under the same metrical conditions, only one name plus epithet formula can be used to

4

designate a particular hero (or god). The exceptions to this principle of economy are very rare. Out of forty name-plus-epithet formulas in the second hemistich of the epic hexameter designating a god or hero in the subject case, only six are not unique. Thus with the same rhythmic schema ∪ - - - ∪ ∪ - - we find 'Hera the cow-eyed goddess' or 'Hera the white-armed goddess'. In the same way two formulas refer to Aphrodite or Apollo; but such doublets are the exception. If one hero answers another or goes into battle, the same phrase half a line long is always used and the line is completed by a series of metrically equivalent subjects. A first hemistich 'Then replied to him/ . . .' may be followed as necessary by 'the blue-green goddess Athene' or 'divine Odysseus the enduring', etc. Each of these subjects may itself be linked to various verbal expressions of the same metric value: 'seeing her rejoices / divine Odysseus the enduring.'

This explains the repetition of phrases such as 'rosy-fingered Dawn' or 'swift-footed Achilles', which are regularly employed, in the same metrical circumstances to refer to important characters. These phrases form a system of great simplicity and flexibility, suited to many different contexts: a hemistich can easily be completed with a phrase chosen for its metrical convenience rather than for its meaning.

This notion of formulaic unit which was defined in relation to diction, could then be extended to scenes[2] and themes. Such a system which has no equivalent in the epics of Virgil or Apollonius of Rhodes is typical of Homer's poems. It is linked to the oral nature of heroic poetry: the traditional formulas provided the bards with aids to memory and improvisation.

Parry's theses were confirmed by a modern, real-life instance. In Yugoslavia he and his student Albert Lord listened to an illiterate Serbian bard reciting a long poem, made up on the spot with a respect for versification. It was observed that this type of poetry implies the existence not only of a mythical heritage built up by preceding generations and orally transmitted, but also rhythmical patterns and formulas.

These discoveries put an end to the argument of the Analysts and Unitarians without settling it in favour of either. For while the Analysts; attempt to isolate an original text by Homer from the later additions was now impossible, it was equally pointless to try to emphasise the author's originality. The oral tradition must have developed over at least three centuries (from 1100 to 800 BC) and it is impossible to reconstruct the history of the transformations which the epic underwent within that tradition. However, the subtlety of the poetic art of the *Iliad* and the *Odyssey* makes it equally impossible to suggest that these two epics are exclusively oral in character. For, although Homer may reflect a tradition, he also plays with it, deviates from it and does not hesitate to make innovations.

The existence of traditional elements cannot be denied; these are the typical scenes (combatants arming themselves, feasting, making sacrifices, fighting in single combat or swearing of oaths) and formulas from which the poet selects what he wants. However, one need only consider several arming scenes from the *Iliad* to gauge the freedom with which the poet plays with the formulas. The basic schema of the arming scene is given in Book III with the description of Paris' gear: his greaves, breastplate, sword, shield, helmet and lance are all soberly mentioned (III, 330–8); Agamemnon's weaponry is described with far more ceremony and pomp in Book XI. Images abound and the accent is on the magnificence of his breastplate and shield and their sumptuous decoration (XI, 17–46). The arming of Patroclus (XVI, 130–44) and Achilles (XIX, 364–91) similarly echo each other significantly.

Formulas too are subject to variation, since the same rhythmical pattern can be preserved when one or two words, or even a whole hemistich, are changed. Thus on eight occasions in the *Iliad* in the second half of the line after the formula 'illustrious son of Atreus', we find the words 'Agamemnon, protector of his people'; but when Achilles pours invective on the king in Book I he cries: 'Illustrious son of Atreus, you the most grasping of all', thereby introducing a significant variation into the line. He returns to the usual phrase in Book XIX (cf. Line 146 or 199), when Agamemnon honourably makes amends.

The intentional refinement which can be discerned in these repetitions and variations and the lucidity and coherence of these two long poems – the *Iliad* contains 15,000 hexameters and *Odyssey* 12,000 – leads today's critics to believe that Homer's poems were contemporary with the appearance of the alphabet and belong to a period of transition between a technique of oral composition and a truly literary technique using writing. Far from being a beginning, Homer can thus be seen as an end.

We can now attempt to identify the main stages in the transmission of Homer's poetry. Following a long period of oral transmission the text was written down in Athens – if we are to believe the Alexandrian scholars – in the sixth century BC on the initiative of

Pisistratus, in order to be recited at the Panathenaeic festival. It may be that the Homeridae of Chios – a clan of rhapsodes who claimed descent from Homer and are mentioned by Plato in the *Phaedrus* (252B) – acted as the guardians of the original text, but we do not know this. The first scholars to seriously edit the poems were the grammarians of the Alexandria library.

The first head of the Alexandrian Museum, Zenodotus (early third century BC) was Homer's first editor. Aristophanes of Byzantium improved the punctuation of the text and Aristarchus, who died in Alexandria in 144 BC, wrote commentaries on the *Iliad* and the *Odyssey* in which he sought to distinguish Homer's usage from Attic or Hellenic usage, thereby providing a starting point for the analysts' researches into the stratification of the text. Lastly, it is also to the Alexandrians that we owe the division of the text into twenty-four Books.

Since that time Homer's poems have been continually edited, commented on and imitated. Let us now consider the magical charm of the Homeric world.

Homer's world

The coexistence of forms belonging to different periods and dialects – notably Ionian and Aeolian – was quickly noticed. Homer's language is a composite which was never actually spoken anywhere; it is purely literary. The same thing is true of the world he depicts, which is made up of elements from different historical periods. This idea, however, was less readily accepted.

The Ancients were convinced that the Trojan War had really taken place and that Homer was describing a precise historical period. In the nineteenth century the German archaeologist Heinrich Schliemann, who also held this view, went to look for the sites mentioned in the epic. He discovered Troy on the Hissarlik hill in Asia Minor (now Turkey) and uncovered the ruins of Mycenae. After this discovery some of the objects which Homer describes were found: Ajax's great shield, made of seven bull skins covered with a layer of bronze (VII, 219–23), the boar's tusk helmet that Odysseus wears in Book X (261–5) and Nestor's cup 'decorated with golden nails' (XI, 633–5). Soon people were convinced that Homer's world was that of the Mycenaean kings and palaces; but this belief faded when the Mycenaean world became better known. In 1953 Ventris and Chadwick managed to decipher the tablets that had been discovered in the palaces of Knossos in Crete, and Pylos and Mycenae in continental Greece. The language of these tablets, which were written in syllabic script, was a form of Ancient Greek (known as Linear B). Mycenaean civilisation would now give us its secrets! However, the deciphering of these documents – accounts and lists – revealed a bureaucratic administration centred on the palace which was reminiscent of the contemporary civilisations of the Near East but had little in common with the Homeric society. The 'Mycenaean thesis' had to be abandoned.

Should we therefore conclude that Homer portrayed the world in which he himself lived, many centuries after the Trojan War? Or is it something in between, the world of the 'dark ages' of the tenth and ninth centuries, as Moses Finley believes? In his landmark book[3] Finley concludes that, a few anachronisms aside, the society described by Homer is coherent and thus existed. Since this society is neither Mycenaean nor that of the city-state, it must be that of the intervening period, the tenth and ninth centuries. At this time the long years of migration and expansion were over; the mixing of races and cultures was complete, 'the catastrophe that brought down Mycenaean civilisation and made itself felt all over the eastern Mediterranean had been forgotten. . . . the history of the Greeks as such had begun' (Finley 1970:48).

Today, Finley's view is questioned, since it assumes, historically speaking, a radical break between the tenth and ninth centuries on the one hand and the eighth and seventh on the other, and is based on the apparent absence of any eighth-century elements in Homer's work. However, recent discoveries, particularly in Euboea, attest to the continuity of certain aspects of civilisation from the tenth to the eighth century. In addition, the presence of elements of eighth-century society, Finley's famous 'anachronisms', has been noted in Homer's work. For example:

- the *Iliad* contains a description of a battle which prefigures the hoplite tactics which were developed at the time when the epic was acquiring its definitive form. This occurs in Book XIII, l 130 ff. (in a group of lines repeated in Book XVI, 214 ff.): 'an impenetrable hedge of spears and sloping shields, buckler to buckler, helmet to helmet, man to man.'
- The chariots which clog the battles of the *Iliad* must have belonged to a distant tradition whose significance was lost to Homer, since, with one exception (IV, 297 ff.), they no longer engage in combat, being used only to carry the heroes to the place where they are to fight. This they then do on foot. Such

a procedure is more readily understandable in the light of the practices of the eighth century, when combatants would travel on horseback to fight on foot.

Both more ancient and more recent forms of war thus coexist in the epic. In the same way the Homeric poems put institutions belonging to different periods side by side. In matters of dowry, inheritance or funerary rites, they portray different practices arising in different societies. It can only be concluded that Homer's is an artificial, composite world in which the most ancient elements coexist with more modern ones. It is a poetic world; it does not give a historically accurate reflection of a society.

This world, so hard to place in time, is not always easily located in space either. Strabo, the late first-century BC historian and geographer, took great pains to show that Homer was a geographer. Following him, many scholars have sought to locate the places described by Homer. Victor Bérard[4] tried to retrace Odysseus' journeys across the Mediterranean and the places where he landed: he identified the island of the lotus-eaters as Djerba, while Stromboli was the island of Aeolus; Circe's cave was to be found in southern Italy, the oracle of the dead near lake Arvernus and so on. Certainly, as J. de Romilly notes, 'visiting the places where Odysseus landed sets one dreaming and gives the Odyssey – as archaeology does the *Iliad* – a heightened presence. Yet the *Odyssey* is no more faithful to geography than the *Iliad* is to history; here too, the poet's imagination was set free by the long work of transmission and adaptation.[5]

So let us end our search for Homer the historian or geographer and turn instead to his poetry.

The Iliad

The *Iliad* describes Achilles' anger and its disastrous consequences.

Book I provides a prologue, describing Achilles' quarrel with Agamemnon. Humiliated by the King of kings, who deprives him of his prize, Briseis the hero retreats to his tent. Zeus promises to make up for the affront he has suffered by arranging the defeat of the Achaeans. Books II to VII describe the first day of fighting (Book II gives a catalogue of the Achaean and Trojan forces and the first set battle between the Greeks and Trojans; Book III recounts the single combat of Paris and Menelaus; Books IV to VII describe a series of battles and duels; during the night the armies retrieve their dead and the Achaeans build a wall around their ships). The second day of fighting (Book VIII) is devoted to the Trojans' victory. Hector, who is Zeus' favourite, sets up his bivouac in front of the Greek ships. Books IX and X provide an interlude: the Greeks take advantage of the night to send an ambassador to Achilles (Book IX) and reconnoitre the Trojan camp (Book X). The third day of fighting begins with Book XI. Despite the exploits of the Achaean leaders (Books XII to XIV), the Greek side is routed; the Trojans penetrate the Achaean camp and threaten to burn the ships (Book XV). Patroclus is horrified by the Achaean losses and puts on Achilles' armour in order to drive back the Trojans (Book XVI), but is killed by Hector (Book XVII). When Achilles hears of his friend's death he decides to avenge him, vowing to kill Hector even if, as Thetis has predicted, his own death follows that of the Trojan hero. Hephaestus makes new arms for Achilles (Book XVIII). The fourth day of fighting opens with Book XIX, which tells of the reconciliation of Agamemnon and Achilles. Achilles drives the Trojans back to the river (Book XX), then into their city (Book XXI). He kills Hector (Book XXII), but the presages of his own death multiply in these four books. Book XXIII describes Patroclus' funeral and Book XXIV, which ends the poem, replaces the climate of violence which has reigned hitherto with one of pity and compassion: Achilles renounces anger and agrees to return his son Hector's body to Priam. In this final book humanity and fraternity in suffering triumph over the warlike values which were uppermost in the poem until this point; a sense of shared misfortune provides the basis for a moment of sympathy between the two enemies:

> Priam had set Achilles thinking of his own father and brought him to the verge of tears. Taking the old man's hand, he gently put him from him; and overcome by their memories they both broke down. Priam, crouching at Achilles' feet, wept bitterly for man-slaying Hector, and Achilles wept for his father, and then again for Patroclus. The house was filled with the sounds of their lamentation.
>
> (XXIV, 508–12)

Rather than a depiction of victory and vengeance, the epic concludes with a scene of mourning: Hector's funeral.

As Aristotle notes (*Poetics* 1451 A 22ff) Homer's great art resides in the fact that, instead of recounting the entire Trojan war or all of Achilles' exploits, he concentrates on Achilles' anger. The violent emotions that fill the hero's heart one after another – anger, friendship, the desire for vengeance, compassion – provide the driving force of the action. Thus the *Iliad* is as dramatic as it is heroic and warlike. Plato was right to call Homer the father of tragedy (*Republic* 598 D). Fate hangs heavy over the whole poem: the end of Troy, Hector's death and the death of Achilles himself are all repeatedly announced from the outset and the gods, who preside over the unfolding of events, constantly intervene in the narrative. Thus the *Iliad* displays all the features and mechanisms which, according to Aristotle, are characteristic of tragedy: the reversal, the recognition of one's fate and the madness which signals the hero's death are all present in Book XVIII, in which the fates of Hector and Achilles are sealed. Finally, the heroic ideal itself is superseded in the finale of Book XXIV, where an obsession with revenge, which nothing should quell, gives way to pity born of a common suffering.

Clearly the extraordinary fascination exerted by Homer's epic springs from the poem's humanity; however, it is also linked to its diversity of tone. For the *Iliad* gives the same reality, the same presence, to domestic scenes as it does to those portraying the deeds of the heroes or the gods. The heroes are so bound up with the business of everyday life – war, hunting, meals, sharing out the spoils and so on – that these activities naturally have a place in the epic. The sublime may thus go hand in hand with an effortless description of daily life, which is thereby itself rendered sublime through the use of poetic formulas. For everything is beautiful in Homer's work, whose descriptions magnify the smallest scene. Thus tragic order, heroic grandeur and everyday realism coexist harmoniously, even in the battle scenes. In his descriptions of fighting, Homer constantly extends or escapes his world by using similes. He may compare warriors to the force of the elements, for example, a tempest, or the violence of wild animals, or again to the most humble activities of the peacetime world, setting up a constant counterpoint between warlike deeds and life in its broader sense. Thus the sight of men running across the camp to answer the call of their kings suggests to Homer the image of a swarm rising: 'like buzzing swarms of bees that come out in relays from a hollow rock and scatter by companies right and left, to fall in clusters on the flowers of spring' (Book II, 87–91).

Here lies the unity of his concrete style, 'which knows only the foreground and an evenly lit, objective present'[6] and reflects a profound acceptance of the human condition and all forms of life.

The Odyssey

The atmosphere of the *Odyssey* is quite different from that of the *Iliad*. The *Odyssey* is not the story of a war in which heroes struggle with each other; it tells of a lone hero, Odysseus, who is trying to get home to his country, Ithaca, after the Trojan War. It has often been suggested that, if the *Iliad* was written by Homer, the *Odyssey* must have been produced by someone who continued his work. Perhaps, as the Ancients believed, the *Odyssey* is the work of Homer's old age, as opposed to the *Illiad*.

The *Odyssey* combines three elements in a complex composition. First there are the adventures of Telemachus, who leaves Ithaca in search of his father. These form the Telemachy (Books I to IV). Then follows the story of Odysseus' return and his subsequent revenge, which occupies Books V and VI and later Book XIII, 285, to Book XXIII, 296. Lastly there are the tales to Alcinous, in which Odysseus recounts his wanderings after the fall of Troy (IX: the tempest, the lotus-eaters, the Cyclops; X: Aeolus, the Laestrygonians, Circe; XI: among the dead; XII: The Sirens, Scylla and Charybdis, the Sun's cattle) and the end of Book XII takes us back to the island of Calypso, which Odysseus left in Book V. The stories of Telemachus and Odysseus meet when the hero and his son both return to Ithaca (Books XIII to XV), with Odysseus, with the help of Telemachus, taking his revenge on the suitors, in Books XIX to XXIII.

This brief account gives an idea of the narrative's complexity and the strange, teeming world of the *Odyssey*. In the *Iliad* things and people usually appear to be what they actually are; in the *Odyssey* everything is double, ambiguous and contradictory.

- The world of war appears in the poem in two forms: the *Odyssey* is haunted by the memory of the Trojan War and draws on reminiscences of the *Iliad*; yet war is also present within Odysseus' house.
- Nature appears fleetingly in similes, which are moreover much rarer than those of the *Iliad*; yet the narrative which carries the reader from one side of the Mediterranean world to the other permits the expression of a feeling uncommon in Greek literature: the sense of nature's beauties. The fairytale 'landscapes of the *Odyssey*' are one of the poem's charms. They have remained famous, and inspired the frescos of the Esquiline in Rome, which convey the same enchanted atmosphere.

- The human world of the *Odyssey* is more varied than that of the *Iliad*. It gives a large place to women, with the figures of Penelope, Nausicaa and the nurse Eurycleia. It gives an important role to the 'divine swineherd' Eumaeus and depicts the noble figure of old Laertes with great feeling.
- Nevertheless, this poem, which offers a more 'realistic' image of human beings, is in many ways a fairy story. The fantastic, which had the most discreet of roles in the *Iliad*, invades the *Odyssey*, which is all sea monsters, sorceresses, automata, enchanted ships, mysterious drugs, journeys to the beyond and metamorphoses.
- Yet – and this is the final paradox – the purpose of this narrative peopled by divinities, monsters and sorcerers is to glorify the mortal condition; it is human life in all its frailty and with all its suffering that 'the enduring Odysseus'; prefers to any form of immortality with Calypso; he wants to return to his mortal wife in stony Ithaca.

Such is the grandeur of this poem which acknowledges the moral needs of human beings. It shows a very new concern on the part of the Olympian gods with justice: the suitors' crimes are punished, Penelope's patience and Odysseus' courage are rewarded. In its emphasis on moral preoccupations, the *Odyssey* turns its back on the pessimism of the *Iliad* and opens the way to Hesiod.

The epic after Homer

Apart from the *Iliad* and the *Odyssey*, the Ancients knew other epic poems attributed to various poets (for example, Panyassis, Arctinus of Miletus or Lesches of Pyrrha) who are but names to us. These works, whose texts are now lost, are today known only through summaries produced by the compilers and scholiasts of the Roman period. Although they are thought to have been written at a later date than Homer's epics, they may be very ancient in origin. With the *Iliad* and the *Odyssey* these poems made a coherent whole illustrating the legends of the Trojan war, known as the *Epic Cycle*. This cycle recounted the origins of the divine race (in the Battle of the Titans or *Titanomachy*), retraced the entire story of the Trojan War: it started from the wedding of Achilles' father Peleus and the judgement of Paris (in the *Cypria*), continued the story of the *Iliad* to the death of Achilles (in the *Aethiopis*) and finally recounted the fall of Troy (in the *Little Iliad* and the *Sack of Troy*). The *Nostoi* ('homecomings') told of the Greek heroes' returns after the fall of Troy and one final epic, the *Telegony*, continued the story of the *Odyssey*. The poems of the Trojan War formed the main part of the *Cycle*, but the three epics of the *Theban Cycle*, recounting the legends of Thebes – *Oedipodia, Thebais* and *Epigoni* – were included in the *Epic Cycle*.

These epics have doubtless disappeared because their literary merit seemed greatly inferior to that of Homer's poems. However, the great number of monuments erected during and after the archaic period which portray legendary scenes from these poems testifies to their popularity with the public. Moreover, we know that the Greek writers of both lyrics and tragedies often drew on the legends of the *Trojan Cycle* and the *Theban Cycle* for inspiration.

The influence of the epic genre is further demonstrated by the existence of parodies. The Ancients attributed to Homer a short parodic poem of 303 lines called *The Battle of Frogs and Mice*, or *Batrachomyomachia*. The humour of this piece stems from the contrast between the elevated epic style and the low subject matter, as in Boileau's *Lutrin*. We should also note the *Margites*, which Aristotle himself attributes to Homer. This satirical epic was famous in Antiquity; according to Aristotle, it 'bears the same relationship to our comedies as his *Iliad* and *Odyssey* bear to our tragedies' (*Poetics* 4, 1448 b 24).

The Homeric Hymns

Apart from the epics of the *Cycle* other poems were composed to glorify a divinity or a sanctuary. The *Homeric Hymns*, so called because they borrow their metre and language from Homer, are a collection of thirty-three poems celebrating various divinities, of which the most important were composed in the seventh or sixth century. The longest of these hymns are also the finest. The *Hymn to Apollo* (which Thucydides mentions under Homer's name in III, 103) tells of the god's birth at Delos and the establishment of his sanctuary at Delphi. The *Hymn to Demeter* recounts Hades' abduction of Persephone, Demeter's long search and the creation of the mysteries of Eleusis. The *Hymn to Hermes* gives a humorous account of the god's childhood and the theft of Apollo's herds by the young Hermes. The *Hymn to Aphrodite* is the most 'Homeric' in its language. The story of the goddess' seduction of the young Anchises is full of Homeric expressions and often refers to the scene of Zeus' seduction of Hera in Book XV of the *Iliad*. These four hymns, many hundreds of lines long, have lengthy narrative developments as well as the traditional appeal to the god and a final prayer and differ from the other hymns, which are simple eulogies to a god, often very short (the *Hymn to Poseidon* is only seven lines long) and would have acted as prologues to a heroic narrative.

The poetry of Hesiod

Hesiod

Apart from the so-called 'Homeric' poetry – heroic narratives and the hymns that introduced them – the other important poet of the period was Hesiod. The Ancients always coupled and contrasted the two names. The *Contest of Homer and Hesiod (Certamen Homeri et Hesiodi)*, which has come down to us, opposed the two poets, each reciting the finest passages from his work, and, in the fifth century BC, the historian Herodotus considered them to be the founders of Greek theology (II, 53). Hesiod's poetry uses the same metre and language as that of Homer; yet, despite these formal similarities, it is the differences between the two poetic worlds that are most striking. Not for Hesiod the pleasure of relating heroic adventures; instead he codifies traditions, both mythological and agricultural, describing the world of the farmers of Boeotia rather than that of Ionia or the aristocratic courts. Nor is he an anonymous poet simply echoing the words of the god. In the two works which have come down to us, *Theogony* and *Works and Days*, he talks about himself.

At the start of the *Theogony* Hesiod tells how, when he was grazing his lambs below Helicon, he received the rhapsodic staff and was consecrated as a poet by the Muses. In *Works and Days* he relates his quarrel with his brother Perses, refers to his father, who left the Aeolian city of Cyme for Ascra, a village in Boeotia, where he worked hard to cultivate the poor soil, and mentions the prize that he himself won for his song in Chalcis at Amphidamas' funeral games (this event, which historians tend to place in the last third of the eighth century BC, gives an approximate date for the poet's most active period). Hesiod is present in his work, seemingly confident in the belief that his poems will be transmitted to posterity under his name and in the form he has given them. This suggests that their texts were fixed in writing.

Hesiod was the first author to introduce his work in this way, bringing a new tone to poetry. Yet in other ways his work is surprising for its archaism. This is particularly true of the *Theogony*.

The Theogony

This 'poem of the gods' celebrates 'the sacred race of the immortals' and scarcely mentions human beings, who appear only in the myth of Prometheus – though it is true that this is in a prime position (lines 506–616) – to receive first the gifts of Iapetos' son (the meat of sacrifices and the fire with which to cook it) and then Zeus' disastrous gift, Pandora, the first woman. This complex work, which may be partially deformed by additions whose limits are not always easy to determine precisely, opens with an extended hymn to the Muses (lines 1–113) and relates, through a series of genealogies and theomachies, the gradual emergence of a just order which coincides with the reign of Zeus.

From a primal state of indistinction incarnated by Chaos (the gaping opening in which the world will be formed) and Gaia (or Earth, the primordial substance), and as a result of the actions of Eros, the principle of all generation, all the elements of nature – Night, Day, Sky, Mountains and Sea – come into being, along with more abstract entities (for example, Sleep, Dreams, Death, Sarcasm, Suffering and so on). At the same time we witness the establishment of Zeus' reign through a double series of confrontations which frame the story of Prometheus. Twice over, the myths of succession tell of a conflict between a criminal father and his youngest son. In the first, Ouranos behaves badly by preventing the birth of his children, whom he shuts away inside Gaia, and is castrated by Kronos (lines 154–210). The story of Kronos (lines 434–506) reproduces that of his father, since he becomes guilty of the same crime: he swallows his children, but is finally vanquished by the 'strength and stratagem' of his son Zeus. After his triumph, Zeus' power is definitively established over the ancient forces of disorder, the Titans (lines 616–735), the sons of Ouranos and Gaia, and Typhoeus, son of Gaia and Tartarus (lines 820–880).

Hesiod's interest in obscure forces and in the powers of darkness contrasts with Homer, whose gods are usually 'gods of light'. Hesiod may have borrowed something of his theological vision from the Near East. His myths have been compared to the Hittite legends of Kumarbi and Ullikummi and to the Babylonian myth of creation, *Enuma Elish*. These myths also combine the theme of the genesis

of the world with a royal epic whose ultimate goal is the establishment of a stable order.

At the end of the *Theogony* Zeus is established as the permanent
master of the universe. Unlike the earlier kings he has been able
to prevent the birth of a stronger son. His power is based on a
combination of strength ('thunder and lightning and the smoking
bolt'), intelligence (he has swallowed Metis, who incarnates
cunning) and, most importantly, justice. Zeus allies himself to the
established order by marrying Themis, who gives him daughters
whose names are significant in themselves: Good government
(*Eunomia*), Justice (*Dike*) and Peace (*Eirene*). Finally he divides the
honours and powers equally among the gods, respecting the prerog-
atives of the divinities of the first generation, such as Hecate and
Styx. His reign thus guarantees a just order.

Works and Days

In this 'poem of men' Hesiod does not recount the stories from a
distant past, but instructs his listeners as to their daily tasks.
Independently of the context – whether invented, traditional or real
– of a quarrel between Hesiod and his brother Perses which provides
the motivation for the poem, here we have a man addressing other
men of his time.

The first lines of the poem celebrate Zeus, god of justice. The
prologue is followed by two mythical narratives designed to explain
the mortal condition: the myth of Pandora, the scourge sent to
earth by the gods for the misfortune of human beings (42–105)
and the myth of races, which describes successive human generations, from the race of gold to the race of iron to which the poet
belongs (106–201). This is followed by the fable of the hawk
and the nightingale – the first fable of Western literature –
illustrating the cruelty of a world governed by pure force, and
by contrasted portraits of the just and unjust city, after which
Hesiod exhorts Perses and 'bribe-swallowing' kings to follow justice.
He then makes an ardent appeal for hard work: 'If your spirit
in your breast yearns for riches, do as follows and work, work
upon work' (381–2). These words introduce the calendar of labour
in the fields (383–617), which is followed by a calendar of navi-
gation (618–94). Lastly the poet lists a number of religious
prohibitions (695–764) and the dates that must be observed, the
days that are propitious for those engaged in agriculture and those
that are not.

This poem, which combines varied literary forms, some of which are very ancient (such as the maxim, fable, myth or admonition) is unique in Greek poetry. Its only parallels are found in Sumer and Egypt (where it is known that there was a tradition of didactic and gnomic poetry from 2500 BC to the first centuries AD). Should this be seen as another indication of the influence of the Near East on Hesiod's poetry? If so, it is particularly noticeable in the 'myth of races', which seems to be Mesopotamian in origin. The poem is also unique in the value it places on work and the dignity which work gives to the farmer. 'Work is no reproach, but not working is a reproach' (311). This idea is not expressed elsewhere in Greek literature before Antisthenes and the Cynics, for the Ancients did not place value on 'work' (*ponos*), preferring 'studious leisure' (*scholè*, the origin of our word 'school').

Finally, one theme of *Works and Days* makes it a perfect stepping stone between Homer and the poetry of the centuries that followed: the plea for justice. We have seen how the need for justice appears in the *Odyssey*. Praise of justice is a central theme in *Works and Days*, where Hesiod inaugurates a tradition that the lyric poets, tragedians and philosophers were all to illustrate after him. It is not surprising that this theme should appear in a world of disorder and conflict. The old order which had broken down had not been replaced. In such a state of confusion the force of Hesiod's call for justice is easy to understand.

The Shield

The last poem attributed to Hesiod is the *Shield of Heracles* (*Aspis*). Although this was transmitted in medieval manuscripts with the other two poems, it must be later (it is usually dated as being written in the sixth century) and undoubtedly composed by an imitator. Written in hexameter, the poem recounts the combat between Heracles and Cycnus, concentrating mainly on a description of Heracles' shield modelled on the description of Achilles' shield in Book XVIII of the *Iliad*. Yet the tone of the description (or *ecphrasis*) is quite different: whereas Homer enlivened his account by describing how Hephaestus made the shield, here the author simply amasses details and fantastical figures.

The poem opens with an evocation of the hero's mother, Alcmene, and begins with the formula ē hoiē. It could therefore be included in the 'Catalogue of illustrious women', which is also often attributed to Hesiod and whose title, the *Ehoiai* (ἢ οἵαι) clearly reflects the very structure of the narrative in which each episode is linked to the next by the transitional phrase, 'like the woman who. . .' (ē hoiē). This formula, repeated like a refrain, introduces the heroine's love affair, which usually ends in the birth of a hero. Such a poem could go on for as long as the audience wanted; the order of the episodes was not fixed and a poem like the *Shield of Heracles* could easily be added to it.

2

THE ARCHAIC PERIOD
(FROM THE SEVENTH
CENTURY TO THE EARLY
FIFTH CENTURY B C)

Early lyric poetry

The seventh century heralded a period of change. Coinage, which had been invented in Croesus' Lydia, was gradually spreading throughout the Greek world, colonisation was increasing cultural exchanges, Greece was opening up on all sides, and land ownership was no longer the only form of wealth, with huge fortunes being amassed through trade. While small landowners, vulnerable to a bad harvest, were getting into debt and losing their independence, land ownership was becoming concentrated in the hands of an oligarchy whose wealth and power were constantly increasing. The power of the old aristocracy was crumbling. In the military sphere, the hoplite reforms had given the advantage to the infantry as opposed to the cavalry, whose dominance had symbolised the strength of the aristocrats, the only ones able to keep a horse. Calls were made for laws to be published. This was the time of the great legislators (who were often mythical) such as Zaleucus in Locris, Charondas in Catana or Pittacus in Mytilene. 'Tyrannical' regimes supported by the people were gradually supplanting the aristocracy.

Throughout the Greek world, in this climate of social conflict and wars between states, there was a huge poetic output which sometimes reflected political struggles. Between 650 and 450 in Asia Minor (with Callinus of Ephesus, Mimnermus of Smyrna and Hipponax of Ephesus), the islands (Archilochus was from Paros, Sappho and Alcaeus from Lesbos), in Greece proper (with Alcman in Sparta, Solon in Athens, Theognis in Megara and Pindar in Thebes) and in Magna Graecia (Ibycus was from Rhegium and Stesichorus from Sicily), poems were being written whose short length and flexible, direct language marked a break with the solemnity of the epic style. They were sung or declaimed to a musical accompaniment, usually the lyre (hence the name 'lyric' which the Alexandrian grammarians gave to such poetry), but sometimes the pipe.

Greek lyric was characterised by its musical dimension rather than the expression of personal feelings provoking an emotional response. For Herodotus, unaware of the 'lyric' label invented during the Hellenistic period, Alcaeus and Sappho were 'melic' poets (from *melos*, meaning 'song'). The definition of a lyric genre, characterised by individual effusion, dates from the German Romantic, who established the hallowed trio of genres: epic, lyric and dramatic. The Greeks, though they made the distinction between poetry that was sung and that which was recited, like the epic, never contrasted the 'lyric' (or sung) genre with the dramatic. On the contrary, they considered the composition of songs (or lyrical sections) to be an essential part of dramatic art.

Although the lyric poems that have come down to us are later than Homer, due to accidents of transmission and, for the most part, earlier than the tragedies, we should not therefore regard Greek lyric as a genre that took over from the epic, 'that expression of the naive consciousness of a people', as Hegel put it, and marked the birth of subjectivity, 'the emergence of the individual', before the arrival of tragedy. For sung poetry is much older than Homer. The epics themselves contained paeans to Apollo (*Iliad* I, 473), threnodies or mourning songs (XXIV, 720), wedding songs (XVIII, 493) and partheneia (maiden songs) (XVI, 182). Furthermore, comparative metrical studies of Indo-European languages confirm that the metres of sung poetry belong to an older tradition than the hexameters of epic poetry.

For the Ancients, lyric poetry meant nine names: Alcaeus, Sappho and Anacreon, who composed 'monodies' (poems sung as a solo) and Alcman, Stesichorus, Ibycus, Simonides, Bacchylides and Pindar, who were mainly famous for their great compositions of 'choral lyrics', in other words, odes sung and danced by a choir. In addition to 'melic' poetry thus defined, there were two related forms of poetry declaimed to a musical accompaniment, which were contemporary with and often dealt with the same themes as sung poetry. These were the iambus, satirical poetry recited to the accompaniment of string instruments, and the elegy, which was declaimed to the sound of the pipe.

Very little of this abundant production has survived. Although when the Alexandrians edited these poets they were able to produce ten books of Alcaeus, nine of Sappho and 8000 lines of Solon, we now have only scattered fragments, cited in later works or preserved on papyri. Complete poems are rare before Pindar.

The most striking thing about this poetry is its diversity. It was written in different rhythms (iambics, dactyls or lyric metres) and dialects (the iambus and the elegy are in Ionian, the choral lyric is in Dorian and the monody in Dorian or Aeolian) with a diversity of themes and audiences: from confessions of the poet's own passions and resentments to celebrations of great men, praise of the gods or entertainment for guests at a banquet.

Yet within this diversity there are some unifying factors. First is the period, since all these poems were composed between 650 and 450 BC. Secondly, this is a poetry of the present. No longer seeking to extol some distant past, it often engages with the conflicts of its time. Lastly, it is first-person poetry, presented as the words of an 'I' speaking to another individual or to a group – usually identified by the poem – and trying to pass on some form of wisdom.

Iambic poetry

The earliest Greek lyric poet is Archilochus, whose most productive time is generally placed around 650. He is thought to have been born in Paros. His father, Telesicles, was said to have been commanded by an oracle to colonise Thasos. Archilochus followed his example and participated in the second colonisation of Thasos. He is thought to have been killed in combat.

Archilochus celebrates war:

> On my spear's my daily bread
> On my spear my wine
> from Ismaros; and drinking it,
> it's on my spear I recline.

Although the meaning of these lines is disputed, it is clear that they place the spear at the centre of the poet's daily activities. Yet Archilochus resolutely rejects the epic idealisation of war. His most famous lines describe the loss of his shield:

> Some Saian sports my splendid shield
> I had to leave it in a wood,
> but saved my skin. Well I don't care –
> I'll get another just as good.

This abandoned shield is the first in a long series that goes from Alcaeus to the Latin poet Horace. It symbolises the distance separating heroic poetry from iambic, realist poetry which cares nothing for glory and the opinion of others. Archilochus declares:

No one here enjoys respect or reputation once he's dead:
In this city we the living tend to cultivate instead
the living's favour;
Once you die you get the worst of everything.

Archilochus also describes his disappointments in love. He rails against the rich Lycambes, who refuses to let him marry his daughter Neobule, and insults the whole family, while describing his love-making in the crudest terms. Lastly his poetry seems to give an important place to fables, which bring human beings down to the level of animals. The fables of the monkey and the fox and of the eagle and the fox were well known in Antiquity. Comparisons with animals which, in the epic, celebrated warlike values are here used to highlight human failings.

The same is to be found in the work of another seventh-century iambic poet, Semonides of Amorgos, who is known above all for his poem *On Women*, the first misogynistic work of our literature. In this poem of 118 lines the poet draws ten caricatures summing up the faults of the eternal feminine: the woman-sow wallows in filth, the woman-mare loves luxury and laziness and so on.

Realistic complaints, recriminations, personal attacks: such is the tone of iambic poetry, illustrated better than any other by Archilochus – the poet whom the Ancients placed alongside Homer and Hesiod; despite the subtlety of Hipponax at the end of the sixth century, however, it soon lost its brilliance.

Elegiac poetry

The archaic Greek elegy is a poetry of war and politics. It is not 'the gentle elegy' with its 'touching grace' that French classicism inherited from the *Roman erotic elegy*.[1] The elegy as it appeared in the seventh century in the work of Callinus of Ephesia and Tyrtaeus in Sparta took the form of a military harangue. The poet addresses his fellow citizens directly, exhorting them to defend their city. 'It is a fine thing, says Tyrtaeus, to die in the front rank for one's country'; it is shameful to wander without a homeland, accompanied by one's parents, wife and children. This praise of heroism is reminiscent of Homer. Indeed, the elegy remained close to the epic in terms of its metre (the elgiac distich consists of a dactylic hexameter – the 'heroic' metre – and a pentameter), of its Ionian dialect rich in Homerisms and of its praise of military valour, seen as the only source of glory. However, the wars that the poets refer to are contemporary; the heroism which young men are called upon to display is no longer that of the individual exploit: it has become the ability to stand firm, 'legs wide apart, feet firmly planted on the ground', holding one's place in the hoplite phalanx. The practice of war has changed: it has become combat in serried ranks, for and with one's city. In exchange, the city confers glory on those who sacrifice themselves for it; the brave man is mourned by all: 'his death puts the whole city into mourning; neither his name nor his noble glory perish; even when he lies under the earth, he is immortal' (Tyrtaeus). It is said that this warlike poetry was the source from which the Spartans drew their courage for centuries. According to the Athenian Lycurgus, three centuries later the Spartan soldiers still assembled on the eve of every expedition to listen to Tyrtaeus' poems in front of the king's tent.

The elegiac genre remained alive throughout the sixth century. Mimnermus of Smyrna is said to have used it to celebrate the victory of his compatriots over Gyges the Lydian, although he is best known for the poems in which he celebrates the joys of love and youth. With Solon and Theognis the elegy became political and moral. We known Solon as a politician. His deeds as archon in Athens in 594 made his name as one of the founders of Athenian democracy and one of the Seven Sages of Greece. Born in Athens around 640, Solon took part in the battles fought for his city in the conquest of Salamis around 612. When he became archon, the unity of the city was under threat; some people were building up massive fortunes while others had nothing but debts. Solon freed the land, abolished slavery for debt, established laws that were equal for all, then travelled for ten years so that they should not be changed.

The political reforms of this sage reflect the moral preoccupations that echo through his poetry: justice must reign, combating all forms of excess (*hubris*). A famous poem describes 'order' or *eunomia* which 'makes the rough smooth, curbs excess, effaces wrong, and shrivels up the budding flowers of sin'. Although the poet denounces 'the unprincipled mob-leaders' who 'know not how to prosper modestly', he was in no way a revolutionary. He says:

The commons I have granted privilege enough,
not lessening their estate nor giving more;
the influential, who were envied for their wealth,
I have saved them from all mistreatment too.
I took my stand with strong shield covering both sides,
allowing neither unjust dominance.

Solon's politics illustrates the golden rule of archaic morality – the desire for the 'fair mean': 'I marked the frontier in the No Man's Land between these warring parties.'

The tone of the elegies of Theognis of Megara is quite different. His poetry directly reflects the bitterness of an aristocrat landowner who has been deprived of his land. A collection of 1,200 lines has come down to us under his name, though it doubtless contains pieces of different origin. Along with virtuous advice addressed to a certain Cyrnus, it contains complaints about the misfortunes of the times. Theognis curses a world in which money is valued more highly than moral worth, in which nobodies, who 'used to wear old goatskins on their flanks . . . are [now] the gentry, while yesterday's gentry are dregs.'

Thus the sixth-century Greek elegy was above all a poetry of morality and politics. However, as it was often performed at banquets, it also gives a place to themes directly linked to that context. Theognis describes the pleasures of wine and love, and Solon himself celebrates the gifts 'of Cypris'. These themes also inspired Alcaeus' monodies in the same period.

Monody: Alcaeus, Sappho and Anacreon

These three names represent a fertile genre; however, of the nine or ten books written by each of these poets, we have only 450 fragments of Alcaeus, fewer than 300 fragments of Sappho and fewer than 200 by Anacreon. Their poems appear as the product of a brilliant and refined society under threat from the rise of tyranny, which depended on the people. All three poets were exiled.

Alcaeus, like Theognis, was a politically active commentator on a troubled period. Born into the aristocracy of Mytilene, he opposed the tyrant Myrsilus and has remained famous for his lively attacks on Pittacus (one of the Seven Sages). This poet of political struggles could also give a Homeric brilliance to 'the high hall . . . agleam with bronze'. Moreover, he was a poet of feasting: his drinking songs praised 'getting drunk' – 'the best cure' – and wine, which 'puts cares out of the mind' and goes hand in hand with truth.

The masculine world of Alcaeus contrasts with the feminine world of 'chaste Sappho of the violet curls and gentle smile'. She is the only example we have of women's poetry in archaic Greece, since her contemporary women poets, Telesilla of Argos and Praxilla of Sicyon, are nothing more than names to us and, despite the papyrological discoveries of Hermoupolis, we still know little of Corinna, who was the rival of Pindar.

In her poetry, Sappho, who lived in a society of women – she taught the arts of music and singing to girls – often celebrates marriage, that major event in women's lives. She is said to have written a whole book of epithalamia (of which barely twenty lines remain) and her depiction of the transports of love, which we know about thanks to pseudo-Longinus' treatise *On the Sublime* (first century AD), made her famous among the Ancients as among the Moderns. Indeed it is to Sappho that we owe the first description of the physical symptoms of the lover's emotions in the first person singular:

> . . . speech fails me,
> my tongue is paralysed, at once
> a light fire runs beneath my skin
> my eyes are blinded, and my ears drumming
> the sweat pours down me, and I shake
> all over, sallower than grass:
> I feel as if I am not far from dying.

The force of this description comes from the realism of its depiction of the physical effects of love, a realism which Sappho borrowed from Homer. But in describing lovesickness rather than the panic of war, Sappho founded lyricism in the modern sense.

Anacreon of Teos is the last great name of archaic Greek monody. This court poet and friend of the tyrants Polycrates (in Samos) and Hipparchus (in Athens) was the bard of feasting, wine and love. But love is not a tragic passion in his work; it provides the opportunity for refined genre pictures whose strength lies in their detail. The charm and delicacy of this elegant art full of wit and innuendo seduced the Alexandrians, who imitated it in 'anacreontic poems', as did the Latin poets after them, and indeed later writers up to and including Ronsard.

The choral lyric

There is nothing in modern poetry that resembles the Greek choral lyric. When, in the sixteenth century, Monteverdi tried to rediscover the laws of this lost art, he created opera. Yet in opera it is the musical element that dominates; in the odes, which were sung and danced by choirs of young people, led by a conductor draped in a long red robe and to the sound of the cithara or a type of reeded pipe called the *aulos*, poetry, music and dance were of equal importance.

This poetry was both religious and civic. It brought the community of citizens together to celebrate one of its divine protectors or illustrious sons. The classification of the odes refers to the circumstance of their performance: hymns, paeans and dithyrambs celebrated the gods, while the epinician odes did the same for men who had triumphed in the great Panhellenic Games. But the victories they hailed were inseparable from religious festivities and the life of the sanctuaries. The earliest exponent of this genre is said to have been Arion of Methymna, whom we know today by name only, like Terpander of Lesbos, who is said to have founded a school of choral lyric in Sparta. It was in seventh-century Sparta that Alcman composed the *Partheneia* sung by choirs of young girls, of which a few fragments were discovered on papyri about a century ago. This explains why Dorian is the language of the choral lyric.

We have only a few scattered fragments of Alcman's successors. Stesichorus is said to have used his talents in Sicily in the mid-sixth century. His narrative odes give an important place to mythical stories and the tragic poets frequently drew on them for inspiration. However, Stesichorus is best known as the author of the *Palinode* for Helen, a poem in which he withdrew the attacks on Helen, made in an earlier poem. Helen, now divine, then gave him back his sight, which she had taken from him in her anger. As for Ibycus of Rhegium, who wrote his odes in the court of the tyrant Polycrates of Samos in the mid-sixth century, almost nothing of his has survived.

It was not until the late sixth and early fifth century that the genre blossomed with the work of two Ionian poets, Simonides of Ceos (556–467) and Bacchylides of Ceos (*c.* 510 to *c.* 410), and most importantly the Theban Pindar (518–438). These three poets composed many kinds of odes; however, the main elements of their work that we read today are the epinicians celebrating the victory of the athletes at the Panhellenic games.

27

Epinician odes

The athletic competitions of Olympia (which date, according to tradition, from 776 BC), Delphi, the Isthmus and Nemea, were true Panhellenic celebrations to which no barbarians were admitted. They appear to have reached their height between 500 and 475 BC, at the time of the conflict with the Persians. Members of the top aristocratic families competed with each other at running, jumping, wrestling, boxing, fist-fighting and throwing the discus or javelin. The most glorious contest, the chariot race, was often the preserve of the richest tyrants, Arcesilaus of Cyrene or Hieron of Syracuse, who were the only ones wealthy enough to bear the costs of training the teams. Victory covered not just the winner and his lineage but also his city with glory. Sculptors would put up statues to commemorate him, poets would write epinicians. These odes celebrated the athlete's return to his city. Some would be recited all along the triumphal route taken by the winner; but they were most frequently presented as part of the ceremony with which the whole city would celebrate its victorious son. These poetic eulogies followed set rules and generally included praise of the victor, his family and city, a mythical narrative and moral and religious maxims; for the ode to the victor was also a hymn to the divine patrons of athletic contests and, like the games themselves, as an expression of religious feeling.

If tradition is to be believed, Simonides was the first to celebrate men in his poetry. He was born in Ceos near Athens, lived to a great age and left an extensive body of work. He was most famous for his songs of mourning (in which he emphasised man's fragility and powerlessness) and his epigrams, which were much admired by the Alexandrians. He celebrated the glorious death of the Thermopylae fighters in vigorous lines: 'The urn which holds their ashes has taken Greece's most splendid light . . . Leonidas' valour shines with immortal brilliance.'

Only fragments of his epinicians are left to us. It seems that Simonides was not greatly interested in the concrete details of athletic feats; he tended to celebrate the gods who had made such feats possible and heroes whose memory he invoked. The high tone of his choral lyrics prefigures Pindar. After living in Athens, Simonides ended his days at the court of Hieron of Syracuse, where his successors in the art of the choral lyric, Pindar and Bacchylides, also spent time.

Pindar gave unrivalled breadth to the epinician ode. We know very little about his life. He is said to have been born around 518 into an aristocratic family at Cynoscephalae near Thebes. He started

28

writing triumphal odes very early: his first, *Pythian X*, was composed in 498 when he was 20. His fame soon spread throughout Greece and he celebrated athletes from the entire Greek world. His last ode, *Pythian VIII*, dates from 446, when Pindar was 72. He is thought to have died in 438 at the age of 80. The four books of epinicians which have survived are only a small part of his poetic *oeuvre* which, according to his biographers, amounted to seventeen books and included, among other things, hymns to the gods, processional hymns and songs of mourning.

Pindar praises the merit of men who obtain divine favour through their own efforts. He is not interested in the anecdotal aspects of victory; instead, he sees the athlete's success as a sign of his worth and that of his lineage, turning him into a symbol of human greatness through a combination of celebration, myth and religious and moral teaching. In addition to these three obligatory ingredients of the epinician, Pindar includes comments on his art or on the role of the poet. The themes are not organised according to any fixed plan and his odes move freely from one motif to the next; Pindar himself praises this aspect of his art: 'The light of the holiday song / darts from one thought to another like a bee' (*Pythian X*, 53). If we add to this his taste for ellipsis and abrupt transitions, it is understandable that some people – Voltaire for one – found the complexity of Pindar's lyrical outpourings off-putting.

Pindar is the poet of movement, constantly creating images of extraordinary density:

> Water is preeminent and gold, like a fire
> burning in the night, outshines
> all possessions that magnify men's pride.
> But if, my soul, you yearn
> to celebrate great games
> look no further
> for another star
> shining through the deserted ether
> brighter than the sun, or for a contest
> mightier than Olympia –
> where the song
> has taken its coronal
> design of glory, plaited
> in the minds of poets
> as they came, calling on Zeus' name,
> to the rich, radiant hall of Hieron.[2]

In these opening words Pindar gives to the Games he is celebrating the splendours of water, gold fire and sun; the tone of the epinician rises to that of the hymn, praising man, hero and gods in a fusion of brilliant light.

The eulogy unfolds on three levels: divine, heroic and human. The ode celebrates both the Olympian gods, source of all delight (*charis*), who grant success to the athlete and the gift of hymns to the poet, the hero, whose former glory is reawakened in the present victory, and the victor whose feat demands a hymn of glory, the only form that can make the fleeting brilliance of victory last. For 'even high deeds of bravery / Have a great darkness if they lack song' (*Nemean VIII*) and 'men forget / whatever has not been yoked to echoing streams of song / to come to the topmost peak of art' (*Isthmian VII*). Through his fusion of the present victory with the legendary past, placing myth at the centre of most of his odes, Pindar lifts athletic prowess above the level of anecdote and the confines of time. The mythic hero is the victor's double: in *Olympian I* the glory of Pelops prefigures that of Hieron and gives it its meaning. The myth weaves together the human and the heroic world, lifting athletic success to the level of the eternal and bestowing a form of immortality on the victor by ensuring that his memory will survive. Thus although the event that gives rise to the poem is different every time, the epinician remains the poetry of eternal values and atemporal truths. Each new feat is another illustration of heroism and an exaltation of human greatness.

This constant reference to the world of the gods and heroes gives Pindar's poetry its brilliance; for while Pindar shares a sense of human frailty with all the poets of the archaic period, he also knows the heights which man can attain thanks to the gods:

> Man's life is a day. What is he?
> What is he not? A shadow in a dream
> Is man: but when God sheds a brightness
> Shining light is on earth
> And life is sweet as honey.
>
> (*Pythian VIII*)

The poet's role is to do justice to these flashes of greatness and beauty, thereby conferring ultimate perfection on the world. When we measure the importance that Pindar gives to poetry we understand why, so often in the odes, he chooses to break the illusion to speak of his art, to bring the activity of poetic creation on to the stage as well. It is because he wants to bring everything into the epinician. This poetry, which operates in several registers at once, is a precious jewel, gift of the Muse and fruit of poetic genius; its blazing images make abstractions visible, ideas concrete or matter spiritual; it strives endlessly to 'exhaust the field of the possible'.

Pindar's young rival was the poet Bacchylides. The two competed with each other, sometimes both celebrating the same victory. Thus Pindar's *Olympian I* and Bacchylides' *Poem V* both commemorate the victory of Hieron, tyrant of Syracuse, in 476.

Like Simonides, whose nephew he was, Bacchylides was from Ceos. Six books of hymns to the gods and three of poems celebrating human beings, including a book of epinicians, are attributed to him. It was not until 1896 that some of his poems were revealed to us by two rolls of papyrus. His epinicians contain the same elements as those of Pindar, with myth fulfilling the same role of mediation between men and gods; but Bacchylides's mythical stories unfold in serene compositions. His narratives present the salient facts clearly and with feeling lingering here and there on melodramatic tableaux. However, Bacchylides' likeable talent, his smooth and pleasant art, seems superficial in comparison to the gravity and intensity of Pindar's genius.

Today, Pindar's work thus remains the high point of the lyric tradition. His achievement nevertheless also represents an end. Although younger by a few years than Aeschylus, Pindar belongs entirely to the generation moulded by the sixth century: he glorifies a way of life that was already passing. After him, during the second half of the fifth century, the world of the Games lost its glory, falling into the hands of professional athletes, while the religious traditions at the heart of the choral lyric were challenged by the critiques of the Sophists, and lyrics soon became confined to the choral sections of tragedy.

The birth of philosophy: the Presocratics

Philosophy was born in the sixth century, at different ends of the Greek world: in Ionia, native land of the Milesian philosophers, and Magna Graecia, where Pythagoras found refuge in Croton, while Xenophanes settled in Elea in Lucania to the south of Paestum. Whether of the Milesian, Eleatic or Pythagorean schools, all these thinkers tried to explain the origins and nature of the universe without recourse to the solutions proffered by mythology or the anthropomorphic imagery proposed by Hesiod in his *Theogony*, which they rejected in favour of a more impersonal and general explanation. Convinced that the tangible world forms an ordered whole – a *cosmos* – and that it therefore has a rational, intelligible order which human reason can and must discover, these 'physiologists' (from the Greek word *phusis* meaning 'that which grows', i.e. 'nature') sought a universal principle that would explain everything, a causal, 'physical' explanation of nature and the human beings who live in it.

This intellectual revolution began in Miletus in the sixth century, with Thales, Anaximander and Anaximenes, whose philosophical research consisted largely of 'enquiries into nature' (*peri phuseos*). In order to make a clean break with preceding literary traditions, which were almost exclusively poetic, Anaximander and Anaximenes chose to write in prose.

Thales (640–550?) produced no written works and is known to us only through anecdotes. Plato made him the symbol of the absent-minded sage: he is said to have fallen down a well while absorbed in contemplation of the stars. Yet Aristotle presents him as a wise man: when his astronomical observations enabled him to predict an abundant olive harvest, he hired all the oil presses in the region and later, when they were needed, rented them out himself on his own terms, thereby proving that the philosopher can get rich when he wants to. He is said to have taught that water is the primal substance from which all things were derived. He is best known as an astronomer however (he was able to predict the total eclipse of the sun of 28 May 585) and mathematician. He is considered to be the founder of Greek science.

Anaximander, born in 610 and younger than Thales, was the first to write a treatise, *On Nature*. He stated that the primal substance is infinite (apeiron). Like Thales, he was interested in astronomy and was the first to draw a map of the world.

His successor Anaximenes, of whose writing we have only a single fragment, seems to have thought that air, the primal substance, is infinite: 'Just as our soul, being air, holds us, so do breath and air encompass the whole world.' This doctrine of air as the principal constituent of the world was taken up by Diogenes of Apollonia in the fifth century.

According to Aristotle, Heraclitus of Ephesus (*c.* 540 to *c.* 480) was also part of the Ionian school in the early fifth century. This philosopher, known as 'the Obscure', described the world in his sibylline aphorisms as an ever-living, ever-changing fire, for he believed fire to be the basic element. He taught that everything is unstable, constantly shifting, an idea reflected in his adage: 'Everything flows' (*panta rhei*) and his assertion that it is not possible to step twice into the same stream. For Heraclitus everything is in a state of continuous transformation perpetuated by conflict (*Polemos*), 'father of everything', seen as an inherent tension which maintains the harmony of opposites. Life and death, youth and old age, night and day, sleep and wakefulness, are one, each born of the other in a continuous cycle. Heraclitus' insights inspired his disciple Cratylus' thinking on the instability of the tangible world and were the point of departure for Plato's thought. The elevation of Heraclitus' thought was admired by Hegel and Nietzsche and caused André Breton to hail him as a philosopher close to surrealism.

In 546 Ionia was conquered by the Persians and in 494 Miletus was destroyed. Many Greeks emigrated from Asia Minor and philosophy left Ionia for southern Italy with Pythagoras and Xenophanes.

Pythagoras was born in Samos, but had to leave the island around 530 to escape the tyranny of Polycrates. He settled in Croton, where he founded a politico-religious sect and was soon seen as a semi-divine being. As Pythagoras himself left no writings and since his disciples observed a cult of secrecy, we have no ancient texts and it is hard to identify the historical facts in the later biographies written by the Neopythagoreans, Porphyry and Iamblichus.

The first of the Pythagorean theoretical positions is that number is the informing principle of the universe. Pythagoras is said to have carried out mathematical research, established the table that bears his name and did much for the development of exact science. Noting that every number has a spatial representation (3 is represented by a triangle, 4 by a square, the decad or tetractys, sum of the first four numbers, by another triangle), the Pythagoreans thought that, conversely, every shape must have a number. They also laid the foundations of acoustics by showing that musical harmony rests on numerical proportions. It is the same for the distances between the planets; hence the idea of the music of the spheres, which they believed accompanied the movements of the stars. Plato, in the *Republic*, congratulated them on having discovered that astronomy and harmony are related sciences. These mystics also believed in the transmigration of souls (metempsychosis), were vegetarians and practised purification rites, all of which were ideas that influenced Plato in the fourth century and which would later inspire the Neoplatonists.

Like Pythagoras, Xenophanes of Colophon (570–474) had to leave Ionia for southern Italy. He settled in Elea and founded a philosophical school which later became very important. His desire to purify mythology makes him a forerunner of later thinkers. In his poetry this strange bard criticised the anthropomorphic conceptions of divinity found in Homer and Hesiod. Denouncing the immorality of the Homeric gods, he substituted the idea of a single, undying and supreme god whose thought gave life to the whole universe. For posterity he remains the first critic of Homer. He is also the latter's rival, since philosophical message and poetry are once more united in his work. Parmenides and Empedocles followed him on this point, being similarly concerned to give their work the dignity of revelation.

From Parmenides to Democritus

Parmenides of Elea (515–450) is seen as the disciple of Xenophanes. In the early fifth century he wrote a metaphysical poem in which he states that what is real is immobile: 'No, you will never force nonbeing to be.' With him and his disciple Zeno of Elea (whose 'paradoxes' are still famous) comes the idea that the only reality is a hidden absolute, the one unique existent behind sensible appearances.

The problem of philosophy then becomes one of explaining the changeability and multiplicity of appearances while respecting the principles of ontology, in other words the principles of the immutability and eternity of Being. In the fifth century Anaxagoras of Clazomenae and Democritus of Abdera offered two different solutions to this problem.

With Anaxagoras, philosophy came to Athens, where he spent many years and was a friend of Pericles, although he was born in Ionia around 500. Anaxagoras was regarded as the typical scientist, enemy of all superstition. Almost nothing remains of his treatise *On Nature*, but we know from Plato that he saw the Mind (*Nous*) as the organising principle of the cosmos. According to Anaxagoras this *Nous*, 'the lightest and purest thing', organises the elements which are mixed together and swirl in a circular movement, by separating them. Anaxagoras is said to have been the first to suggest a natural explanation for lunar eclipses and to have taught that the moon and the sun were simply fiery stones, which caused him to be prosecuted for impiety.

The 'atomists'

In the thought of Democritus of Abdera (*c.* 460 to *c.* 370) and the man traditionally regarded as his teacher, Leucippus of Miletus, the unity of being advocated by Parmenides is fragmented into indivisible atoms, moving in a void, which necessity drives to weld together to form the diversity of reality.

The unusually large body of work left by Democritus reflects his taste for encyclopaedic knowledge and people have seen him as the precursor of Aristotle. Apart from his interest in physics – Democritus' atomist theories lead, through Epicurus, Lucretius and Gassendi, to the physicists of the twentieth century – he was interested in mathematics, music, psychology and ethics and wrote a great number of technical texts. This scientist, who would have given "the whole of the Persian empire for one causal explanation" was the first to try to explain the universe without recourse to an external motor force. Thus, like Anaxagoras, Democritus removed the sacred element from his depiction of the universe.

Empedocles of Acragas was younger than Anaxagoras, yet his thought seems more archaic. This philosopher was born around 490 and is thought to have left almost 5,000 lines of poetry, of which a few hundred have come down to us. He expounds his concept of the world in his poem *On Nature*, in which he says that there are 'four roots to all things': fire, water, air and earth. These elements are animated by two forces, love (philotes) and strife (neikos), which successively combine and separate them. Yet Empedocles the philospher, astronomer, physicist and biologist was also a prophet performing miracles and a mystic. In his poem on *Purifications* (or *Katharmoi*), he comes across as a disciple of the Pythagoreans and Orphics, describing the cycle of reincarnation of the soul and asserting the need for abstinence and purification.

Empedocles is said to have ended his life by throwing himself into the purifying fire of Mount Etna. The mysterious personality of this philosopher-poet, scientist and mystic fascinated the German Romantics. Hölderlin wrote a play about him and Nietzsche, who admired him, perceived Empedocles' ambivalence with his customary acuity: 'Two centuries meet in him . . . Pythagoras or Democritus, he floats between them.'

How can we evaluate the contribution of the Presocratic philosophers? Should we follow Isocrates and criticise these ancient sages, 'one of whom claimed that there is an infinite number of beings, whereas Empedocles saw only four with Strife and Love between them, Ion said there were only three, Alcmaeon only two, Parmenides and Melissus one'?[3] Were they, on the contrary, the first Western scientists and precursors of our own scientific thinking?[4] Or theologians who placed the problem of divinity at the centre of their speculations?[5] Should we see them as the only true philosophers of Antiquity, as Nietzsche and later Heidegger said, since they were the only ones to pose the problem of Being? The debate continues.

Part 2

THE CLASSICAL AGE AND THE FLOWERING OF ATHENS (FIFTH TO FOURTH CENTURIES BC)

INTRODUCTION:
The new spirit

A new Greece arose from the Persian wars. The victory of Greek 'freedom' over the Persians was accompanied by an unprecedented intellectual revolution. In Athens this was the start of what is sometimes called 'the Age of the Greek Enlightenment' because it shares two characteristics with the European eighteenth century: rationalism and an enthusiasm for intellectual discovery. Aristotle himself bears witness to this enthusiasm, though not without irony: 'Since they were filled with pride after their exploits in the Persian wars, they began to engage in all sorts of studies, indiscriminately, but always seeking new knowledge.'

A number of different factors encouraged the blossoming of this new spirit. At the end of the sixth century the influences of an increasing use of coinage, more and more cultural exchanges and the criticism of traditional beliefs by thinkers like Xenophanes or Heraclitus all combined to undermine the old ideal of aristocratic education based on the cultivation of hereditary natural virtues and imitation of the examples of the past. This was also a time of political change: the 'tyrannical' regimes were gradually disappearing. In Athens, after the tyranny of Pisistratus, the reforms of Cleisthenes, completed by Ephialtes, established a democratic regime. Every Athenian citizen was invited to be involved in the life of the city, to have an opinion, in other words to adopt a political role. However, the need to get one's view accepted in the assembly required new qualities of thought and expression which only an intellectual education could provide. The Sophists took it upon themselves to supply this education.

The Sophists were itinerant teachers who went from city to city, offering paid lessons. Their teaching had a practical aim: rather than seeking to understand the universe as the Ionian philosophers had, they tried to teach people how to administer their property and to conduct state business most effectively. 'The object of my teaching' said Protagoras, 'is prudence for each man in the administration of his house and, as for city matters, the skill to conduct them to perfection in both speech and actions.'

The Sophists were above all masters of rhetoric: they taught the art of speaking well (*eu legein*, which means expressing oneself well, but also right thinking for the Greek word *logos* means 'speech' in the sense of spoken word, what is spoken, and 'reason' or 'reasoning'). Gorgias tried to elevate prose to the dignity of poetry. Prodicus attempted to distinguish synonyms from each other with a subtlety which often stimulated Plato's irony; the same goes for Hippias (although his polymath ideal goes far beyond the sphere of the *logos*) and Protagoras himself, whose study on *orthoepeia* (correct speech) is mentioned by Plato in the *Phaedrus*.

Two tendencies can be observed: Gorgias seems to have been primarily concerned with form. In the *Encomium of Helen*, one of the few speeches of his that we have, he extols the power of speech as a tyrant that bewitches the listener's soul. To charm his audience the orator plays with sonority and rhythms, utters a great many clauses of the same length with a final rhyme, constantly uses chiasmus and antithesis, metaphor and poetic language, and abuses rhetorical devices. Thus he intoxicates his listeners rather than persuading them with reasoned argument. He does not so much analyse facts as alter their meaning to suit the demands of audience and circumstances; the most important things are the suitability of the ideas and their expression. Prose thus becomes the rival of poetry, with the latter's magic power to seize hold of the listeners' souls. Rhetoric – in other words a technique that could be learned – replaced the divine gift of inspiration.

Protagoras was interested in dialectics. He is seen as the instigator of the rhetorical debates, of which the works of Thucydides and Euripides provide many examples. In his major work, *Antilogiae* (contradictory arguments) he is said to have proclaimed that on any subject two opposing arguments can be made, adding that he was able to make the weaker cause triumph. Aristophanes and Aristotle were horrified, yet one can see how, for Thucydides, this art of -antilogy and contradictory debate provided a valuable method for analysing historical situations. The practice of antilogy involved new intellectual tools, including the argument based on probability (*ta eikota*). This argument is based on what public opinion believes to be possible, referring to the general rather than the universal (which alone is necessary), and can thus deal with exceptions and contradictions.

To gain an idea of the subtlety of the reversals which the manipulation of this kind of reasoning permitted, we shall turn to Thucydides' master Antiphon. Three judicial speeches have come down to us under the name of Antiphon the orator, and three exercises of rhetorical virtuosity, the *Tetralogies*. As its name suggests, a tetralogy was a series of four speeches – two of accusation and two of defence – supposedly to be delivered during the trial of someone accused of a violent crime. The orator's art consisted in drawing opposing conclusions from the same facts from one speech to the next. The arguments based on 'the probable' therefore have a vital part to play in this exercise.

In the first speech the accuser bases his argument on the enmity between the accused and his victim, seeing this as a sign of the defendant's guilt. The latter however inverts the argument: 'If the violence of my hatred is a likely clue in your eyes, it is even more likely that, before acting, I should have seen the suspicion that would fall on me: even if I thought someone else was premeditating the murder, I should have stopped him.'

This examination of 'the probable' rests on psychological observations and analyses of human motivations, implying an attempt to classify human behaviour. The same trend can be seen in the use of maxims, which was widespread in fifth-century texts. This was the time when what we call the 'social sciences' (psychology, sociology, politics and ethics) were founded.

All these discoveries were made in a climate of great intellectual enthusiasm; 'arts' (*technai*) were being developed in every field: besides the art of oratory there were the arts of flute-playing, cooking, building war machines or architecture, and above all, as we shall see, medicine. Everywhere people sought to understand, to know, to evaluate and see clearly. Everything was a subject for argument; nothing was taboo and all traditional beliefs were closely examined. It was the end of the religious concept of the world which had held sway until then. 'With regard to the gods,' said Protagoras, 'I cannot feel sure either that they are or that they are not, nor what they are like in figure; for there are many things that hinder sure knowledge, the obscurity of the subject and the shortness of human life.' People put their trust in human intelligence.

There was a belief in progress; concepts of human history were turned upside-down. The pessimistic view of a golden age followed by decadence which we find in Hesiod was replaced by a history of human progress from civilization. The stages of humanity's material progress and successive discoveries were celebrated by the three tragedians. In *Prometheus* Aeschylus praises the gifts of the Titan, while Sophocles exalts human greatness in a famous chorus from *Antigone*, 'There are many wonders in this world, none is greater than man', and Euripides echoes them in the *Suppliant Women*. This resolutely rationalist and humanist approach, which makes of man, according to Protagoras, 'the measure of all things', is also to be found in the medical writings of the Hippocratic collection.

The Hippocratic collection

This was also the period when medicine, which had long been no more than a rudimentary practice combining magical treatments with a few natural remedies, became a rational art and sought to define the rules of empirical practice. The sixty or so medical treatises in Ionian dialect which have survived under the name of Hippocrates demonstrate this clearly. It is not easy to determine which of these writings are the work of the 'father of medicine', Hippocrates himself, who was almost certainly born in Cos around 460 into a school of physicians who called themselves 'Asclepiadae'; however, the majority of the treatises seem to date from the late fifth or early fourth century and their all-pervading concern with rationality gives them their unity. The analysis of the causes (or aetiology) of illnesses, their prognosis and treatment were all subject to rational enquiry; explanations involving divine influence and all recourse to magic were rejected. The author of the treatise *On the Sacred Disease* strongly criticises the errors of those who attribute this illness to the influence of a god and states that, far from being a 'sacred' disease, epilepsy has natural causes like other illnesses. From the observations that they amassed, doctors sought to discover the laws of human nature (*phusis*), to analyse the components of *The Nature of Man* (the title of a treatise) and to identify the influences to which it is sensitive. The concept of 'nature', which the Milesians applied to the entire universe, was transferred to human beings, who were thenceforward considered as a structured, organised whole which had to be understood to be treated and kept healthy. Thus the treatise *On Airs, Waters and Places* is a treatise on Environment, and discusses the influence of climate on health and temperament; other treatises pose problems of method or the definition of the art of medicine (*On Ancient Medicine* or *On the Art*). In the early nineteenth century, Laënnec was struck by the admirable sense of clinical observation to be found in treatises such as the

Epidemics, to the extent that he gave Hippocratic empiricism as his model in his thesis on *The Doctrine of Hippocrates* (1804).

We know that Gorgias had a brother who was a doctor. We know from Plato's writings that the doctor Eryximachus never missed a single one of Protagoras' lectures. Like the Sophists, doctors went from city to city offering their services. They all knew each other and lived in the same intellectual climate. It was in Athens that this new spirit found a home. It is true that Protagoras came from Abdera in Thrace and Gorgias from Leontinoi in Sicily, while Hippocrates was from Cos; yet Sophists and doctors came to stay in Athens, which became the centre of Greek cultural life. Whereas, before the fifth century, Solon was the only Athenian author who has passed into posterity, between 450 and 350 everything came from or converged on Athens. It was in Athens that the tragedy and comedy competitions, launched within fifty years of each other, were at their most brilliant with the names of Aeschylus, Sophocles, Euripides and Aristophanes; it was in Athens that history came into being (Herodotus spent time in Athens and was involved in the foundation of the Panhellenic colony of Thurioi, which Pericles established and whose laws were drawn up by Protagoras); it was in Athens that the Sophists discussed philosophy and made advances in rhetoric; and it was in Athens that Socrates was born and died. All of Greece was, for a time, contained in Athens.

3

THEATRE

The Athenian theatre, which was popular and national in the full sense, was closely bound to the city and its gods. Its productions were staged for all the citizens in the context of a state-run festival. The state decided which authors would be allowed to compete (three tragedians, who each presented three tragedies and one satyrical drama, and between three and five comic writers, who each put on a single play), required rich citizens to pay for the shows, gave money to poorer ones to ensure that they could attend and set up a panel of judges representative of the entire community to name the winners. Fifth-century theatre was thus a highly political genre. This can clearly be seen in Old Comedy, which mocks contemporary statesmen and claims to give useful advice to the city. However, it was also true of tragedy; though this genre held the present at a distance and generally took its subjects from myth, it centred on the problems of communal life in fifth-century Athens.

The theatre was also closely bound up with the cult of Dionysus. The plays were staged during the Dionysian festivals (the Lenaia around the end of January, the Great or City Dionysia near the end of March), in a theatre that bore Dionysus' name and in the presence of his statue and priest; they were also preceded and followed by processions and sacrifices in honour of the god. In this light the importance of ritual elements in both tragedy and comedy are easier to grasp.

The plays were staged in the open air. All parts were acted by men, who wore masks (painted white for women). The acting area was split into two areas, with the stage platform, where the actors performed, raised a little above the orchestra, where the chorus stood. Tangent to the orchestra circle was a wooden edifice, the *skēnē*, with a terraced roof (where the actors could also appear). This wooden building might represent a palace, temple, house or even a cave.

What happened there was usually out of sight of the spectators; however, a moveable platform, which could be pushed through the doors of the *skēnē* (the *eccyclēma*), enabled the audience to be shown the results of the actions which were taking place inside the building. Besides this, a kind of crane called 'machine' (*mēkhanē*), made it possible for the characters to appear in the air. The combination of all these elements made Greek theatre a highly stylised art.

Tragedy

Greek tragedy as we still know and read it today can be summed up in three names, Aeschylus, Sophocles and Euripides, and is entirely contained within the seventy or so years between the staging of Aeschylus' *Persians* (472) and Sophocles' *Oedipus at Colonus* (401).

However, the tragic genre came into being before these works and survived long after them. Tragedies intended for the stage were still being written at least until the first century BC and we know of more than two hundred tragic poets from fragments. Among these was Phrynichus, who invented historical tragedy before Aeschylus, Ion of Chios, contemporary of Sophocles, and Agathon, whose reputation in his own time was as great as that of Euripides.

The origins of the genre, which is itself so well defined in space and time, are obscure and disputed. They may have been religious (according to some, *tragoedia*, literally 'goat song', grew out of songs honouring Dionysus and sung by a chorus of satyrs clad in goatskins). According to others it was connected to funerary cults and cathartic rituals during which a goat was sacrificed, political (the first tragedy competitions were set up under the tyranny of Pisistratus) or literary (the rhapsodes' competitions were the ancestors of those for tragedy). Scholars still disagree on this.

In one sense tragedy was heir to the epic. For Greek tragedy, like epic, took its subjects from myth rather than history (historical tragedies like Phrynichus' *Capture of Miletus* or Aeschylus' *Persians* are exceptions that prove the rule). However, unlike epic, it focuses on a single episode, replaces the alternation of narrative and speech characteristic of Homeric poetry with the opposition between speech and song, and between collectivity (the chorus, formed first of fifteen and later of twelve people) and individuals (the actors, who were originally two and later became three). The tragic text is rigorously structured by the alternation of parts spoken by the actors and songs sung by the chorus.

Thus there would be a (spoken) prologue, followed by the *parodos* or entry of the chorus (sung), the (spoken) episodes separated by 'stationary songs in one place' (*stasima* in Greek) and the exit (*exodos*). The rigidity of this division was sometimes moderated by songs alternating between the chorus and the actors (such as the *kommos*, a lament shared by the chorus and those on stage) or recitatives sung by the actors. Greek tragedy was thus both dramatic and lyric in nature: the action was performed by the actors while an ever-present, ever-powerless chorus gave it a public dimension (judging it according to collective values) as well as a heightened pathetic intensity (the chorus as 'ideal spectator' acted as a mediator between the actors and the audience, to whom it communicated its emotions).

As well as its fixed structure, the tragic genre also had a history, illustrated by the three great names of Aeschylus, Sophocles and Euripides.

Aeschylus (525–456) was the true 'creator of tragedy'[1] His productive career (seventy-three plays according to some, ninety according to others) covered the first half of the fifth century and was very successful (thirteen prize-winning plays). All we have left of his work, apart from some fragments, is seven tragedies. We should note that only four of these are truly complete: the *Persians* (472) and *Agamemnon*, the *Choephori* and the *Eumenides*, which together form the *Oresteia* (458). The remaining three are the opening (the *Suppliant Maidens*, c. 463, and almost certainly *Prometheus*) or closing (*Seven Against Thebes*, 467) sections of trilogies that have not been preserved.

Aeschylus lived through the main stages of Athens' transformation into a democracy. According to ancient biographers, he belongs to the glorious generation of Marathon fighters; ten years later he fought at Salamis and may even have participated in Plataea, the last great battle of the Persian wars. In the *Persians* he evokes the battle of Salamis, showing to the victors those whom they have recently defeated. It is easy to imagine a partisan work on this theme; however, the tragedy sets up these contemporary events as an example: the misfortune of a king who had burnt the gods' temples and violated natural order proves to all that 'pride (*hybris*), ripening, bears its crop, the wheat-ear of disaster (*atē*); and reaps harvest of all tears' (820–822).

The *Persians*, which does not separate individual misfortune from a people's disaster, best exemplifies a theatre which gives exceptional importance to the chorus and always emphasises the collective dimension of events. For Aeschylus' characters are not isolated individuals: they belong to a city; they are part of a lineage, as the form of the trilogy itself demonstrates in uniting the destinies of three generations (Atreus and Thyestes, Agamemnon and Aegisthus, Orestes and Electra in the *Oresteia*); lastly, they are closely connected to the gods.

For the gods are everywhere. They are in the foreground of *Prometheus*, in which humanity is presented only by Io. They also play a central role in the *Eumenides*; Apollo and the Furies struggle over Orestes, who owes his acquittal to the deciding vote of Athena. Even when they do not appear on stage, the gods constantly and mysteriously guide the action and make their presence felt by divine signs such as omens and dreams.

Aeschylus' theatre, which binds individuals to groups and human beings to gods, also links the present to the most distant past. This connection is marked in structural terms, in both the *Persians* and *Agamemnon*, by an important scene in the middle of the play in which a flashback to the most distant past is followed by a prophecy concerning the future. It also manifests itself through the workings of a retributive principle which causes the present to mirror the past. Lastly, it is reflected in the conclusion of the *Oresteia*, which asserts that a new order is only viable if it integrates some elements of the old order. This can be seen both at the political level – the 'new' council of the Areopagus, which replaces the 'ancient' Furies in judging cases of murder, adopts their principles – and at the cosmic level – an agreement is reached between the Moira and 'Zeus the all-seeing' and a final procession reunites the Furies and Athene, the old and the new.

These ideas are translated into a highly concrete art, which always reveals the essence of a character or situation in an immediate way, through spectacle, image or myth. Appearance is never misleading and words do not belie the expectations created by the face, as demonstrated by the character of Power in *Prometheus*. Tableaux have a symbolic value: punishment duplicates the crime and the end of the *Cheophori*, when the corpses of Cassandra and Aegisthus are brought forward on the *eccyclēma* is the counterpart of the end of *Agamemnon*, showing the corpses of Clytemnestra and Agamemnon. Images take the place of explanation: the truth of tyranny which treats men like animals is shown in the image of the yoke in the *Persians, Prometheus* and the *Oresteia*. Myth replaces theory: by making the Furies daughters of Night, and Night alone, Aeschylus places them on the side of darkness, femininity and negativity.

It is often impossible to separate the visual from the verbal images in an art in which all levels converge. The purple carpets that Clytemnestra spreads under Agamemnon's feet are not simply decorative; they symbolise the riches of a royal house destroyed by the king who tramples on them and prefigure the cloths in which Agememnon is later trapped by his wife. Lastly, their colour is that of blood, recalling the blood previously spilt by Agamemnon in Aulis and Troy. Such extraordinary integration of levels no doubt explains the impact of this theatre, whose archaic grandeur struck the Ancients themselves.

Sophocles (497–405) was the second of the great tragedians, but his exceptional longevity enabled him to compete against both Aeschylus and Euripides. Of his vast and constantly successful *oeuvre* (he wrote 123 plays, won first prize eighteen times and was never placed last), we have only seven tragedies plus some fragments.

Only two of the plays have been dated with any certainty: *Philoctetes* (409) and *Oedipus at Colonus* (staged in 401). We also know that *Antigone* was staged a little before 441. The following order, based on a combination of information given by ancient biographies and scholia, stylistic criteria and literary criticism, is generally accepted: *Ajax*, *Antigone*, *Women of Trachis*, *Oedipus the King*, *Philoctetes*, *Oedipus at Colunus*; but the date of *Electra* and above all its relation to Euripides' tragedy of the same name are still a matter of debate.

The little information that tradition has passed down to us about Sophocles' life does not help us to grasp the complexity of his plays. If we are to believe the comic poet Phrynichus, this painter of suffering was in fact a 'happy' man. The poet who gives us a most enigmatic image of the gods was pious (he contributed to the establishment of the cult of Asclepius in Athens and was himself honoured as a hero after his death) and political events do not seem to have marked his work, although he was closely involved with the history of Athenian imperialism as *Hellenotamias,* that is, 'treasurer of the league of Delos', *strategos* 'general' and *proboulos*, that is, member of the committee on public safety responsible for taking emergency measures after the Sicilian disaster.

In order to understand the work of an artist who was so conscious of his art (he is said to have written a treatise on the chorus), it is more useful to turn to literary history and Aristophanes, who saw Sophocles as a poet 'apart' and kept him out of the conflict between Aeschylus and Euripides in the *Frogs*.

Aristophanes' view is borne out by a comparison between Sophocles' *Electra* and the two tragedies of Aeschylus and Euripides dealing with the same subject (the return of Orestes and his murder of his mother Clytemnestra). Unlike Euripides, Sophocles changes neither the setting of the action nor the status of the characters; yet his innovations, though more discreet, are none the less real. He dispenses with the connected trilogy and concentrates the action in a single play at a moment of crisis (the day of Orestes' arrival in Argos). He profoundly transforms the structure of the play by delaying the moment of recognition between brother and sister, placing it in the last third of a play dominated throughout by the heroine. The gods also become more distant; in the *Choephori* the gods had the initiative: Apollo ordered Orestes to avenge his father; in *Electra* the incentive comes from human beings: Orestes asks the oracle at Delphi how he can avenge himself against his father's murderers. Even the human universe seems to shrink: Agamemnon's murder is no longer an affair of state leading to the establishment of a tribunal, but simply a family affair which ends in the palace of the Pelopids.

Attention is thus concentrated on individuals and their decisions. Rather than paying for the crimes of the Labdacids, by dying, Antigone is fulfilling a resolution that she has taken alone and maintained to the end, against all advice and threats. She goes down to Hades 'of her own will'. And all the greatness of Sophocles' heroes stems from their desire to place honour above life and to bear the consequences of their choices to the end.

But the heroes' actions have their place in an order which is obscurely dominated by the gods. In *Ajax* a number of troubling coincidences suggest a mysterious link between the death of Ajax, who kills himself with the sword he has been given by Hector, and that of Hector himself, who was tied to Achilles' chariot with Ajax's baldric; they seem to demonstrate that 'all things at all times are contrived for mortals by the Gods' (1037).

Compared to the Gods, Sophocles' heroes are nothing but ghosts or a fleeting shadow. Ajax is led astray by the gods; Deianeira, the heroine of *Women of Trachis* 'did altogether wrong, but her intent was good' (1136): trying to regain Heracles' love by use of a philtre, she poisons him instead. In *Oedipus the King* Oedipus is constantly unable to keep a hold on his investigation and is destroyed by the very intelligence which makes him great.

This theatre, in which things are always understood 'too late', after the event, when it's no longer any use, makes constant use of irony and insistently contrasts appearance and reality. Sophocles' heroes do not always do as they want: for example, Ajax wants to re-establish his honour by killing those who have insulted it, but loses it when he massacres sheep and cattle. They may be trapped by the words they say without understanding their true meaning, as Oedipus condemns himself to the most terrible exile when he curses Laius' murderer. Lastly, they sometimes unwittingly rejoice in the cause of their own downfall, as Aegisthus looks with joy at the veiled corpse, believing it to be that of Orestes, when it is in fact Clytemnestra.

Indeed, Sophocles' art is one of contrast through and through. We can see this in the characters, in pairs of sisters such as Antigone and Ismene or Electra and Chrysothemis, where one embodies the 'heroic temper'[2] and the other conventional values, or in the juxtaposition of the ambitious, ungrateful sons of Oedipus and his daughters who are models of filial piety in *Oedipus at Colonus*. It can also be found in the confrontation of opposites in *Antigone*: there is conflict first between the decrees of the sovereign and the gods' unwritten laws, then between the seer's wisdom and the king's power. The dramatic structure of the plays too is governed by a series of oppositions. Sophocles' first three tragedies, *Ajax*, *Antigone* and *Women of Trachis*, are diptych-plays which are clearly divided into two parts by the death of a major character. In *Oedipus the King*, the contrast between the prologue and the *exodos* provides a stark manifestation of the tragic reversal of fortunes: the king, surrounded by a suppliant people on their knees, has become a blind man from whom people shrink in horror. Moreover, in this tragedy, as in *Ajax*, the catastrophe's horror is emphasised by the joyful song of the chorus which immediately precedes it.

This art of contrast is sober, economical with words and scenic effects. The images are discreet, almost banal, and details apparently insignificant most anodine are in fact vitally important. Even the silences are meaningful: the speechless despair of Eurydyce and Deianeira on hearing the news that kills them is more eloquent than a long tirade. Few objects are displayed on stage, but those that are have a particular symbolic power, for example, the bow Philoctetes inherited from Heracles, which is the visible symbol of his fame.

Finally, Sophocles' art is harmonious. Formal balance introduces order into chaos; the very misfortune of Oedipus, bears witness to the order of the world (since it proves the truth of the oracles) and to human greatness (by revealing human intelligence and endurance). This paradoxical combination no doubt explains the traditional view of Sophocles as 'the most Homeric' of poets and his work as the most perfect form of tragedy.

Euripides (484–406) is the last of the great tragedians. He took part in a competition for the first time in 455, three years after Aeschylus' *Oresteia* and thirteen years after the first plays of Sophocles, who survived him by a few months. He was thus Aeschylus' heir and Sophocles' rival.

His *oeuvre*, less extensive than that of Sophocles, is by far the best preserved. Of the ninety-two plays he is said to have written, nineteen have come down to us under his name, although his authorship of two of these, the satyrical drama *Cyclops* and the tragedy *Rhesus*, is contested. This abundance testifies to the extraordinary diffusion of his work in the Hellenistic period.

Seven of Euripides' tragedies can be dated with certainty: *Alcestis* (438), *Medea* (431), *Hippolytus* (428), *Trojan Women* (415), *Orestes* (408), *Iphigenia in Aulis* and the *Bacchae*, which were staged after the author's death. As far as the others are concerned, the following chronology is generally agreed: the *Heracleidae* (430–28), *Andromache* (425), *Hecuba* (424), the *Suppliant Maidens* (423), *Ion* (418–14), *Electra* (417–15), *Heracles* (417–15), *Iphigenia in Tauris* (413), the *Phoenician Women* (412–8). In addition to these complete works we have more and longer fragments than for either Aeschylus or Sophocles. Euripides' posthumous success contrasts with the semi-failure he experienced in his lifetime (he won only four prizes) which doubtless explains his departure for Macedonia and the court of the tyrant Archelaos near the end of his life.

His work was deeply influenced by the development of the Peloponnesian War. His early political tragedies, the *Heracleidae* and the *Suppliant Women*, depict an Athens fighting for justice and confident of victory. Yet even in the *Suppliant Women*, and more so in the early Trojan tragedies (*Andromache* and *Hecuba*), there is pity for the vanquished and criticism of war's absurdity. These themes lie at the heart of the *Trojan Women*, which was staged shortly after the Melian expedition and the massacre which followed. Three years later *Helen* shows the pointlessness of a war in which the two sides fought for 'an idol of the clouds' (706). A little later, the *Phoenician Women* shows a fratricidal fight reminiscent of the conflicts of 411 between the Athenian oligarchs and democrats.

Euripides' work, with its characteristic innovation and dissonance, is usefully illuminated by the high-contrast portrait of its author that tradition has given us. If we are to believe the comedies of

Aristophanes and the ancient biographies that drew on them, this democratic poet who gave voice even to women and slaves was a lonely man who lived in a cave. He was both a passionate man and an intellectual, connected to everyone and everything of importance in the Athens of his time, from Anaxagoras to the Sophists and Socrates. It seems he was also one of the first Athenians to have a library.

Euripides experimented with everything. He modified the traditional organisation of the tetralogy at least once: with *Alcestis*, he replaced the satyric drama that usually followed the three tragedies with a work that has elements of both tragedy and comedy. His treatment of myths was often innovative, and he was undoubtedly the first to stage Hecuba's revenge. He invented a whole plot for the *Orestes*, profiting from the silence of tradition, and when he did use a traditional plot he profoundly changed its meaning, as the example of *Electra* shows.

In this tragedy, which returns to the subject of the *Choephori* and shows Orestes' revenge, Euripides transports the action to the countryside and introduces an unexpected character in the Prologue (the peasant to whom Aegisthus has given Electra in marriage). He also changes the social status and personality traits of the traditional characters, marrying Electra off, turning Aegisthus into a welcoming host and presenting a less negative image of Clytemnestra, who 'is far from happy at what she has done' (1105–6). Finally, he rewrites the scene of the brother and sister's mutual recognition, entirely transforms the circumstances in which revenge is carried out and emphasises the horror of matricide.

Euripides enjoyed inventing paradoxical situations: in the *Trojan Women*, Cassandra celebrates the glory of the vanquished in a new kind of funeral oration. In his *Heracles*, he even shows a goddess of madness preaching wisdom (855–7). Lastly, and perhaps most importantly, Euripides introduced significant changes into dramatic technique: in the *Suppliant Women* and the *Orestes* he brought human beings in at a level previously reserved for the gods; he developed lyrical exchanges between chorus and characters and ever freer monodies in addition to, or in place of, the chorus' songs; in *Orestes* he even has the messenger's narrative sung by a Phrygian slave.

This resolutely new theatre is rich in contradictions. It juxtaposes realism and exoticism, unites the comic with the pathetic and is at once both intellectual and irrational. On the one hand, Euripides brings tragedy closer to reality, placing his heroes in a contemporary world, surrounding them with ordinary characters and removing them from their pedestals: their language is close to that of daily life (Euripides makes the iambic trimeter more flexible and uses less elevated language than Aeschylus); they carry out everyday tasks – Ion sweeps the area in front of the temple of Apollo at Delphi – and some are even dressed in rags. We only know *Telephus*, the most famous of Euripides' 'kings in rages', from fragments; however, we still have the shipwrecked Menelaus of *Helen* and the old men with withered bodies who people the plays from the *Heracleidae* to the *Bacchae*. Such physical degradation accompanies the heroes' moral decline: in *Iphigenia in Aulis* Agamemnon is a coward, Odysseus a demagogue and Achilles a young man concerned for his reputation.

While depicting everyday life, Euripides was also in love with the exotic and beautiful. He places his Helen, who has never been to Troy, in a fairytale Egypt, where girls 'by the shining blue / water, and on the curl of the grass / there laid out the coloured wash / in the bed of the young rushes / to dry' (179–82). In these richly elaborated lyrics, which contrast with the prosaic dialogue, Euripides evokes the splendour of the heroic world. Yet such aestheticism is never gratuitous: Egypt counterbalances Troy in *Helen* and the beauty of the goddesses who come to give themselves up to Paris' judgement in 'the luxuriant vale, in a mountain pool/ cooled by springs' (*Andromache*, 284) stresses by contrast the atrocity of the play's present.

Euripides sometimes approaches comedy, yet he is also the most tragic of poets, as the example of the *Bacchae* shows. The play contains a scene verging on the burlesque, where two old men, kitted out in fawn skins and each carrying a thyrsus, dance in honour of Dionysus. Yet there are pathetic narratives and horrifying tableaux: through a messenger's speech Euripides spares no details of the scene in which Agave and her sisters tear Pentheus limb from limb with their bare hands. He even lays the horror of a dismembered corpse before his audience's eyes: Agave, who enters carrying her son's head in her arms, is soon followed by her father Cadmus, bearing the remains of his grandson, whose 'body lies – no easy task to find – scattered / Under hard rocks, or in the green woods' (1219–20).

Euripides speaks directly to the emotions through a great many violent images and concrete descriptions: he shows the death of Hippolytus, Polymestor's bloody eye sockets and Heracles sleeping surrounded by the dead bodies of his children; he luxuriates horribly in the details of the death of Creusa and her father, victims of Medea's poison. The pathos is often heightened by the victims' powerlessness:

innocent children pay with their lives for their father's crimes (Jason's children in the *Medea*) or, worse, their heroism (Astyanax in the *Trojan Women*); old men can only groan over their miseries and old women weep for their sons who have died in war.

Euripides' work is also an intellectual feast. His plays show us heroes who use trickery and persuasion to achieve their ends, whether in *Hecuba*, *Iphegenia in Tauris*, *Helen* or indeed the *Medea* since the heroine is a 'clever' woman, as good with words as she is with poison. The plays echo the discussions current in intellectual circles at the time: in *Hippolytus* Phaedra seems almost to be answering Socrates when she maintains that it is possible to do evil while knowing what is good. Their form reflects the intellectualism of the author and his period, as can be seen from the prologues, whose 'clarity' and 'precision' were praised by the Ancients, the debates in which each argument is rigorously answered by another, or the 'sentences' which draw general truths from particular cases.

Yet this intellectual theatre also provides the finest demonstration of the power of irrational both within and outside human beings. Euripides depicts madness: he describes with almost clinical precision the sudden hallucinations (in *Orestes*) or the mad person's slow return to reason after a terrible crime (in *Heracles* and the *Bacchae*). He also shows people dominated by their passions, such as Phaedra. Finally, he stages a series of irrational changes of mind, particularly in *Iphigenia in Aulis*.

His gods are no more reasonable than his men. The Apollo of *Electra* takes 'unwise' decisions (1246), while other characters, such as Aphrodite in *Hippolytus* or Dionysus in the *Bacchae*, are 'like mortals in vindictiveness' (*Bacchae*, 1348) by exacting excessive revenge on those who have dared to deny their power or their divinity. In *Heracles*, Hera goes so far as to ruin, on a whim, a hero who 'alone held up the honours of the gods / when they wilted at the hands of men' (852–3). These changeable gods who 'leap at random between love and hate' (*Trojan Women*, 67–8) are like fortune, which 'has a habit of leaping about in different directions, like a capricious man' (1204–6).

All in all, in Euripides' world 'There is much disorder among Gods and among men as well' (*Iphigenia in Tauris* 572). This disorder explains Euripides' poetics in his late plays, with the chaotic movement of plots full of sudden and unexpected events, the abrupt juxtaposition of formally heterogeneous scenes and the fragmented psychology of the heroes, which makes Euripides the most 'modern' of the tragedians.

Comedy

Ancient comedy was an Athenian creation. The genre came into being in the early fifth century – the earliest rankings we have for the comedy competition date from 486 – died with Aristophanes and is illustrated today only by the nine comedies he wrote during the Peloponnesian war: the *Acharnians*, the *Knights*, the *Clouds*, the *Wasps* (which Racine imitated in *The Litigants*), *Peace*, the *Birds*, *Lysistrata*, *Thesmophoriazusae* and the *Frogs*.

Of the poets who preceded him we have only names – Magnes, Cratinus, Crates, Pherecrates, Phrynichus and Eupolis – and fragments of varying length, none of which date from before 450 BC. When, in the fourth century, Aristotle sought to retrace the origins of the comic genre in his *Poetics*, they had already been forgotten. He could say nothing precise about them: 'Nor is it known who introduced masks, or prologues, or a plurality of actors, and other things of that kind' (*Poetics*, 1449, B4). He suggests however that comedy had its 'first beginnings in improvisation' and that it was linked to 'the leaders of the phallic songs (*phallika*) which still survive today as traditional institutions in many of our cities'. In its origins comedy appears linked to the cult of Dionysus and in particular one of its most ancient forms, the country Dionysia.

These were organised around a phallophoria (processions with the phallus) which was originally a propitiatory rite intended to encourage fertility in gardens, field and homes. This agrarian rite, whose origins were lost in the mists of time, was associated in Greece with the honouring of Dionysus, god of exuberant vegetation, joy and orgiastic feasts that broke down all social hierarchies. In the fifth century the country Dionysia took place during the month of Poseidion (approximately December) in all the rural communities of Attica (the demes).

Aristophanes (*Acharnians* 241–83) gives an idea of what the Country Dionysia might have been like: a troupe of peasants, masked or daubed with wine lees, would go in procession through the village and across the fields, singing comical and bawdy songs, some improvised, some traditional (*phallikon*, see e.g. lines 261 and 263–79). They would carry a phallus (243), which was a fertility symbol, and the ceremony would continue with a sacrifice to Dionysus and end with drinking and a *kômos* (264).

Among other things, the Greeks used the name *kômos* for a group of more or less drunken revellers who wandered through the streets after a banquet, singing, dancing, shouting jibes at anyone else who was still out and ransacking their friends' houses for more drink. The work *kômos* also applied however to the racket made by a vengeful mob, including verbal and sometimes physical violence (Aristotle, fragment 558 Rose). Actors (*kômôdoi*, hence the derivation *kômôdia*, 'comedy') were therefore literally 'singers of the *kômos* which, at the country Dionysia, had something of both carnival and the French Charivari.

However, it is not possible to say when dramatic fiction was included in the celebrations, giving rise to a primitive form of comedy. To help us to understand how this may have happened, we can compare the parallel process by which farces and popular comedies emerged out of carnivals in early France. Aristotle thought that, like tragedy, comedy went back to Homer, who was also the author of a comic epic, the *Margites*. This is thought to have been in the same vein as the iambic poetry of satire and invective, or the Sicilian poetry of Epicharmus.

The Alexandrian critics divided the development of the comic genre into three stages: Old Comedy, into which category were placed the first nine of Aristophanes' comedies that had been preserved; Middle Comedy, illustrated for us only by Aristophanes' *Assembly of Women* and *Plutus*, and New Comedy, whose chief representative was Menander. A certain number of structural characteristics distinguish old comedy from later comic forms.

The original *kômos* was partly reflected in the structure of Attic comedy in the fifth century (as we know it through analysis of the eleven preserved plays of Aristophanes). Following the Prologue (introductory scene and start of the action) came the *eisodos* (or *parodos*), 'entry' of the chorus, consisting of twenty-four choreutae who danced and sang. In its canonical form an old comedy contained a *parabasis* in which the chorus leader (the coryphaeus) 'introduced himself' (*parabainei*) to the audience and addressed them directly in the name of the poet. The 'parabasis', which interrupted the action, was reminiscent of the *kômos* leader's calls to the peasant crowd that surrounded him. Comedy also frequently had a scene of *agôn*, a 'combat' or 'debate' between two theses, each upheld by an actor, in which the chorus participated. Lastly, a series of scenes illustrated the consequences of the hero's victory before the tumultuous exit of the chorus (*exodos*), which provided an echo of the unruly mob of the *kômos* at the end of the comedy.

However, as Zielinski[3] showed in the nineteenth century, the *agôn* and the *parabasis* followed precise rhythmic forms and used set metres. The parabasis was divided into seven parts: the *kommation*, a short transitional piece in which the actors were dismissed and the audience invited to listen to the 'anapaests', was followed by the *parabasis* proper, in anapaestic tetrameter (hence its name 'anapaests'); in this section the poet expressed his personal views on such things as his art or political life. This development was closed by the *pnigos* or 'suffocation', a brilliant finale carried along by a rapid rhythm. After this, sung and spoken sections were alternated. The songs, *ōdē* and *antōdē*, often highly poetic couplets, had their spoken counterparts in the *epirrhēma* and the *antepirrhēma*, generally written in trochaic tetrameter.

In this way old comedy reconciled two apparently opposite characteristics: a formal structure and rigorous metric framework on the one hand[4] and, on the other, within these set forms, almost total freedom of pace, tone and language and an unbridled and fantastical imagination. This element of the fantastic appeared from the outset in the role reserved for the chorus, which was one of the main actors in the comedy and often gave the play its title. It might comprise very colourful characters (exotic Babylonians or coal merchants from Acharnae), animals (birds, wasps, storks, goats, ants or bees, all titles of comedies), or more abstract entities (clouds, demes, cities) and its appearance was doubtless eagerly anticipated every time. The progression of each play was similarly fantastic: following a tenuous dramatic thread and indifferent to plausibility, old comedy brought together various comic forms, from farce to satire and personal invective, and all kinds of tone, from flights of lyricism to crude speech, acts and situations. Such is true of Aristophanes' comedies, anyway.

Aristophanes, whose family may have come from Aegina, was almost certainly born in Athens around 445. Little is known about him. He was barely 20 when he wrote his first play; the last to have survived, the *Plutus*, dates from 388, and it is believed that he died shortly after this date. Of the forty-four plays known to the Alexandrian scholars, only eleven have been preserved, most of which are contemporaneous with the Peloponnesian War (431–04). He is said to have put on the *Banqueters* in 427 and the *Babylonians* in the following year, both of which are lost. In 425 he staged the *Acharnians,* in which he attacks warmongers. Next came the *Knights* (424), a play criticising Cleon the 'demagogue'; the *Clouds* (423), a satire on Socrates, buried in his 'reflectory', and the Sophists, who were the leading thinkers of the day (we know that this caricature of Socrates was countered by Plato's marvellous pastiches: in the *Symposium* he pits Socrates against Aristophanes and Agathon, i.e.

the comic author and the tragic author); and the *Wasps* (422), a violent critique of the Athenian law courts. *Peace* (421), in which Aristophanes celebrated the end of hostilities, was followed in 414 by the *Birds*, a fantasy full of invention and poetry and, in 411, by *Lysistrata*, another plea for peace, and the *Thesmophoriazusae*, in which he attacks Euripides and condemns the return to war. The *Frogs*, which ridicules Euripides and praises Aeschylus, dates from 405.

Of course comedy, like tragedy, tells a story. Unlike tragedy, however, which took its subjects from the distant past of myth, comedy located its action in the most contemporary of settings. It constantly alluded to characters and events of the day (not necessarily a good thing for the survival of the plays, since the comic element disappears when the allusion is no longer obvious), doing its utmost to draw the audience into a wild game of Aunt Sally led by the master of ceremonies, the comic hero. For old comedy was not concerned with creating dramatic illusion; it made no claims to being anything other than a play. The conditions of representation themselves were mentioned on stage: in *Peace* Trygaeus asks the crane operator to be careful; in the *Knights* the audience is brought into the dialogue: 'shall I explain the trick to the audience?' a servant asks his associate.

Any means might be used to make people laugh, starting with what was on stage. The comedy stage was cluttered with objects, providing a very colourful image of daily life in Athens:[5] street scenes were followed by scenes at meetings, markets or, more often, kitchen and banquet scenes. For the hero of the play was first and foremost a belly concerned with satisfying his appetites abundantly and in peace. He would grope the girls who came within his reach, belch and defecate at will, gaily stuffing himself with food and emptying flagons of wine. His ultimate success at the end of the play was a vitalist triumph of bodily reality and its functions: he proclaimed that natural life was good.

This Rabelaisian character with his cunning and cynicism was also a discontented citizen, quick to criticise everything. The comedy would attack all kinds of bores with the briskness of a satirical review: warmongers, Lamachus the ridiculous bully, profiteers who went off on missions at the city's expense, public informers, sycophants – the scourge of Athens – politicians such as Cleon, Cleophon or Phormisios, Socrates and Euripides, the intellectuals in vogue, lyric poets and soothsayers. All of Athens would file past to be jeered at, much to the delight of the audience.

Should we look for a political 'message' behind Aristophanes' satire? Many have thought so; we, however, do not. The comedy was used to deride well-known characters; contemporary situations provided a pretext to vituperate in the name of the good old days against those who seemed to be plotting against the happiness of the greatest number. Rulers, current celebrities, women, all take a drubbing; crude words and easy jokes abound. This is part of the pleasure of these plays.

But Aristophanes' comedies are above all the creations of a free fantastical imagination. In them the craziest schemes are realised, such as a separate peace (the *Acharnians*), a city in the clouds (the *Birds*) or a sex-strike (*Lysistrata*). In this world, which makes free with the laws of reality, everything is possible: characters are carried up to Olympus by a beetle – a cheap substitute for Pegasus – or move in with the birds; poets are brought back to life. The whole universe is invited to the celebrations: not just Athens and Greece, but Olympus, heaven or the swamps of hell, where Dionysus loses his way while looking for a tragic poet. The most unlikely characters twirl like puppets in this ballet and any concern with psychological or social realism is outlawed.

This fantastical universe is supported by extraordinary verbal comedy. Aristophanes, like Rabelais, had a taste for endless lists, bringing together the most unlikely elements. He might name all the game and fish of the Greek world, creating a land of plenty on stage by the sheer force of his words, or provoke gales of laughter with his unexpected combinations: bizarre neologisms, puns, contrast between rhythm and content and parodies of tragic poetry. All these elements made the audience laugh and contributed to create a paradoxical, distorted, unreal world.

Though he plays with reality, Aristophanes takes language absolutely literally: metaphors become real and images incarnate. In Greek the same word – *spondè* – signifies both 'libation of wine' and 'truce'. In the *Acharnians* Dicaeopolis tastes the three flasks of wine that are brought to him to decide which truce he prefers. The demagogue who protects the people is often compared to a good dog; this is the origin of the burlesque trial in the *Wasps*, during which the Dog of Cydathenaeon (Cleon) is prosecuted by the Dog and Labes (Laches).[6]

The ability to make metaphors come to life and *Clouds* to take human shape: perhaps this is the greatest secret of the journey to the lands of Utopia and Nonsense on which the master of ancient comedy takes us.

The plays Aristophanes wrote during the ten years following the defeat of Athens have not come down to us. In the last two of his plays that we have – the *Assembly of Women* and *Plutus* – the humour starts to grate, and the creative vitality and talent for bringing metaphors to life seems diminished. In *Plutus* the links between chorus and action are gone: the chorus' songs are simply interludes. These two plays have been classed as Middle Comedy. By the time they were written, Ancient Comedy was definitively dead.

.

4

HISTORY

History before Herodotus

Our word 'history' comes from the Greek, from the Ionian word *historiē*, formed on the Indo-European root **wid-*, meaning 'see' and in the perfect, 'knowledge from sight'. The origins of history in the West lie in the taste for enquiry which expressed itself in every sphere in Ionia at the end of the sixth century (and was still inspiring the activities of Aristotle and the Lyceum at the end of the fourth century). Thus it has its source in the same curiosity as early science.

Prior to this the Greeks had satisfied their desire to know about the past with religion and myth. The epic served as history. In the sixth century the first 'historians', who were simply called 'prose-writers' (*suggrapheis* from *graphein*, 'to write') or 'logographers' often contented themselves with simply continuing the epic tradition of mythical narratives in prose. They would retrace the genealogy of the heroes and traditions concerning the ancient founding of cities. The work of Hecataeus, at the turn of the sixth and fifth centuries, illustrates this orientation of Ionian curiosity.

Hecataeus carried out geographical and ethnographical research in addition to his investigations of the past. His *Peregesis* (of which about 300 fragments have been preserved) was no doubt intended as a commentary for a map of the world, thought to have been similar to the earliest known map, which was drawn by Anaximander. Hecataeus also wrote four books of *Genealogies*. The first sentence of this collection made him famous: 'I write things as they seem true to me, for many of the tales of the Greeks are, in my opinion, ridiculous'. The results he obtained do not always reach the heights of his ambitions, for the subject matter of Hecataeus' *Genealogies* is the same – mythology and epic legends – as that of the epic poets. He was, however, the first to seek to establish a rational chronology for the heroic period, linking it to the historical period by a continuous chain of generations.

Thus, in the work of Hecataeus, history had already chosen its form, prose, and its dialect, Ionian.

Herodotus, 'father of history'

Herodotus was born around 485 in Halicarnassus in Asia Minor and had to go into exile very early on. He spent time in Athens and died as a citizen of Thurioi around 420 BC. He was a great traveller, who seems to have journeyed to almost all parts of the known world of his time. Besides the Greeks he was interested in the Lydians, the Massagetae, the Egyptians, the Babylonians, the Scythians and the Ethiopians, describing their countries (in terms of such things as climate, soil, vegetation and fauna) and customs (eating and sexual habits, religious beliefs, rites and political organisation). Continuing Hecataeus' research, he thus founded the Greek ethnographical tradition and outlined its field of study.

From the opening lines of his work, Herodotus proclaims himself to be the rival of Homer: he wants to preserve the memory of 'the astonishing achievements of both our own and the Asiatic peoples'.[1] Yet this search for the 'memorable' is undertaken in relation to a particular event from the recent past: the Persian wars, a conflict between the Greeks and the Barbarians, the West and the East. After recalling the Persian and Phoenician traditions according to which hostility between Asia and Greece dated from the mythical period, Herodotus resolutely turns his back on legend: 'I have no intention of passing judgement on its truth or falsity. I prefer to rely on my own knowledge, and to point out who it was in actual fact who first injured the Greeks' (I, 5). With these words Herodotus founded history. His *Histories* begin with the story of Croesus, the first barbarian to rule the Greeks of Asia.

The *Histories* consist of nine books, each bearing the name of a Muse, in what is undoubtedly a later division carried out by the Alexandrians. The first four recount the advance of the Persian empire after its foundation by Cyrus in 549, detailing Cyrus' victories over Croesus, king of Lydia, and Assyria and the Massagetae in Asia Minor (Book I), followed by Cyrus' son Cambyses' conquest of Egypt (Book II), the reign of Darius and his campaigns against Scythia, Thrace and Lydia (Books III and IV). Each new conquest by the Persian kings provides an opportunity for ethnographic discussions, of which the most famous and frequently referred to is the description of Egypt in Book II. The account of the Persian wars themselves opens with the Ionian revolt, whose beginnings are recounted in Book V. There are then a number of digressions devoted to the recent history of Sparta and Athens, the two main Greek cities of the time. Book VI describes the increasing number of Persian incursions into the Greek world and the victorious response by the Athenians, who repelled the Persians at Marathon. Finally, Books VII to IX tell the story of the second Persian war, Xerxes' mobilisation of the Barbarians and Greeks under Persian rule, the invasion of Greece, the heroic resistance of the Spartans at Thermopylae, the victory of the Greek fleet at Salamis in 480, followed by that of the land army at Plataea. The entire work concludes with the taking of Sestos by the Greeks and ends with an edifying fable illustrating the wisdom of Cyrus, the founder of the Persian empire, who remained attached to his people's ancient virtues.

Herodotus' *Histories* cover a great amount of time as well as space. His narrative is not structured according to chronology and goes back to the earliest periods whenever a people or an important character appear in the story: thus in discussing Croesus he goes back to Gyges, founder of the Mermnad dynasty. His chronology is limited to the establishment of reference points, based on the principle that one century corresponds to three generations.

Despite his vague chronological framework, Herodotus proves himself to be a historian in his concern to establish the facts and his effort to understand and analyse the causes of events. He has often been criticised for his 'naivety'; but this is to forget that, although he frequently refrains from deciding between the different oral traditions on which he relies to reconstruct the past, at other times, when faced with many versions of the same event, he does choose the one he considers to be most trustworthy. In his own way, Herodotus undertook historical criticism. Similarly, he seeks to complement the narrative with explanations, trying, for example, to uncover the causes of the conflicts between the Greeks and the Barbarians (Book I, 1). Yet his explanations are far from systematic: a smile from the tyrant of Corinth, a baby at the time, is enough to save him from death. Among the causes of the first Persian war Herodotus identifies Darius' wife Atossa's wish for Greek servants. Although there is some political analysis, the prime motive for action in the *Histories* is revenge.

Why did Croesus attack Cyrus? Because he 'had a craving to extend his territories, but there were two other reasons ... namely his trust in the oracle and his desire to punish Cyrus for his treatment of Astyages' (Book I, 73). Herodotus thus combines various levels of causality. Divine causes are superimposed on to considerations of a political or psychological order which lend themselves to rational calculation. For the world of Herodotus was one still dominated by the will of the gods, who maintained order and punished all forms of excess.

Herodotus' philosophy of history guaranteed his impartiality: he would write about small cities as well as large ones, for 'in this world nobody remains prosperous for long', and cities that were once great had often lost their importance and those which were currently great were once small (Book I, 5). It also conformed to the wisdom shown in the famous conversation in which Solon, the Athenian sage, teaches Croesus, who thought himself to be the happiest of men, that it is impossible to assess a man's happiness before his death (Book I, 30–3).

This rich, dense work has given rise to many different interpretations. Some see Herodotus as another Hecataeus, presenting a series of ethnographical discussions artificially stitched together; others stress the unity of his project and of the mode of analysis underlying his entire work; yet others prefer to see the coexistence of ethnography and history in the *Histories* as a sign of the gradual formation of a genre whose parameters were still not fixed. It is true that the narrative follows a firmer line in the last three books, where the information is more precise, the tone more clearly political and where there is more direct effort to provide an understanding of events. In its diversity Herodotus' work thus appears as a transition between Homer and Thucydides.

Thucydides and political history

With Thucydides we are no longer travelling into the cities of the wide world, enjoying their diversity or contemplating the fickleness of fortune. The focus of history is narrowed to an extraordinary degree: Thucydides only describes the war pursued by his own city in his own time.

An Athenian, born around 460, Thucydides belonged to an illustrious family, who had links with Thrace and owned gold mines in the region of the Strymon. It may have been this that resulted in his being a strategist in that region in 424. He was unable to prevent the Spartan Brasidas from taking Amphipolis and was exiled from Athens following this defeat. He did not return until after the city fell in 404. He is thought to have died in the first years of the fourth century BC, perhaps around 396,[1] leaving his work on the history of the Pelopennesian war unfinished.

Thucydides' work tells the story of the war of 431 to 404 between the two most powerful Greek cities, Athens and Sparta. The author is careful to justify his choice of subject, noting the conflict's importance, 'with more far-reaching effects than those of earlier wars' (Book I, 1), and his position as a privileged observer, since he was able, during his twenty-years exile, to find out what was happening on both the Athenian and the Lacedaemonian sides. His eight-volume narrative is unfinished. The first book describes the events leading up to the war and analyses the causes. Hostilities begin with Book II. Books II, III and IV each recount three years of war, leading up to the Amphipolis campaign, which ended the Ten Years' War. The peace of Nicias was signed in 421 (Book V, 24) and the end of Book V describes the following years of uneasy peace. Books VI and VII recount the Athenian expedition to Sicily (415–13) and Book VIII, whose structure is less clear, suddenly breaks off during the events of the winter of 411–10.

Thucydides was a contemporary of Hippocrates and pupil of the Sophists, whose prime concern was to relate the facts exactly. This concern led him to adopt a rigorous chronological order based on seasons, instead of following the order of succession of the eponymous magistrates of either city, which is a less precise method. Aware that versions of the same event 'differ according to the sympathies and memories of their witnesses', he drew up precise rules for historical criticism. This desire to be accurate is also apparent in the words which Thucydides uses. He does not try to relay the actual words used, seeking instead to remain faithful to the general idea of what was said. Lastly he does not allow any fantastical embellishments into his narrative. There are no gods in Thucydides' history:

> And it may well be that my history will seem less easy to read because of the absence of exotic detail. It will be enough for me, however, if these words of mine are judged useful by those who want to understand clearly the events which happened in the past and which (human nature being what it is) will, at some time or other and in much the same way, be repeated in the future.
>
> (Book I, 22)

The corollary of this new methodological rigour was an immense advance in the explanation of historical evolution. The analysis of the causes of the Peloponnesian war in the well-known Chapter 23 of Book I is admired by modern historians, who see it as the source for the model of causal explanation in history. For, beyond the incidents and quarrels which preceded the war, Thucydides distinguished 'the most true, but also the least admitted cause', which was the Lacedaemonian fear of Athenian expansion. It was Athenian imperialism that forced Sparta to war. Herodotus' juxtaposition of heterogeneous causes, including the gods, has been replaced by a rigorous distinction between apparent and fundamental causes, with no place left for supernatural causation. Thucydides restricts his considerations to the world of phenomena, seeking to 'see clearly' and provide understanding, he restricts his considerations to the world of phenomena, seeking to provide an exhaustive and acute analysis. Each fact mentioned is accompanied by explanatory elements such as material data, strategic or economic aims and psychological motivations. In this way Thucydides reconstitutes a rigorous chain of causality in which each fact appears as both the effect of a series of earlier events and the origin and cause of a series of later events. The result is perfect continuity and a narrative that acts as a kind of demonstration. This passion for causality excludes everything else: there is no room for anecdote, expressions of personal feelings or moral judgements, characteristics which again distinguish Thucydides from Herodotus.

To increase the rigour of his exposition, Thucydides provides the calculations and assumptions of the various protagonists of the action, putting words into their mouths. The tactical discussions attributed to the generals before a battle fortell its outcome. Political speeches respond to each other and to the narration in the manner of Protagoras' antilogies. They reveal the forces at work in history and contribute to the intelligibility of the narrative.

Intelligibility is not, however, synonymous with rationality. Thucydides accords a place to chance (*Tukhē*); he acknowledges that 'the event that occurs may, by chance, take a turn no less unexpected than human dispositions themselves'. He knows that human beings – the efficient cause of historical change – are not only notional beings, they are often driven by irrational impulses. He does not fail to describe the blindness of the mob, the rashness and errors of their leaders. Yet Thucydides' moral pessimism, which has been called his 'realism', has its counterweight in his analysis of the powers of reason, which makes effective action possible, as shown by the success of Themistocles and Pericles. Thus this historian who eschews anecdote, descriptions of physical and moral particularities or details of the private lives of the statesmen, grants an essential place to psychological causality. According to him the prosperity of Athens was partly due to the qualities of Pericles, while Alcibiades' failings 'largely contributed to his ruin' and 'the truest cause' of the war was Sparta's fear on seeing the rise of Athenian power.

Yet beyond these analyses, Thucydides' narrative makes it possible to grasp the logic of political development, which requires that once an empire has been formed, it must face the hostility of its subjects and is soon obliged to maintain itself by force; he also shows how boundless expansionism can lead an empire to its destruction. In this light the analysis of Athenian imperialism functions as an example and is, as its author wished it to be, 'a possession that will last forever'.

History in the fourth century

Herodotus's accomplishments and Thucydides were remarkable, each in their own way. Their successors in the fourth century did not remain at these heights. It should perhaps be noted in their defence that between 404 (the year when Athens was forced to bow to Sparta) and 323 (the year of Alexander's death), the history of the Greek cities was all 'trouble' and dissent (Xenophon, *Hellenica*, Book VII, 5, 27). During this time writers would produce sequels to Thucydides or *Hellenica*. Some of these were Theopompus, a student of Isocrates, Xenophon and the (unknown) author of the *Hellenica of Oxyrhynchus*, named after the town where the text was discovered in 1906.

However, other species of history came into existence. Local histories were still being written: Androtion wrote a chronicle of Athens (as Hellanicus had done in the fifth century). An interest in great men, which can even be seen in the *Hellenica*, gave rise to biographical writings: Xenophon wrote an *Agesilaus* and, after his twelfth book *Hellenica*, Theopompus wrote the fifty-eighth volume *Philippica*, a history of the Greek world centred on the person of Philip. Constitutional history[2] was also gaining independence; whereas, in Book III of his *Histories*, Herodotus had presented a debate on the comparative merits of various regimes, Xenophon wrote a whole treatise on the *Constitution of the Lacedaemonians*. Lastly with the first *universal history* Ephorus of Cyme, a student of Isocrates, the historical genre underwent a radical transformation. Unlike earlier works, this history, written by a scholar and compiler, was not based on the political experience and oral investigations of its author. Instead, it drew on archive materials and required the interpretation of historical documents. Unfortunately, like Theopompus' work, that of Ephorus is lost to us.[3]

The only historical work to have survived, that of the Athenian Xenophon, illustrates many of the trends described above. Xenophon was an Athenian from the deme of Erchia, born around 426(?). He had certainly been a member of Socrates' audience, if not actually a disciple (and perpetuated the memory of Socrates in his *Memorabilia*, *Oeconomicus*, *Symposium* and *Apology*). In 401, on the invitation of his Boeyotian friend Proxenus, he participated in the expedition of the ten thousand Greek mercenaries led by Cyrus against his brother Artaxerxes II, whom he wanted to replace at the head of the Persian empire. Then he fought for Sparta, whose king, Agesilaus, had greatly impressed him. At Corona he even went so far as to take up arms against his own country, which is said to have resulted in his being exiled from Athens (although the dates of his exile are disputed). He went to live in Scillus, near Olympia, on a property given to him by the Spartans. Shortly after the battle of Leuctra, which established the hegemony of Thebes, Athens and Sparta made peace and Xenophon's banishment was lifted. The great number of encomia and epitaphs dedicated to his son Gryllus, who died fighting for the Athenians at Mantinea in 362, testifies to Xenophon's own renown. Xenophon ended his days in Athens and died around 355.

In his major work, the *Hellenica*, Xenophon continues Thucydides' history, taking up his narrative from where Thucydides left off with the words' After that . . .'. Xenophon's first two books relate the events of the end of the war up to the fall of Athens in 404. He then continues his account until the battle of Mantinea of 362, which created even more confusion and disorder in Greece. However, this work 'in the manner of Thucydides' does not in fact remain true to its model.

Very early on in the work the chronology loses its precision and the historical explanations become more simplistic. Xenophon was more interested in individual psychology than the analysis of political forces. The many speeches in his work reflect the orators' personalities in their tone and style, but make little contribution to a political understanding of events. Above all, Xenophon's vision is religious in the way that Herodotus' was. He sees the decline of Sparta's power as a matter of divine will: the Spartans broke their oath to allow the Greek cities their independence and this betrayal was punished by the gods. Finally the author is obviously biased in favour of Sparta. Thus he remains silent on such important events as the battle of Cnidus or the formation of the Second Athenian Confederacy, yet uses numerous speeches to emphasise the reconciliation between Sparta and Athens (in 371) of which he personally approved.

Xenophon's qualities can be seen more clearly in the seven books of his *Anabasis*, in which he gives a third-person account of the campaign of the 10,000 Greek mercenaries who enlisted in Cyrus the Younger's army in 401 and their long retreat through the empire of the great king. In this work, summed up for generations of students in the Greeks' shout of *'Thalassa, thalassa!'* ('The Sea, The sea!') on finally seeing the Black Sea (Book IV, 7, 24), Xenophon proves himself very knowledgeable on military matters, fascinated by details and interesting little facts. In Book III the author sacrifices the historian's glory for that of the man of action and brings himself into the picture. He identifies with the ideal of the good general who knows how to win his men's affection and respect, can organise his army's training and supplies down to the finest detail and also manages not to upset the gods by paying attention to signs and omens. In these war memoirs, reminiscent of Caesar's *Commentaries* in their elegance and those of Montluc in their cheerful tone, history meets autobiography.

With the *Cyropaedia*, which recounts the life of Cyrus the Great in eight books, Xenophon gives us a historical novel rather than a work of history. This narrative shows scant regard for historical truth, providing instead a portrait of the ideal monarch.

The *Cyropaedia* enjoyed a lasting popularity. Cicero translated part of it at the end of his *Cato the Elder* and, as recently as the seventeenth century, Mlle de Scudéry drew inspiration from the memory of the great Cyrus' virtues and the loves of Abradates and Panthea for her famous novel *Le Grand Cyrus*.

Xenophon's varied, multiform work also includes treatises on the finances of Athens (the *Poroi* or *On the Revenues*) and on the Athenian cavalry (the *Cavalry Officer*), a manual covering the household organization of a wealthy landowner (the *Oeconomicus*), a meditation on tyranny (the *Hiero*) and handbooks on hunting and riding.

Yet this likeable memoir-writer did not content himself with contemplating the ideal leader in his work. He was the source of literary genres destined to have a brilliant future: biography with the *Agesilaus*, the historical novel with the *Cyropaedia* and, with the *Memorabilia*, which, despite their title, are not a work of history but perpetuate the memory of Socrates, he created a new philosophical genre, which Arrian imitated in his *Discourses of Epictetus*; in recounting the sage's words and activities from one day to the next, he was the first to bring philosophy into daily life. He thus reminds us that ancient philosophy was a search of wisdom, an art of living more than a written *oeuvre*.

5

PHILOSOPHY

Socrates (469–399)

Socrates did not write anything at all. We know him only through the indirect and sometimes contradictory accounts of Aristophanes, who caricatures him in the *Clouds*, and Plato and Xenophon, both of whom paint equally admiring pictures, the former making Socrates the mouthpiece for his philosophical inquiries, while the latter describes the sage of every day life.

The philosophical schools which sprang up in growing numbers from the fourth century onwards all claim Socrates as their own. The Megarians, Cynics and Cyrenaics (the 'minor Socratics'), Platonists, Aristotelians and even Stoics all saw Socrates as the prototype of the sage.

Born in Athens around 469 to a sculptor father and midwife mother, Socrates left his native city only for military campaigns (Potidaea in 431, Delion in 424). He was a just man, who refused to obey an unjust order from the Thirty Tyrants and was accused of corrupting the young and introducing new gods into the city in 399. He chose to drink hemlock rather than break the city's laws by following the advice of his friends and escaping.

Socrates continually said that he knew nothing, yet the oracle of Delphi marked him out as the wisest (*sophos*) of men. In order to understand what the god meant, until his final moments Socrates pursued what he saw as a sacred mission. He talked with his fellow citizens in the streets of Athens, the market or the gymnasium, questioning them about what they thought they knew, about their work, their ideas of beauty, wisdom, piety or courage, always keeping to the Delphic precept 'know thyself'. Socrates thus broke with the enquiries 'on nature' (*peri phuseos*) of the Presocratics. He was interested only in human beings. His philosophy was summed up in a way of life and a method of speaking and thinking,

71

the art of dialogue in which Socrates occupied the position of questioner. This was the maieutic method.

Socrates and the Sophists have sometimes been linked, although they disagree on fundamentals. Nothing could be more different from Gorgias' artfully worked rhetorical speeches than the brief questions and answers of the Socratic dialogues, while sophistic relativism is the opposite of Socrates' efforts to give ethics a solid foundation. For Socrates' enquiries are not a game of words whose aim is victory over the other side; they are searches conducted with the interlocutor and guided by the demands of reason.

The figure of Socrates dominated the Western philosophical tradition. Aristotle acknowledges his gratitude for Socrates' search for universal definition and his refinement of the technique of inductive reasoning. For Cicero, Socrates was the man who 'brought philosophy down from heaven to earth'. For us, he remains the man who exhorted everyone to 'know thyself'.

Plato (428–347)

The 'prince of philosophers' was also the inspired writer who, in the *Phaedrus*, defined literary creation as a 'game in honour of the gods'. In fact it is impossible to differentiate between the literary form of the dialogues, from the philosophical core. Plato's style is of a piece with the philosophical essence of the dialogues; it is a subtle, aristocratic writing which makes high demands on its readers. Only the best are admitted into a work which is similar to the Silens described in the *Symposium* (215B): 'On opening them in the middle one sees that they contain figurines of the gods!' Plato thus has a rightful place in a history of Greek literature.

Born into an aristocratic family in 428, Plato was 23 years old when Athens fell and the oligarchy of the Thirty Tyrants was established, with its procession of murders and extortions. Two of the oligarchs were Plato's relatives, Critias and Charmides. 'Naturally enough' he says in the Seventh Letter, 'I expected that this government would bring about a change from corrupt to upright administration . . . I found that it had taken no time at all for these men to make the previous government look like a golden age' (1973, 113).

Democracy was restored, yet in 399 Socrates was condemned to drink hemlock, proving that the sage cannot survive in an unjust state. Plato abandoned thoughts of a political career, went into exile in Megara with other disciples Socrates, then began travels which, according to some, took him to Egypt and Cyrenaica, and certainly to Magna Graecia (southern Italy and Sicily), where he was in contact with the Pythagorean circles. In Syracuse, where his friend Dion invited him to stay with the tyrant Dionysius I, he initially thought that he had found a laboratory in which to test his political theories. When this idea came to nothing he returned to Athens and, in 388, founded a philosophical school, the Academy, in the gardens of the hero Academus. The Academy way frequented by many great minds, including the mathematician Eudoxus and the young Aristotle.

In 367 Dionysius the Younger succeeded his father and Plato returned to Syracuse at the request of the new ruler's uncle, Dion. However, Dion was quickly exiled and Plato returned to Athens in 365. After one final failed attempt in Sicily in 361, Plato returned to the Academy for good, dying there in 347, about ten years before Chaeronea, while writing the *Laws*. The philosophical tradition of the Academy remained alive for nine centuries, however, until Justinian ordered the dissolution of the Neoplatonic school that was its heir in 529.

Plato's writings, which have been preserved in their entirety, consist of thirty-five dialogues (of which all but a few are certainly by Plato) and thirteen letters of doubtful authenticity (although today it is generally accepted that Letters VI, VII and VIII could be by Plato).

'If someone could reduce Plato to a system, he would do a great service to the human species.' This hope, expressed by Leibniz in 1715, has remained unfulfilled. The 'reduction' has not been made, though many have tried.[1] The first step towards this aim has been an attempt to establish the chronology of the dialogues.

Among the efforts to arrive at a satisfactory classification of Plato's work, Schleiermacher's attempt marks an important advance. In his view the succession of dialogues follows a didactic plan, firmly established from the outset, and the dialogues themselves, our only means to understanding Plato's thought, are thus closely linked to each other. In each one Plato then develops one of his main ideas. Armed with this belief, Schleiermacher concludes that the first dialogue is the *Phaedrus*, because it presents the whole programme which is then realised in the other dialogues and shows the full range of Plato's talents as a writer: the choice of a symbolic spatial setting and the skill of dialogue, rigorous dialectical developments and the creation of myths. The *Phaedrus* thus sets out the whole programme.

In its day, this position had the virtue of reminding Plato's readers that they must never lose sight of the dynamic tension which galvanises his entire work. Today, however, it is generally agreed that Plato's thought developed as he wrote the dialogues. Using stylistic criteria, stylometric tests, literary criticism and philosophical considerations, it has been possible to determine at least approximately a broad chronological grouping which is generally agreed upon.

The first group is made up of the so-called 'Socratic' dialogues. Thought to have been written in the ten years following the death of Socrates, these dialogues defend his memory (*Apology, Crito*) or echo his conversations. In the *Hippias Minor*, the *Charmides*, the *Laches*, the *Lysis* and the *Euthyphro*, Socrates and his interlocutors seek to define a value or a virtue: truth and falsehood, wisdom, courage, friendship or piety. The *Hippias Major* (on beauty), the *Alcibiades* and the *Ion*, whose authenticity is disputed, should perhaps also be placed in this group. These dialogues lead to a dead end – they are aporetic dialogues – and conclude without a solution being found to the question they raise. The *Protagoras*, the *Gorgias* and the *Meno*, which should perhaps be joined by the *Euthydemus*, *Cratylus* and *Menexenus*, represent a transition between the first dialogues and the dialogues of Plato's maturity, which followed the foundation of the Academy: the *Symposium*, the *Phaedo*, the *Republic* (in ten books) and the *Phaedrus*.

On his return from his second visit to Sicily, Plato wrote the great metaphysical dialogues: the *Parmenides*, *Theaetetus*, *Sophist* and *Politicus*. Socrates' role gradually lessens, but the retention of the dialogue form suggests that the discussions of the Academy are a continuation of the Socratic conversations. Whether examining Parmenides' theses on the unity of being or those of Heraclitus on universal change, or trying to define the sophist or the politician by using the method of division, each dialogue is above all a dialectical exercise.

Plato's last works include a projected trilogy, the *Timaeus*, the *Critias* and the *Hermocrates* (we only have the *Timaeus* and the beginning of the *Critias*), and the twelve books of the *Laws*, which were not published until after Plato's death. According to tradition, Philip of Opus edited the *Laws* and wrote the *Epinomis*, which is sometimes seen as the thirteenth book of the *Laws*.

In the two major works in the group, the *Republic* and the *Laws*, Plato sought to define the necessary conditions for the establishment of a just city, a city which would not kill Socrates. We shall confine ourselves here to a succinct analysis of the *Republic* in which we will try to convey the way in which, for Plato, morality and politics are inseparable from the theory of knowledge, which is itself inseparable from ontology. The result is that each Platonic dialogue is both a protreptic, an exhortation to philosophy, and a dialectical exercise.

In recent years the paraenetic aim of Plato's dialogues has been forcefully stressed by the Tübingen school;[2] however, this had already been noted by Aristotle's disciple Dicaearchus in his *Life* of Plato: 'By writing his dialogues, Plato exhorted a mass of people to philosophise.' In the case of the *Republic* this is historically proven: Themistius relates in his twenty-third discourse how, after reading the *Republic*, a woman from Phlious came to Athens disguised as a man in order to become a disciple of Plato.

The first book of the *Republic* examines the validity of the most widely accepted definitions of justice: 'Rendering to each his due owed' or 'do good to one's friends, harm to one's enemies'. When examined, none of the proposed definitions proves satisfactory. The Sophist Thrasymachus then breaks into conversation, maintaining that justice is merely the interest of the strongest. His demonstration does not stand up. In its procedure and closing failure to resolve the problem this opening is reminiscent of the aporetic dialogues of the first period. Here Plato may have been using an old draft dialogue, a *Thrasymachus*.

The discussion picks up again in Book II on new bases. In order to define justice more easily, it is seen first in the context of the city, where it is written 'in larger lettering'; this analysis is then used to deduce what justice is in the human soul. The stages of a city's foundation are therefore described.

A city is born of many human needs, whose satisfaction requires a division of labour: people get together in one place and help each other (Book II, 369B sq.). Since needs are always increasing, more and more people come, and this can lead to territorial encroachment and cause wars. The city thus needs guardians to defend it, and these in turn need leaders to tell them what to do (Books II–III).

Where is justice to be found in a fully virtuous state? It is clear that in such a city all rulers should have wisdom, all guardians courage, while temperance should be a characteristic of the three groups which make up the city. Justice is the virtue that keeps each person in their place and guarantees the order of the three classes; from this point of view, injustice is an 'encroachment on the functions of others' (Book IV, 434A-C).

The definition of the three classes in the city (producers, warriors and supreme magistrates) makes it possible by analogy to discern the three parts of the human soul. These are the appetites (bodily desires), the spirited (the self-assertive elements) and the rational. Justice is present in the soul of an individual when these three parts are ordered hierarchically and when each fulfils its proper function. (This idea of a tripartite soul, which underlies Plato's definition of justice, reappears in the *Phaedrus* with the image of the winged chariot which, via neo-Platonism and Marsilio Ficino, was still inspiring Florentine art in the mid-fifteenth century).[3]

Justice has now been defined, but Adeimantus asks Socrates to describe the conditions necessary for such a state to exist (Book V, 449A sq.), of which there are three:

- equality between men and women, who should receive the same education;
- wives and children held in common;
- rule by the philosophers.

This last point is essential and is justified at length in Books V, VI and VII of the *Republic*, in which Plato describes the education that the philosopher-magistrate should receive and the process by which he raises himself from observation of the sensible world to the contemplation of 'ideas' or 'forms' and, beyond these, the idea of the Good, foundation of being and the knowledge of ideas, organising principle of the universe, sun of the intelligible world, supreme object of the goal's desire and ultimate end of the world's order.

Thus a dialogue which set out to define justice and gave an outline of the just city now turns to pure philosophy. The famous allegory of the cave at the start of Book VII presents human beings as prisoners in chains with their backs to the light, who see only the shadows of passing objects. Freed from their bonds, they perceive both the objects themselves and the fire which illuminates them.

Those who leave the cave see all that is illuminated by the sun as well as the sun itself; however, they have to return to the cave to tell those who have remained inside what they have seen. Similarly the philosopher, having contemplated the idea of the Good, must strive to realise this ideal in his life and in the government of the city.

Books VIII and IX pursue the parallel between city and soul and consider the four imperfect forms of government and their corresponding souls.

The start of Book X returns to some of the points made in Books II and III and condemns artistic creation – *mimesis* – from an ontological point of view. The dialogue closes with an eschatalogical myth: the Pamphylian Er's story of the soul's fate after death. The *Republic* thus shows how, in order to act, thought must first disengage itself from the world around it. The contemplative life is for Plato the necessary condition for action: intellectual progress is indissociable from moral (or political) advance. This conception, in which science is the foundation of politics, constitutes the underlying difference between Plato and Isocrates; for although both believe that *philosophia* must lead to political action, Isocrates, convinced that human beings cannot attain absolute knowledge, is content to educate citizens in the proper use of 'opinion' (*doxa* in Greek). For Plato, only the philosopher who has contemplated the idea of good can serve good.

Each dialogue follows this rising movement by which the soul seeks to rid itself of the 'lead plates' dragging it down, to detach itself from the sensible world and turn towards the forms and, beyond them, the Good (the aporetic dialogues are those which do not get there); for all human beings are illuminated by the same principle of the Good, from which everything proceeds, including the forms, and whose contemplation alone satisfies the soul and ensures happiness. Like Pythagoreanism, Platonism reveals itself to be politics, science and religion rolled into one.

Finally, the *Republic* makes it possible to assess Plato's talent as a writer and to analyse his dialectical style. In the Platonic dialogue all means of expression are made to serve a pedagogy of the soul. The aim is to make the style of conversation display the movement of the soul's conversion towards the ideas described by the allegory of the cave, without which there can be no act of knowledge. To do this, Plato uses both tragic mimesis and Sophistic rhetoric.

The dialogue is carefully staged: the place, circumstances of the meeting and the protagonists are described each time. Socrates is surrounded by rich young men concerned for their own education, from the most famous Sophists like Protagoras, Gorgias, Prodicos, Hippias, Polos and Thrasymachus, to poets like Aristophanes or Agathon, exegetes and rhapsodists, generals like Laches and Nicias, doctors like Eryximachus. The entire Athenian elite passes before our eyes, with an intensity of life worthy of Aristophanes. The dialogues often follow a dramatic progression marked by crises: aporetic situations are ended by sudden reversals, which launch the conversation/conversion in new directions. The 'playwright of the soul', as Plato has sometimes been seen, is no stranger to the peripeteia as defined by Aristotle. These are the 'psychagogical' powers which Plato steals from tragedy, a genre he criticises so strongly elsewhere.

His major borrowing from Sophistic rhetoric is the mythical narrative. In Plato's work, however, myth is no longer simply ornamental; it is a precious tool of persuasion for the soul, which is still a prisoner of the body, held fast in the world of sensual perception. It is also sometimes a model, as in the *Timaeus*, which is entirely 'mythical'; in other words, 'a likely fable which mimics the event of the birth of the God-world', as Hadot puts it. In such cases myth takes on the function of truth and may even be the only means of access to ineffable realities.

Discussion or dialectic remains fundamental; yet here too there is a complete 'transposition'.[4] At no time do we find a contest from which participants emerge as winners or losers. Platonic dialectic rejects all violence: it is neither the Sophists' means of refutation current among the 'eristics', nor the art of persuasion by clever argument as taught by rhetoric. It is a search for knowledge, undertaken in common, in an atmosphere of gentleness and mutual goodwill; it is a means to progress, proceeding by stages. Plato takes the Sophistic mode of refutation and turns it into a positive method.

We should add that these highly complex dialogues, which borrow, combine and transpose various literary forms in the service of the soul's conversion, are perhaps only a propaedeutic to Platonic philosophy when the latter's development is taken as a whole. In the *Phaedrus* Plato himself stresses the incapacity of writing to teach truth (276C); only living and animated speech can sow the seeds of truth in the soul. This remark is echoed in the Seventh Letter (341C). We also have eye-witness accounts of Plato's oral teaching on the One, which seems to have drawn heavily on mathematics, conforming to the precept inscribed on the Academy's pediment: 'Let none enter here who is not a geometer.' Thus in his oral teaching Plato pursued the enquiry into causes, principles and ultimate elements of reality which had been started by the Presocratic philosophers. Far from representing a break in the Greek philosophical tradition as Socratism was, Platonism thus appears as an attempt to 'explain, from the smallest number of principles, the diversified structure of reality',[5] and as a stage between Parmenides and Plotinus. This philosophy, whose later development has been so broad and vast, can thus be seen as having itself absorbed all the earlier trends.

Aristotle (384–322)

Of Plato's works we only have those that were destined to be read by the public at large – the 'exoteric' works – and questions are still being asked about the form his teaching took. For Aristotle, on the other hand, we have only the 'esoteric' writings; in other words, his course notes, intended only for his students and which were doubtless retouched by the school before being published by Andronicus of Rhodes in the mid-first century AD. Aristotle's literary works, which were admired by Cicero (*Academica*, Book II, 38) are lost to us. We shall therefore confine ourselves here to a brief survey of his work, concentrating on the treatise whose influence on aesthetic and literary debates can still be felt today: the *Poetics*.

Aristotle was born in Stagira, Macedonia, in 384 and spent his childhood in Pella. He was the son of a Greek physician, Nicomachus, who was attached to the court of Amyntas, king of Macedonia. In 367 he was sent to Athens to follow Plato's teaching at the Academy, where he stayed for twenty years, until Plato's death. After 347 he spent some time with the tyrant Hermias of Atarneus, until Philip called on him to be tutor to the young Alexander in 343. He did not return to Athens until 335, the year in which he founded his school, the Lyceum (named after the gymnasium where it was located). He taught there until 323. As he was in the habit of strolling when giving his lessons (*peripatein*, 'to stroll'), his school was called 'Peripatetic'. After Alexander's death, threats from the anti-Macedonian party forced him to leave Athens; he went to Chalcis, where he died in 322.

Aristotle was a logician who, in works collected later under the title *Organon*, developed the theory of the syllogism as a method of deductive proof and created formal logic. This 'tool' – the meaning of the word *organon* – is not attached to any particular branch of knowledge, but establishes the method applicable to all. Knowledge is divided (according to the division established by Aristotle himself in Book E of the *Metaphysics*[6]) into the theoretical sciences, which consider objects that do not depend on us, and the practical sciences, whose objects of study do depend on us. The latter are divided into the practical sciences and the poetic or productive sciences, according to whether they generate an internal change or a product which is external to us. This division of knowledge inspired the classification of Aristotle's works. The studies of nature (which contains the principle of its own movement) came under the category of theoretical works: biological treatises (such as *Parts of Animals* or *On Generation and Corruption*), the *Physics*, which studies the general principles of movement, the treatise *On the Heavens*, a central text of ancient and medieval cosmology against which modern science had to construct itself, and the twelve books of the *Metaphysics* (meaning 'what comes after physics'), which deal with primary philosophy. The ethical works (*Eudemean Ethics*, *Nicomachean Ethics*) and the *Politics* are examples of 'practical' writings. Among Aristotle's 'poetic' writings are the *Rhetoric*, in which he studies the means of persuasion available to the orator, and the *Poetics*, whose influence on literature was immense. To this list we can add one of the 158 constitutions collected by the peripatetician school, the *Athenian Constitution*, revealed to us by an Egyptian papyrus in 1891.

Clearly Aristotle was driven by an insatiable curiosity, which led him to try to produce an encyclopaedia of the knowledge of his time, with a single exception, mathematics, to which Plato had given such importance. Thus, in both spirit and form, Aristotle's *oeuvre* as it has survived contrasts with that of his teacher. Plato sought to explain the sensible world in terms of intelligibility; Aristotle cannot believe in the existence of an intelligible world of ideas separate from the sensible world and thinks that there could be no knowledge without sensation. Raphael emphasises this contrast in his fresco for the Vatican chambers, *School of Athens*, in which he represents Plato, the idealist, pointing his finger at the sky while Aristotle stretches his own hand towards our sublunary world.

Aristotle was a scholar as well as a philosopher and he believed, as he states in the opening lines of his *Metaphysics*, that 'all men naturally have a desire for knowledge'. This belief inspired his enquiries into biology and natural history, for 'if some [creatures] have no graces to charm the sense, yet even these, by disclosing to intellectual perception the artistic spirit that designed them, give immense pleasure to all who can trace links of causation, and are inclined to philosophy' (*Parts of Animals*, Book I, V, 645A).

Such a belief also lies at the heart of his analysis of tragedy in the *Poetics*,[7] a treatise neglected by philosophical commentators, both ancient and modern, but which inspired a number of aesthetic and literary debates from the sixteenth to the nineteenth century.

The *Poetics*

The plan of the discussion is clear. In chapters 1–5 Aristotle deals with poetry in general, characterising it as one of the arts of imitation, which he then divides into different species. Tragedy is analysed in chapters 6–22. Aristotle defines its parts, emphasising the importance of the 'plot' (*muthos* in Greek) which is, in his eyes, 'the essential of tragedy and something like its lifeblood'; he elucidates the emotions it rouses among the audience – fear and pity – and the characters which are likely to stir them. In the final chapters (23–6) he compares tragedy with the epic, concluding that tragedy is superior.

The definition of tragedy given in Chapter 6 has remained famous:

> Tragedy . . . is a representation (*mimesis*) of an action that is worth serious attention, complete in itself, and of some amplitude; in language enriched by a variety of artistic devices appropriate to the several parts of the play; presented in the form of action, not narration; by means of pity and fear bringing about the purgation (*katharsis*) of such emotions
>
> (1965, pp. 38–9)[9]

This definition, which combines the two concepts of *mimesis* ('imitation' and 'representation') and *katharsis* ('purgation' and 'purification') has been much discussed. However, by replacing it in its context, we can see that in this treatise Aristotle was going against Platonic conceptions and turning tragedy into a means of education.

In defining poetry as an imitative art (*mimesis*), Aristotle seems to be following Plato; in reality his perspective is altogether different. He replaces Plato's ontological disparaging of imitation in Book X of the *Republic* with a 'physical' description of an activity natural to human beings, since all men take please in imitation (1448 B 6–8). This pleasure is not purely aesthetic: it is a pleasure linked to knowledge. Noting that '[man] learns his earliest lessons by imitation; (1448 B 7–8), Aristotle concludes that learning can be achieved through the pleasure of imitation; thus tragedy itself can lead people to the path of philosophy by means of the 'purgation of emotions'. For problems of behaviour and regulation of emotion – ethics in general – relate not to a science but to a practical knowledge acquired by exercise and imitation. A tragedy that stages a complex of events, relationships, reversals and emotions which the human gaze cannot comprehend as a whole anywhere else, makes it possible, through a phenomenon of spontaneous abstraction, to perceive models of intelligibility or behaviour. Like painting, tragedy sharpens perception and facilitates recognition. By staging a metaphorical representation of ethical situations, it enables analogies to be understood and provides an equivalent of the process of abstraction. Tragic imitation thus draws 'universal' from particular situations; in this sense it can be seen as 'more philosophical than history'.

At the end of the discussion the relationship between *poiesis* and *mimesis* has been elucidated: poetry is 'imitation–representation' since it rests on reality (it is well known that the notion of creation *ex nihilo* was foreign to Greek thought); yet this 'imitation' is also creation (*poiesis*) since it does not content itself with reproducing a model, but organises its materials in order to construct a general meaning. Hence tragic imitation does not betray the object it imitates, as Plato believed; rather, it interprets it. Far from being a technique of trickery, it is a pedagogical method.

This is the treatise that was marginalised by the philosophical tradition and given over to the interpretation of artists and literary critics. Since 1498, when the first Latin translation was made by Giorgio Valla, this work has constantly been quoted, commented on and thought about. French classical tragedy took from Aristotle its precept of the 'imitation of nature', the rule of the three unities (of action, time and place) and the theme of the 'purgation of the passions', which provided the seventeenth-century poets with an excuse for depicting passionate love in front of a court in the grip of the Counter-reformation. A century or so later German Romanticism hailed the *Poetics* as a founding text. For in this slim treatise Aristotle the philosopher not only continues his dialogue with his teacher Plato, but provides a condensed version of his thought and more or less founds aesthetics.

6

RHETORIC

Fénélon's view that 'among the Greeks everything depended on the people and the people depended on speech' is particularly appropriate to classical Athens. The art of speech had been an important element of the hero's education in Homer's work; but in the democratic city the art of speaking proved indispensable to those who wanted to make themselves heard, whether before the law courts (where the decision was in the hands of popular juries) or in the assembly, where the citizens' vote was sovereign. Thucydides regarded the relation of 'what was said' to be as important as 'what happened'. Finally, in some circumstances – such as the funerals of citizens who died in combat – the city delegated one of its members to commemorate it in a funeral speech.[1] The three canonical forms of the oratorical art were judicial or dicenic oratory, political or persuasive oratory and ceremonial or epideictic oratory. Many of these speeches did not enter into literature: they were intended simply to be spoken, and not to be published. It was not until the last third of the fifth century that any orator thought of publishing his speeches.

A comic fragment proclaims that 'alone among orators, only Pericles left his sting in the souls of his listeners'; yet we have no authentic speeches of his. Those that Thucydides puts into his mouth bear the hallmark of the historian himself.

The first legal defence speeches to be published were those of the speech-writer Antiphon. Athenian law stated that defendants had to plead their own cause before the court; those who mistrusted their own abilities would turn to a 'maker of speeches' (logographos in Greek), who would write them a speech. Antiphon, Thucydides' teacher, was one of these; we have three of his speeches, all concerned with homicide cases, as are the rhetorical exercises which bear his name, the Tetralogies. Known for his anti-democratic views,

Antiphon was executed for his participation in the oligarchic revolution of the Four Hundred, after giving a defence speech which Thucydides tells us was 'the most perfect ever heard in a capital case'.

Andocides was not a professional writer. The three speeches of his that we have relate to his life and, in the case of the two *On Mysteries* and *On his Return*, to the unfortunate affair of the mysteries, which shocked Athens in 415 and in which Andocides was implicated.

Lysias and judicial oratory

Lysias was incontestably the most gifted orator of the fifth century. He was a metic (resident alien) born around 440, the son of a rich man, Cephalus, who had come from Sicily and set up a weapons factory in Athens. Lysias strongly supported the democratic regime. After the murder of his brother Polemarchus by the Thirty Tyrants, he escaped to Megara, joined the exiled democratic forces and partic- ipated in the re-establishment of democracy.

Lysias tried his hand at grand oratory, writing a *Funeral Oration* and an *Olympiacus*, but his talent blossomed to the fullest in his defence speeches for the civil courts, a genre which was in no way considered lesser in Greek eyes, since Demosthenes himself was later proud to be one of its exponents.

Of the 233 speeches circulating under the name of Lysias at the time of Dionysius of Halicarnassus (first century BC), we have only about thirty. Most of these are speeches written for clients, and the skill and flexibility with which Lysias adapted the style of his speeches to the character and condition of the person for whom he wrote it have often been admired. Whether he is writing for a deceived husband (*On the Murder of Eratosthenes*), an invalid who wants to continue receiving his pension (*On the Cripple*) or a family ruined by an unscrupulous tutor (*Against Diogeiton*), a new char- acter comes to life in each case; the different tones – naive, crafty, pathetic – are always conveyed in simple, clear language.[2] His most famous speech is doubtless his *Against Eratosthenes*, the only one which he delivered himself. In it Lysias attacks Eratosthenes, who was one of the Thirty Tyrants and jointly responsible for the death of his brother Polemarchus; it is a statement of his democratic beliefs.

However, while all are united in praising Lysias' faithful portrayal of character (*èthopoiia*), tight argumentation was not his strong point. Plato, who wrote a pastiche of Lysias in the *Phaedrus*, criticises him for piling up arguments. It is not until Isocrates and Demosthenes that one encounters full mastery of all the aspects of rhetoric.

Isocrates and Epideictic oratory

Isocrates lived for nearly a hundred years. He was born in 436 BC and died in 338, just after Philip of Macedon's victory at Chaeronea put an end to the independence of the Greek cities. He came from a wealthy family and was able to follow the teachings of the Sophists in Athens, possibly studying under Gorgias. But the Peloponnesian war brought about the collapse of the family fortunes and Isocrates had to become a writer of forensic orations. This activity, which he later disparaged, was not enough to fulfil his ambitions. Since his shyness and poor memory prevented him from becoming a great political orator, he opened a school of rhetoric in 393. The speech *Against the Sophists* is seen as this school's manifesto. From that time until his death Isocrates was primarily a teacher.

Isocrates always emphasised the distance that separated him from both his Sophist contemporaries, with their pointless wranglings, and from Plato, whose taste for abstract speculations he criticised. His education, to which he gave the name *philosophia*, aimed at training good leaders and citizens through rhetoric. For Isocrates the art of speech implied a total intellectual education: the art of speaking well (*eu legein*) was inseparable from the art of thinking well (*eu phronein*). Three criteria must be fulfilled to ensure success as an orator: natural qualities, a good teacher and a long period of training. Isocrates' ideal was based on a conception of the *logos* as a civilizing power. It found its perfect embodiment in the city of Athens, which Isocrates, like Thucydides (Book II, 41), regarded as the 'school of Greece'.

Founded on these principles, Isocrates' school soon became famous and attracted many fine minds from all over Greece. The king of Cyprus, Nicocles, the historians Ephorus and Theopompus, the general Timotheus and the orators Lycurgus and Hyperides all attended. To give an idea of its influence, Cicero compared it to the Trojan horse filled with the hero elite (*On Oratory*, Book II, 94).

Isocrates intended his speeches to illustrate his ideal. Apart from the early speeches he wrote as a *logographos* (*Against Euthynous*, *Against Callimachus*, *Against Lochites*, *On the Team*, *Trapeziticus* and *Aegineticus*), all Isocrates' speeches were fictitious and were never delivered in law courts or assemblies.

As well as *Against the Sophists* and *Antidosis* which were directly linked to his work as a teacher, there are the encomia: the *Encomium of Helen* and the *Busiris* reflect the Sophists' taste for paradoxical eulogies. The *Evagoras* (365) reveals Isocrates' desire to raise prose to a level where it could compete with poetry.

However, the main part of his work consists of political manifestos. When he deals with Athenian politics, as in *On the Peace* (356), in which he urges for peace between Athens and some former members of the Second Athenian League, or in the *Areopagiticus* (354?), which discusses problems of internal politics, Isocrates advocates a policy of justice and moderation. In his speeches on foreign policy, addressed to the whole of Greek public opinion, he defends two fundamental ideas with great conviction: Greek unity and the need for a Panhellenic expedition against the Barbarians. He remained faithful to these two principles, from the *Panegyricus* published around 380 to the *Panathenaicus*, his last speech, written between 342 and 339, calling first on Athens (*Panegyricus*), then on Sparta (*Archidamus*, 365–362), and finally on Philip of Macedonia (in the *Philip*, 346) to put them into practice.

All in all, Isocrates' long career was not without its paradoxes. The fall of Athens (404) occurred when he was still young, his adult life was spent under the domination of Sparta (404–379), he lived to see the renaissance of Athens and the creation of the Second Athenian League (377), the advance of Theban power under the influence of Epaminondas (379–362), the end of the Second Athenian League and the war of the allies (357–355). Although he witnessed the growth of Macedonian interference in Greek affairs – against which no voices were raised except that of the ardent Demosthenes, with his desperate calls for unity against Philip – Isocrates continued to regard Persia as the Greeks' main enemy. For us he belongs to the period of the decline of independence, since he was entirely cut off from the order of things he had known in his early life and most of his work dates from after 380. The final paradox lies in the contrast between the inadequacies of the man himself, whose lack of originality and creative imagination are blindingly obvious in comparison with his great rival Plato, and the influence of his school, whose principles set the canons of education for the Western elite until the early twentieth century.

Demosthenes and political oratory

'With Demosthenes, oratory sent up its last sparks in an Athens which was soon to lose its independence.' Born in 384 BC,

Demosthenes lost his father, a wealthy armourer, when he was 7 years old. He saw his fortune eaten away by his tutors and when he came of age he had to plead against them to recover some of his property. He is said to have been a student of Isaeus (an orator by whom we have eleven speeches on inheritance cases) and, during the first part of his career, he was a speech-writer. About thirty speeches for the law courts have come down to us in his name, but the authenticity of a number of these is doubtful.

After the 350s, Demosthenes fought against the menacing power of Philip of Macedon. His *First Philippic* dates from 351 and was followed by the *Olynthiac* (349–348) and the second and third *Philippics* (344). With Philip's advance, which soon threatened Elatea in Boeotia, Demosthenes managed to bring about peace between Athens and its perennial enemy Thebes. However, the Greek coalition was defeated at Chaeronea in 338. This did not prevent the Athenians from giving Demosthenes the task of delivering the funeral oration for their war dead. Athens acknowledged the Macedonian king as leader of the Hellenic League; however, it rebuilt its fortifications and Demosthenes, who was appointed to oversee the works, contributed some of his own money. The following year, in 337, Ctesiphon proposed that he should be given a golden crown in recognition of services rendered. Aeschines attacked this idea. We have the speeches of either side: Aeschines' *Against Ctesiphon* and Demosthenes' *On the Crown*. Aeschines won less than a fifth of the vote and had to leave Athens. Unfortunately, Demosthenes was himself accused of corruption in 324, given a heavy fine and exiled. Recalled to Athens by popular decree on Alexander's death (323), he was once more obliged to flee the following year in order to escape Antipater's troops, who were conquering Attica. He poisoned himself in 322.

Just as the Ancients called Homer 'the poet', so they called Demosthenes 'the orator'. Cicero gave him the first place in his canon of Attic orators and the Treatise *On the Sublime* makes him one of the great figures remembered as an object of emulation to future writers. Yet Demosthenes' oratory 'does not care about rhetorical rules,' and often does the opposite of what the 'rhetorical treatises' recommended. At a time when the different parts of a speech – exordium, narration, proof and epilogue – were precisely codified, Demosthenes overturned traditional rules, following a different kind of logic.[3]

Thus the composition of the *First Philippic*, for example, proceeds by using terms, themes and images which present Athens as 'a world upside-down' in which power is only 'on paper': 'its armies are transformed into forces which harm its allies and thus Athens itself, they obey Philip's order than the Athenian generals'.

He uses metaphors and similes to highlight the important ideas and does not shrink from paradox (in the *First Philippic* he even upholds Philip as an example to the Athenians). But his greatest quality is his variety. Sometimes his tone is familiar, studded with proverbs, interjections and pressing questions, elsewhere he uses periodic sentences. He appeals to the emotions, inciting fear and anger, and does not shy away from invective or pathos. Yet he also speaks to reason in an abstract and rigorous style similar to that of his model Thucydides.

These qualities, instantly apparent in the political harangues, can also be found in the courtroom speeches of the same period, *Against Meidias* (which was never actually delivered) and the speech *On the Embassy*, given during the trial of Aeschines in 343. But it is perhaps in the speech *On the Crown* that the orator surpasses himself. In this speech, written several years after the defeat, Demosthenes proclaims that there is no shame in failure, when fighting for the sake of principle and that success should not be the measure of human actions. All the resources of rhetorical art are here made to serve passionate belief, tragically dramatised by the contrast between the ideal he reaffirms and the misery of experience.

Other fourth-century orators

Among Demosthenes' contemporaries, Hyperides and Lycurgus belonged to the same party and also fought against Macedonian expansion.

Aeschines, on the other hand, wanted peace and dreamed of an understanding with Philip. He was Demosthenes' direct and constant adversary. Doubtless because he was self-taught, Aeschines respected the traditional rules of speech-writing as well as chronological order. He demonstrated his knowledge of poetry and laws; his work often lacks flights of oratory, but never irony: he was good at stigmatising his adversary's departures from good style. Thus in a famous passage from *Against Ctesiphon* (166), he parodies Demosthenes' metaphors, putting incoherent and ludicrous images into the mouth of his adversary: 'They are removing the republic's buds; they have suddenly cut the nerves of democracy; we have been sewn up, tightly plaited.'

We should also mention Dinarchus, whom the Ancients included in their canon of the ten Attic orators. He was a speech-writer, born in Corinth in 361, who put his talents at the service of the pro-Macedonian party. He wrote an *Against Demosthenes* for one of the latter's accusers in the Harpalus affair.

But the end of Greek independence also marks the end of great oratory. Gone were the 'isegoric' speeches with which one citizen would seek to persuade his fellows on an equal footing. The brilliant oratory of the Empire, at the time of the 'second sophistic', was of a quite different nature.

CONCLUSION

After this brief panorama, we should like to hazard a few observations. Most of the extraordinary diversity of works written between the seventh and fourth century BC are linked to the city. Whether they magnify its praise (like the great odes of the choral lyric, the tragedies, epideictic speeches or Herodotus' history), relate to its life (such as the political speeches to the people), describe its crises and difficulties (as do the comic theatre, many of the harangues, or indeed the works of Thucydides or Plato), the city is the soil from which they grew. The thinkers' eyes never stray beyond its limits. When seeking to resolve the contemporary political crisis, both Aristotle and Plato are entirely concerned with strengthening the barriers which protect the city and ensure its unity. To this extent they are always looking to the past.

And yet, at the end of the fifth century, the poet Euripides revealed other aspirations. Was he the first to understand that this inward-looking community was doomed to die? He left Athens for Macedonia, where he was welcomed by King Archelaos and, in the choral songs of his last tragedies, expressed the desire to open up his city's frontiers in a movement towards broader horizons. In the fourth century, and in their own way, the Athenian Isocrates and the laconizing Xenophon bore witness to the incapacity of the civic institutions to solve current problems: they dreamed of the man who could save them, meditated on the qualities of leadership and sought a broader definition of Hellenism.

Alexander's conquests opened up new territories to Greek culture. It may be that the Hellenisation of a large part of the world proved so quick and easy as a result of the cultural synthesis that Athens had brought about, by attracting people from all the regions of the Greek world and managing to blend elements taken from the entire Greek tradition into a harmonious whole. The Greek language soon spread from the Crimea to Egypt, from Marseille to the frontiers of India; many cities built gymnasia and theatres, set up philosophical schools and invited rhetors, poets and scientists, thus upholding the Greek cultural model which had been so brilliantly embodied in Athens. Paradoxically, although the Macedonian conquests marked the end of the city state as a completely independent centre of power, in so doing they increased the vitality of the cultural form that the city had created.

Part 3

THE HELLENISTIC PERIOD

The Age of Distinction

INTRODUCTION

Philip's victory over the united forces of Athens and Thebes at Chaeronea (338 BC) and the conquests of his son Alexander (334–323 BC) marked a break in the political history of Greece. A Greek world centred on the Aegean and made up of autonomous city states gave way to the much larger Hellenistic monarchies. This political change resulted in a genuine transformation of mentalities. 'The city state did indeed still exist . . . however, it declined to the level of municipal importance; it was not replaced by the framework of the state, which was too vast and ill-defined, and, from this time on, the problem . . . of the human individual took centre stage.'[1] More isolated from one another, more dependent on themselves, men and women increasingly devoted their time to private life and 'care of the self'.[2]

A new era of Greek culture emerged from these changes. The cities founded by Alexander – more than seventy according to Plutarch[3] – and his successors extended their cultural influence from the Indus valley to the island of Sicily, from the shores of the Black Sea to the land of Egypt. A few years ago, archaeologists discovered a genuine Greek city at Ai Khanoum, complete with monuments and inscriptions, which attests to the penetration of Delphic maxims such as 'know thyself' into the heart of Afghanistan.

However, this culture was not open to foreign influences: it considered itself to be uniquely Greek. The presence of the gymnasium betrays the will of Greek settlers to maintain the distinctive characteristics of Hellenism. A mixed civilisation that would have harmoniously combined Hellenism and oriental culture, 'uniting and mixing in one great loving-cup, as it were, the lives, the characters, the habits' of the Greeks and Persians only existed in the mind of Plutarch, or, more recently, the nineteenth-century German historian Droysen, who invented the concept of 'Hellenism'[4].

Even the centres of literary production shifted. Though Athens was the home of New Comedy and remained an intellectual capital, a place where members of the elite came to complete their education, in all domains other than philosophy it lost the pre-eminence it had had during the fifth and fourth centuries. The more lively cultural centres were now the cities of Asia Minor, the islands that were thriving on the intensification of trade between Egypt and the Orient and, most importantly, the capitals of the new Hellenistic kingdoms. Like the tyrants of the archaic period, Hellenistic sovereigns attracted intellectuals from all corners of the Greek world. More broadly, they took the culture in hand both to cement a sense of unity among immigrant groups of diverse origins and to define more clearly what distinguished them from the non-Greeks among whom they lived. They created centres of research and libraries modelled after the Lyceum, such as Alexandria and its famous Museum, Pella, Antioch, and, most importantly, Pergamum, whose library vied with Alexandria's in its wealth.

The public to whom this literature was addressed also changed. Up until the fourth century, poets and orators had composed their works for a live audience. From the Hellenistic period onwards, writers were primarily addressing readers. Because of the extension of Hellenism and the intense circulation of intellectuals and their writings, this public was more dispersed. It was also more homogeneous due to the diffusion of a 'common language' (the *koine*) that gradually supplanted local dialects and evolved at the same pace throughout the Greek world. Common literary references such as Homer and the classics also contributed to this homogeneity, since it was at this time that canons or lists of the best authors were created for each genre. The Hellenistic public was also less diverse. Unlike the productions of archaic lyric poetry and classical theatre, which were performed for the entire body of citizens, Hellenistic works excluded the popular masses and non-Greeks, who were denied access to the gymnasium. They addressed a cultivated elite, who alone could appreciate their subtle erudition.

It is difficult however to give a complete and accurate image of the literature produced during the Hellenistic period. The hazards of transmission and changes in taste, which from the Imperial period onwards favoured the Attic style, have deprived us of the near totality of Hellenistic prose. Our knowledge of the poetry of this period is undoubtedly better, but nevertheless deficient. None of the hundreds of poems celebrating the deeds of sovereigns, the greatness of cities or the exploits of heroes are extant. We therefore cannot attempt to write a literary history of this period, but we only present the works that have survived.

7

POETRY

Menander and New Comedy

In this changing world, the Athenian bourgeoisie seems to have prolonged the old dream of the autonomous city state. However, civic solidarity was dissolving and the gulf between rich and poor was widening. While important political decisions were made elsewhere by the all-powerful kings of Macedonia, a small group of landowners controlled municipal life, constructed public buildings and organised the festivals. It was for these people that Menander wrote his plays.

We have little information on Menander's life other than the fact that it coincided with a troubled chapter of Athenian history. He was born a short while before Chaeronea (c. 342 BC) and is thought to have died around 292 BC. He thus experienced the moderate oligarchy of the peripatetic philosopher Demetrius of Phaleon. The two may have been close enough friends that Menander's life was endangered during the 'liberation' of Athens by Demetrius Poliorcetes in 307 BC. Some sources claim he was a student of the philosopher Theophrastus (Diogenes Laertius, V, 36) and bring him into close relationship with Alexis, a major representative of the so-called Middle Comedy (*Souda*). He was perhaps acquainted with Epicurus (Strabo, 14, 638).

Menander is thought to have composed his first play, *Anger* (*Orge*) when he was aged about 20. During the next thirty years he wrote more than a hundred plays – ninety-seven titles have survived – that seem to have been instantly popular throughout the Greek-speaking world, though he was victorious only eight times at the Athenian festivals. Until the end of the nineteenth century only citations and Latin imitations by Plautus and Terentius were extant, but papyrological discoveries of the twentieth century have since vastly increased our knowledge of his work. The papyrus brought from Cairo by G. Lefevre in 1907 and the Bodmer collection of papyri published in the 1960s contain important fragments of his plays. We are now better acquainted with the *Arbitration* (*Epitrepontes*), the *Samia*, the *Rape of the Locks* (*Perikeiromene*), the *Shield* (*Aspis*), the *Sicyonian*, the *Hated Man* (*Misoumenos*), *Twice a Swindler* (*Dis Exapaton*) and, most importantly, the *Bad-tempered Man* (*Dyskolos*) which is almost complete.

In Menander's work, characteristic elements of Old Comedy such as scathing attacks on politicians, obscene jokes, padded costumes and enormous phalluses, all disappeared. His plays, divided into acts (usually five) by musical interludes unrelated to the action, were domestic and bourgeois comedies bearing more resemblance to the tragedies of Euripides than the comedies of Aristophanes. The influence of the last of the great tragedians can be felt in both the themes (in Euripides' *Ion* there are abandoned children, seduced girls and moving scenes of recognition) and forms (for instance, monologues and messenger scenes). Scholars have recognised a scene of the *Sicyonian* as a rewritten version of a scene of Euripides' *Orestes*. This taste for virtuosity and literary games is typical of Hellenistic poetry.

Unlike Old Comedy, New Comedy relied on plot and character portrayal. One of the anecdotes reported by Plutarch[1] reveals Menander's capital interest in plot. To one of his friends enquiring with concern whether his new comedy would be ready for the upcoming festival, Menander is said to have replied: 'I most certainly have composed it: I have my treatment of the theme worked out – I just have to set the lines to it.' Plots did not vary much from one comedy to the next. Love holds a central place: a young man falls in love with an unknown beauty and various obstacles prevent their union, such as the social position of the young girl, the opposition of a father or tutor or lack of money. These are overcome by an ingenious slave, who comes to the aid of the young lover, or by the discovery that the young woman is of noble birth. All ends happily in marriage. Menander composed 108 variations of this basic plot. Part of the pleasure of the audience therefore stemmed from the recognition of traditional elements repeated and transformed. These games of love and chance – for blind fortune (*Tukhē*) wildly complicates the plot – reflect the spirit of the times. They reveal the growing individualism of a society whose foremost preoccupation was personal fulfilment, and betray anxiety about the future, an anxiety over which comedy triumphs by showing that in the end happiness always springs from misfortune.

The appeal of Menander's theatre also stems from his skill in depicting colourful characters with accuracy and humour. Even though he uses stock characters such as the bullying soldier, the parasite, the boastful cook, the bashful lover, the hot-tempered father, the resourceful *hetaira* or the slave, often bearing the same names (Daos, Smicrine, Moschion and so on), his talent resides in the fact that he varies the traits of each character from comedy to comedy and plays with the (always undermined) expectations of the spectators. Menander surprises his audience by creating the unusual combination of the bullying soldier who is also a bashful lover. He also adds unexpected traits to liven up his portraits: the courtesan Habrotonon of the *Arbitration* displays the opportunism commonly found among her colleagues, but is the only one possessing a repressed maternal instinct. Her love of babies distinguishes her from the stereotype and gives life to her character.

These portraits are drawn in dialogues whose rapidity and ease have always baffled critics. While all the characters speak the same language – the *koine* – whether man, woman, rich, poor, educated or slave, many of them have tics and idiosyncrasies that make them unique. Thus we find a cook who relishes vivid metaphors and a misanthrope who has no time for nuances, but sees the world in binary oppositions so that everything is all or nothing. Yet Menander avoids caricature as he avoids conventionality. Despite his stock-in-trade plots, he succeeds in giving an illusion of psychological and social realism which was absent from Old Comedy. While Aristophanes used contemporary figures to mock the Sophist, the bad poet and the bully (Socrates, Euripides and Lamachos respectively), he deprived them of any personal traits and made them symbolic puppets. Menander succeeds, by the inverse procedure, in investing even the most traditional comic types with life and individuality.

Throughout his plays, this disenchanted observer of human folly defends the values shared by the cultivated elite of his time and advocates an ideal of urbanity, tolerance and friendship. His plays were immensely popular. The Mytilene mosaics dating from 300 BC are all illustrations of his comedies. Plautus and Terentius imitated him, Quintilien and Plutarch praised him. With Menander the Greek *vis comica* sent out its last sparks in Athens.

Hellenistic poetry

Hellenistic poetry developed in the first half of the third century, after New Comedy, and elsewhere, in Alexandria. It was composed in the shadow of the largest library in the Greek world, which comprised more than 500,000 scrolls. Its authors benefited from the enormous labour of philologists such as Zenodotus and Aristophanes of Byzantium, who spent their lives editing and producing commentaries of classical texts. They were often eminent scholars themselves. Eratosthenes, who headed the library of Alexandria for a time, was not only a mathematician and a geographer; he also composed a long poem in hexameter, the *Hermes*. Others, such as Callimachus, divided their time between poetry and scholarship. All wrote for the kings, who in turn prided themselves on their love of literature (Ptolemy Philopator composed a tragedy), and for an audience of cultivated men. Hellenistic poetry is therefore first and foremost scholarly poetry.

It borrows its language and metre from Homer and archaic poetry and displays a partiality for rare expressions collected in glossaries. Lycophron's *Alexandra*, which made lavish use of enigmatic formulas and *hapax legomena* in order to report the prophecies of Cassandra, has remained famous for its obscurity. Such poetry delights in little known legends and local rites. It also refers to contemporary knowledge of geography, astronomy (the *Phenomena* of Aratos of Soloi) and natural sciences (the *Theriaca* and *Alexipharmaca* of Nicander of Colophon).

However, erudition is not synonymous with servile imitation. Poets often used citations to better reveal the distance that separated them from their predecessors. They might borrow the metre of an Archaic poet but not imitate his dialect or remain faithful to his spirit. Such a 'croning of genres' is a characteristic of Hellenistic poetry. When Hellenistic poets borrowed a theme, they would treat it in an unexpected fashion, not hesitating to renew traditional genres by introducing farmers and simple folk who represent the height of exoticism to their cultivated and urban public. Theirs was also an art for a coterie. It was developed behind closed doors where men of letters all knew one another, dedicated their works to one another and cited and quarrelled with one another. For instance, Callimachus replied with an epigram (46) to Theocritus' *Cyclops*, which was addressed to another poet, the doctor Nicias, who in turn answered him in verse. In the Prologue of the *Aetia*, Callimachus violently attacks those who reproach him for not composing a long epic poem, calling them *Telchines* (malevolent wizards). The famous quarrel that he is supposed to have had with Apollonius of Rhodes is probably a legend, but it is nevertheless revealing of the literary ways of the time.

Hellenistic poetry was also a court art, refined, allusive (in polemical writings and encomia, periphrases are preferred to direct style), ironic with a taste for dissonance and brevity (the Hellenistic period was the golden age of the epigram, which treats a theme in a few verses). It was art for art's sake, produced by authors who were conscious of the originality of their approach and quite willing to theorize about their art. Among these poets three great names emerge: Callimachus, Theocritus and Apollonius of Rhodes.

Callimachus (305–240 BC), who spent most of his life in Alexandria, is the perfect representative of Alexandrian poetry. An erudite librarian, he catalogued all the books in the library of Alexandria and wrote scholarly works, whose titles alone have survived. He was also a court poet, who celebrated the Ptolemies and their wives: he sang of the apotheosis of Arsinoë and dedicated the first and last poems of his masterpiece the *Aetia* to Berenice, to her 'victory' and her 'lock of hair'. His poetry, which greatly influenced Latin writers, exemplifies Hellenistic literary taste in its variety, its erudition, and its search for the rare and allusive, as well as in a subtlety that often puts the interpreter to the test.

Callimachus the poet is distinguished above all by his versatility, for he mastered a variety of genres. He composed hymns, of which six are extant, epigrams, and iambi modelled on those of Hipponax. He also wrote a long elegy, the *Aetia* in which The Muses relate the origins of a series of local customs, and an epic poem, *Hecale*, of which only fragments have survived.

Callimachus displays the same versatility within a genre, and even a poem. The *Hymns* use hexameters (I, II, III, IV, VI) and elegiac couplets (V). They are written in Ionian dialect (I, II, III, IV) and in Doric (V, VI). Three of the hymns are 'mimetic' and describe festivals held in honour of Apollo (II), Athena (V) and Demeter (VI). The other three use direct address to celebrate a divinity in the style of the Homeric Hymns. Diversity is also the rule within each poem. Thus Hymn V juxtaposes a series of heterogeneous elements: a lively evocation of an archaic Argive ceremony frames a genre scene, the bath of the goddess, that ends tragically with the story of Tiresias, who is blinded for having seen the naked body of Athena.

The poet's erudition is omnipresent. In the *Aetia*, Callimachus displays an antiquarian's taste for local tradition and obscure rituals. In the *Hymns* he sometimes parades his scholarly knowledge: the enumeration of the rivers of Arcadia in the *Hymn to Zeus* (I) reminds us that Callimachus was the author of a treatise on the rivers of the inhabited world. His allusive style artfully plays with reference to distance from former poems. For instance, the conclusion of the *Hymn to Apollo* borrows its theme from Pindar; however, here Envy does not intervene, as she does in the epinician ode, to ask the poet to cut short his mythic narrative. On the contrary, she asks him to lengthen the tale. It is Apollo, and the poet with him, who opt for brevity.

Callimachus displays a taste for rarity. He boasts of preferring footpaths and springs of pure water to wide roads and muddy rivers. He tends towards the most obscure version of a myth and chooses to develop little know details of legends. For example, in the *Hymn to Athena*, he deviates from the traditional version of the myth when he narrates the blinding of Tiresias and the death of Acteon. In his poem *Hecale* he retains only a minor incident from the exploit of Theseus killing the bull of Marathon: the night that the hero, caught in the rain, spends with the old woman who gives her name to the poem.

Callimachus is fond of abrupt changes of tone. His longest poem, the *Aetia*, is segmented into episodes which greatly differ from one another, including aetiological narratives, love stories and praise for the royal family. He loves incongruity and chooses to portray unusual aspects of the gods. The *Hymn to Artemis* (III) depicts a 3-year-old Artemis on the lap of her father trying in vain to grasp his chin. The *Hymn to Delos* takes the search for the baroque even further: Apollo sends forth his prophetic voice while he is still in his mother's womb.

This ambiguous and allusive poetry, which delights in misleading the reader with digressions which are sometimes longer than the main theme, is understandably disconcerting. In fact, scholars are still perplexed by the intentions of the most known and studied of his poems. Were the Hymns occasional pieces, performed during celebrations for the gods, or erudite works to be read by the literary set? At what level should they be interpreted? The subtle and ironic art of Callimachus continues to hold its secrets.

Let us use epigram 28 as an example:

> I hate the cyclic poem, nor do I take pleasure in the road which carries many to and fro. I abhor, too the promis-cuous beloved, and I don't drink from every fountain. I loathe all common things. Lysanias, you are, yes, fair, fair: but no sooner has Echo said the word, someone says, 'Another has him'.

All the characteristics of Callimachus' art are present: brevity of course; imitation, since this epigram closely follows some of Theognis' erotic verses; an original way of transforming the most banal pederastic epigram, 'such and such a person is beautiful', into a sophisticated word play, which is unfortunately untranslatable (because of Echo's vulgar pronunciation, the last sentence is distorted and creates an echo); an unusual combination of the literary manifesto with crude eroticism; and, last but not least, a biting irony that spares not even the author.

Theocritus (born *c.* 300 BC) was a court poet like his contemporary, Callimachus. He first offered his services to Hiero II of his native Syracuse (*Idyll* 16) and then found a patron in Ptolemy Philadelphus, whom he celebrated in *Idyll* 17. He lived in Alexandria and also in Cos and to this day remains famous for being the creator of the idyll. Some of his epigrams are also extant as well as a poem, the *Syrinx*, the distant ancestor of Apollinaire's *Calligrammes*, which is set out in a form that evokes the shape of Pan's pipes (*syrinx* in Greek).

As their name indicates, the idylls are 'brief forms' (*eidullion* is a diminutive of *eidos*, form). With few exceptions (Idylls 28, 29 and 30), they are 'miniature epics' – the longest comprising 223 verses – written in dactylic hexameter. But the homogeneity of metre should not obscure the diversity of Theocritus' *oeuvre*.

This diversity is in part formal. Most idylls are written in a 'literary' Doric dialect that owes more to the works of Epicharmus and Sophron than to the Doric language spoken by Alexandrians, originated in Sicily and South Italy, but *Idylls* 12 and 22 use Homeric language and *Idylls* 28, 29 and 30, modelled on the poems of Alceus and Sappho, revive Aeolian metres and dialect. Some of Theocritus' poems (1, 4, 5, 10, 14, 15) are dialogues, such as the conversations between a goatherd and a shepherd in *Thyrsis* (1) and the *Herdsmen* (4). *Idylls* 2 and 12 are theatrical monologues; In the *Pharmakeutriai* (2), a forlorn maiden tries to summon back her faithless lover by singing incantations. Like the epic, *Idylls* 6, 7, 11 and 13 place speech or song within a narrative framework. For example, the narrative of *Idyll* 7 incorporates two poems, different in spirit and tone. Finally, some poems such as the *Charites* (16), the *Encomium of Ptolemy* (17) or the *Dioscuri* (22) adopt the form of a hymn.

The diversity is also thematic. As the etymology of their name suggests, the 'bucolic' idylls depict country folk such as cowherds (*boukoloi* in Greek), shepherds, goatherds, woodcutters and harvesters.

Besides these poems, which became especially popular, there are idylls that depict city dwellers. In *The Woman at the Festival of Adonis* or *The Women of Syracuse* (15) two women of Alexandria, originally from Syracuse, visit the royal palace for a festival in honour of Adonis. Some idylls are mythological narratives, such as the *Childhood of Heracles* (24), the *Dioscuri* (22), and encomia of sovereigns (16, 17).

Theocritus' art is therefore diverse, but also refined and ironic, subtly playing with the distance and dissonance between a creator who belongs, like his public, to the urban elite and his humble characters, between the epic verse form and its content, which reflects the world of simple folk, between the social status of the speaker and the style of his speech (shepherds cite Homer and on occasion make a show of their lexicographical knowledge) and finally, and perhaps most importantly, between this miniature epic and its models, the epic poems of Homer and Hesiod.

Theocritus transforms some of the figures of epic: the cannibalistic monsters of the *Odyssey* becomes a love-struck shepherd in *Idyll* 11 (*Cyclops*). He transposes scenes: in Hesiod's *Theogony*, it is the Muses who bestow the gift of poetry, symbolised by the sceptre upon the shepherd poet, while in *Idyll* 7 they are replaced by a goatherd wearing hides that still smell of rennet, who offers the young poet a 'club'. Theocritus also renews traditional epic motifs when the scenes which decorate Achilles' shield are replaced by the vignettes that adorn a drinking cup of sculpted wood in *Idyll* 1.

Dissonance is the very essence of Theocritus' poetic art. It is the key to a mythological poem such as the *Childhood of Heracles*. The first exploit of the greatest of heroes, who strangled the two serpents sent by Hera while still in his crib, is framed by two scenes of daily life: a mother putting her infants to bed after nursing them and being awakened in the middle of the night by the cries of the youngest. *The Women at the Festival of Adonis* (15) also juxtaposes two opposites and leads the reader *petit-bourgeois* world complete with screaming children, tyrannical husbands and crowded streets to a universe of luxury and poetry as the women penetrate the royal palace to listen to the funeral song in honour of Adonis.

This art of dissonance distinguishes the bucolic poems of Theocritus from their often insipid imitations. The countryside of Theocritus is not always idyllic. To be sure, it is often a 'pleasant' world for which city dwellers long, a *locus amoenus* where the air is filled with the chirping of cicadas and the song of birds, where springs are pure, shade is cool and sheep gambol on the tender grass while shepherds turn their thoughts towards poetry and love. Yet realism is not entirely absent. There are also unwatched animals which graze on trees, thorns that stick in people's feet and farmers who frolic with young girls behind the barn, care nothing for love, and express themselves in clichés and proverbs. This oscillation between idealisation and caricature is at the core of *Idyll* 7, which begins as a harmonious and nostalgic song (sung by a smelly goatherd!) followed by a grotesque poem about a lover hanging around waiting for his ageing beloved. The poem ends with the description of a rural banquet which is transfigured by the memory of one of Heracles' mythical feasts.

Theocritus is the most famous of the bucolic poets, but there were others. We must mention Moschus (*c.* 150 BC), who is also a native of Syracuse. His only extant poem narrates Zeus' abduction of Europa. He succeeds in combining motifs borrowed from various sources. The subject, the abduction of a young girl by a god while she is picking flowers in a field, is borrowed from the Homeric *Hymn to Demeter*. The heroine's dream comes from Aeschylus' *Persians*. The description of the basket is inspired by that of the wooden drinking cup, the prize given to the Thyrsis of Theocritus' *Idyll* 1. Bion of Smyrna (*c.* 100 BC) is the last of the bucolic poets included in the canon. His funeral song in honour of Adonis is also a prime example of a mixing of genres. It takes its theme from one of Sappho's lyric poems and develops it in hexameter and Dorian dialect. The number of spurious idylls which were integrated into the Theocritean corpus also attest to the popularity of the genre he created.

Apollonius of Rhodes (born *c.* 295 BC) also lived at the court of the Ptolemies, but he exiled himself to Rhodes for a time. This philologist, who both ran the library of Alexandria and was the private tutor of the king – two functions which often went hand in hand – was the student and possibly later the rival of Callimachus. Of his works, only an epic poem in four books, the *Argonautica*, survives. It narrates the conquest of the golden fleece by Jason and his companions.

After a prelude and a catalogue of the Argonauts (I, 1–233), the poem narrates the departure of the heroes (I, 234–518), their journey (I, 519–II, 1285), their stay in Colchis, where Jason gains possession of the fleece with the help of Medea (III, I–IV, 211), and their return to Greece (IV, 212–1781). This epic, haunted by the memory of Homer, exemplifies the new aesthetic in the same way as the hymns of Callimachus and the idylls of Theocritus.

Like Callimachus, Apollonius was an erudite poet who collected aetiological legends. He also delights in ethnographical digressions, such as the description of the funerary rites of the inhabitants of Colchis in Book III. His geography, endorsed by the historians and geographers of his time, still amazes modern scholars with the accuracy of its topographical indications. His knowledge of the most up-do-date medical theory, which stressed the role of the nerves in the transmission of emotions, is reflected in his portrait of the lovesick Medea. Philological knowledge can be detected everywhere, for Apollonius implicitly takes a stance on problems linked to the editing and interpreting of the Homeric text.

Like Theocritus, Apollonius has a predilection for discontinuity and abrupt tonal changes. He divides the narrative of the journey of the Argonauts into a series of independent episodes which are frequently interrupted by digressions. He mixes several genres in the same book: light comedy in the scenes of Aphrodite doing her hair and the boy Eros playing knuckle-bones with Ganymedes; tragedy in his portrayal of Medea mad with passion, and epic in the description of the combat between Jason and the Spartans. This fight opens with a superb Homeric simile and imputes to Jason an exploit greater even than those of Diomedes, Hector and Aeneas: he brandishes a stone that four men could not lift, in place of the *Iliad's* two. It ends, however, with the image of a hero that is as unheroic as possible. Having thrown his stone, Jason becomes a spectator of the action and hides 'bravely' under his shield (III, 1370).

This episode exemplifies the spirit of the whole poem. Playing with echo and dissonance, it cites epic the better to distance itself from it. Apollonius reminds us that 'the singers of old still cele-brate' (I, 18–19) the construction of the ship Argo, but does not develop the theme himself. He transforms the *Iliad's* catalogue of ships into a catalogue of heroes. He borrows the episode of the Sirens from the *Odyssey*, but introduces Orpheus, who triumphs over their virginal voices with his cithara (IV, 907–9). Apollonius also takes well-known Homeric similes and changes their meaning. In Book III, the apparition of Jason, like that of Achilles in Book XXII of the *Iliad*, is compared to the baneful Sirius. However, this comparison no longer foreshadows the massacres of war, but the torments of love.

This is why the *Argonautica* is referred to as an anti-epic. Men and their actions are subordinated to women and their passions. Among the gods, Aphrodite takes the place of Zeus. The figure of

Medea, who inspired the Dido of the *Aeneid*, dominates the two
last books, and the hero himself is more of a seducer than a warrior
– the splendours of Achilles' shield are therefore replaced by those
of Jason's cloak.

This negative definition of the *Argonautica* is unfair, however. It
does not do justice to Apollonius' masterful *tour de force*, which
creates a constant tension between the archaism of its theme and
the novelty of its form. This work, which is in many ways paradoxical and experimental, questions the genre it professes to
illustrate and explores its limits. It is best described as 'an epic for
modern times'.

To give a more complete picture of Hellenistic poetry we should
also mention didactic poems in hexameter that follow the Hesiodic
tradition, and, first among them, the *Phaenomena* of Aratus, written in
the second half of the third century. This philosophical poem of Stoic
influence attests to the brilliance of the literary circle assembled at the
court of Pella around the Macedonian king, Antigonus Gonatas.
Beginning with a hymn to Zeus, it successively discusses astronomy
(v. 1–757) and meteorology (v. 758–1154), showing divine law at
work both in the regular movement of the constellations and variations in the weather. Aratus uses a subtle archaic style that was much
appreciated by the cultured Greek and Latin public. Cicero translated
him and Virgil often alluded to him in the *Georgics*. The *Theriaca*, a
work on reptiles and venomous insects, and the *Alexipharmaca*, which
deals with antidotes to poisons, written by Nicander of Colophon, are
of a later date. Their author uses epic verse for zoology and medicine.
These poems offer a strange and not entirely successful example of the
mixing of genres in Hellenistic poetry.

The *Mimiambi* of Herondas (*c.* 280–265 BC) are also hybrids,
created from a combination of the 'mime' that is a staged dialogue
written in prose, and the iambic metre. They were intended for a
cultivated audience capable of appreciating their racy mixture of
refinement and realism. In artificial and archaic language, imitating
Hipponax, Herondas describes the less flattering aspects of daily
life in the underworld of Alexandria, using refined language to
depict the world of pimps and prostitutes.

The epigram became a genre in itself during the Hellenistic
period. It was at the end of this period, during the first century
BC, that Meleager of Gadara compiled his *Garland*, which is the
earliest collection of epigrams to have survived, as it was integrated
into the *Greek Anthology*, also called the *Palatine Anthology*
(*Anthologian Palatina*, *AP*) (after the tenth-century manuscript

preserved in the Palatine library in Heidelberg). Thirty-seven of the forty-eight authors cited in this compilation belong to the Hellenistic period.

As their etymology indicates, epigrams were first texts 'inscribed upon' monuments and objects; yet, they are also poems that, for the most part, were never engraved in stone, but only imitate genuine epigrams by their brevity. Like the works of Callimachus, who was regarded as the undisputed master of the genre, the epigram stands out by its diversity. This is reflected in metre: Hellenistic epigrams are not solely written in elegiac couplets like genuine epigrams, but are often in iambic trimeters and in even rarer metres; in dialect, which may be Ionian, Doric or even a mixture of both; in themes: in addition to epitaphs and dedications, there are poems celebrating wine and the love of women and men; and finally, the tone of the epigrams, which ranges from humour to high emotion, from parody to seriousness and from sobriety to the most affected mannerisms. A nostalgic poem by Nicias (AP, 9, 315), which invites the reader to refresh himself at a fountain commemorating a dead man, is no less typical than a comic text by Leonidas of Tarentum (AP, 9, 99) formulated as the echo of a curse hurled by a vine stem against a goat who has come to eat it.

Because of its taste for renewal and variation (we have several epigrams celebrating the memory of the poet Erinna) and its art of bringing opposites together (Leonidas of Tarentum (AP, 7, 452) transforms the formula often used at the beginning of epitaphs 'in memory of the sage Euboulos' into a toast, 'let us drink'), the epigram represents the quintessence of Alexandrianism.

8

PROSE

Philosophy

During the Hellenistic period, philosophy, unlike poetry, remained centred in Athens. The names of the various schools where philosophical thought continued to flourish (the Academy, the Lyceum, the 'Garden' of Epicurus, and the Stoa [*stoa* is the Greek word for portico] of the Stoics) were derived from the areas in Athens where they were created, and attest to the enduring importance of this city. However, the philosophers themselves came from all corners of the Greek world: Theophrastus, Aristotle's successor, was from Mytilene; Pyrrhon, the first Sceptic, from Elis; and the most famous figure of Cynicism, Diogenes, from Sinope, on the shores of the Black Sea.

Their work, of which very little is extant, was both abundant and diverse. The ongoing polemic between those upholding opinions, the so-called 'dogmatics', and those who suspended judgement, 'the sceptics', and the conflicts between the different schools account for a large part of this output. In addition, these philosophers wrote systematic treatises for the members of their schools. They also attempted to popularise their theories by means of letters, discourses, handbooks, aphorisms, and even poetry.

This philosophical literature, which was, in theory, addressed to all, in reality targeted the cultivated elite throughout the Greek-speaking world. In it the investigation of nature is reduced to a secondary level of importance; the treatises on physics, often impressively detailed, represented only one branch of philosophy, which was now also concerned with ethics and logic. The philosophers had become less interested in the problems of the city-state, now incorporated into the kingdoms of Alexander's successors. The search for 'the good life' now dominated philosophical enquiry. In a world subject to political upheaval and sudden reversals of fortune,

philosophy taught how to resist the pressures of external circumstances and to gain independence from internal passions. The search
for *ataraxia*, the absence of disturbance, and *apatheia*, the absence
of passion, was common to all philosophical schools created during
the Hellenistic period.

The importance of these schools in the history of literature
varies. We shall mention the Academy only in passing because its
contributions to this field are relatively few. However, it remained
operative as a school until the first century AD, though not always
faithful to the spirit of its founder, Plato. It borrowed from
Scepticism and then Stoicism under the leadership of Antiochus of
Ascalon (born *c*. 130 BC). Its most brilliant representatives,
Arcesilaus of Pitane (315–240) and especially Carneades of Cyrene
(219–129), who gave back to dialectics its critical function, and
advocated, like the Sceptics, the suspension of judgement, followed
in Socrates' footsteps and did not write anything.

We shall not spend much more time on the Lyceum, simply
noting the name of Theophrastus (372–287 BC), who continued
the encyclopaedic work of his master, Aristotle. According to tradition, he wrote 225 works covering all subjects. He is most famous
for his *Characters* which were used as a model by La Bruyère.
Portraying various types of character flaws and the gestures and
speech of those who embody them, these vignettes may have been
intended to serve a moral purpose; today, however, their value lies
in the vividness and precision of the descriptions. This minor work
must not eclipse the contributions of Theophrastus to botany,
rhetoric, and, most importantly, to the history of philosophy. His
Opinions of the Physicists, of which only the treatise *On the Senses* has
survived, is the first doxography or 'collection of opinions' of
philosophers.

If we were to rely solely on the extant works of the Cynics and the
early Sceptics, fragments of poems and a late summary by Teles, their
importance in Greek literature would also be negligible. The most
famous among them, the founder of the school of Scepticism,
Pyrrhon of Elis (born 365 BC), is believed not to have written anything and the tradition that attributes a series of works to Diogenes
of Sinope (413–327), the ideal Cynic, is far from unanimous.

The cynics owe their name to Antisthenes, a friend of Socrates,
who attended the Athenian gymnasium of the Cynosarges ('white
dog'). They introduced into Greek literature a spirit of radical
opposition to authority which had no prior equivalent. Like the
Hippies, to whom they are often compared, these members of a

counter-culture rejected civilisation, challenged the basic conventions of classical Greek life, and preached a return to nature.

They created two genres that were destined to flourish, the 'diatribe' (which is usually translated as 'conversation' but which literally means 'pastime'), popularised by Bion of Borysthenes (born *c.* 335 BC), and the 'satire' created by Menippus of Gadara (beginning of the third century) who, in order to mock the dogmatic philosophers, mixed the serious with the comic (creating the *spoudaiogeloion*) and combined prose and verse. He strongly influenced the *Menippean Satires* of Varro and the dialogues of Lucian.

The Sceptics refused to make assertive judgements and repudiated the possibility of being either right or wrong. Judging from what we know of the poems of Timon of Phlius (320–230 BC), a student of Pyrrhon, the Sceptics saw the suspension of judgement to be the source of tranquillity of the soul, which they equated with happiness. Timon's *Silloi* (*Invectives*), written in hexameters, parody the *Odyssey* and use narrative and dialogue alternatively to abuse and caricature dogmatic philosophers.

As our vocabulary today still shows, the two philosophical movements of Epicureanism and Stoicism had a profound effect on the history of ideas. They also strongly influenced literature.

Epicurus (341–271 BC) was an Athenian, born in Samos. According to Diogenes Laertius, he settled permanently in Athens in 306 BC, 'was a most prolific author and eclipsed all before him in the number of his writings' (X, 26). Only fragments of technical treatises, aphorisms, and three letters preserved by Diogenes Laertius are extant. In these letters, Epicurus summarised the main dogmas of his philosophy so that its doctrines would be within the reach of beginners.

His school had disciples throughout the Greek world well after the end of the Hellenistic era. In about AD 200, a certain Diogenes put up an inscription of the main principles of Epicurus' doctrine at Oenoanda for the benefit of his fellow citizens. This inscription, which is now one of the most important sources for Epicurean philosophy, testifies to the latter's wide diffusion in Asia Minor. Its influence was soon felt throughout the Roman world. The charred remains of a library in Herculaneum contained the works of Epicurus and Philodemus of Gadara (born *c.* 110 BC), an Epicurean who belonged to the circle of the Pisos. Furthermore, the *De Rerum Natura* of Lucretius (*c.* 54 BC) was probably closely inspired by Epicurus' treatise *On Nature*.

Those who confuse Epicureanism with the search for pleasure do not do justice to the refined ideal of a philosophy which, according to Nietzsche, 'renounced . . . almost everything'. Epicurus even rejected the notion of Providence. His gods, set in an eternal tranquillity, played no part in either the lives of men or the course of the stars. He also rejected 'necessity' as the 'destiny of the physicists'. Embracing the atomism of Democritus, he peopled the universe with uncuttable elements combined through random collisions (the famous 'declension' of atoms). Thus, isolated in an indifferent universe, the Epicurean sage removes himself from the city, conducting business there only in exceptional circumstances, as well as from the family (he avoids marriage), replacing these natural communities by a freely chosen society of friends. His knowledge is rooted in experience, and pleasure, which is 'the principle of every choice and avoidance' (*Letter to Menoeceus*, 129), regulates his life. This pleasure is not to be confused with the pleasures of the dissipated. It consists mainly in 'freedom from pain in the body and from disturbance in the soul' (*Letter to Menoeceus*, 131). Thus the absolute freedom of the sage leads, by a strange reversal, to a withdrawal into a 'static pleasure' and retrenchment into the isolation of the garden.

Unlike Epicureanism, which was essentially the creation of a single man, Stoicism was the result of a progressive elaboration, where prominent disciples played a role equal in importance to that of their masters. The school was founded by Zeno of Citium (332–262 BC), a Phoenician, who, for a time, followed the teachings of the Cynics – his *Republic*, which is known through a summary made by Diogenes Laertius, is clearly influenced by the Cynics, as demonstrated by its rejection of civic institutions such as the gymnasium and marriage (he advocates the community of women). Cleanthes of Assos (332–232 BC) succeeded him at the head of the school. Then came Chrysippus of Soloi (281–05 BC) who is regarded as the second founder of the Stoa. Our knowledge of these 'Early Stoics' and their abundant literary production – tradition attributes more than seven hundred treatises to Chrysippus alone – is limited to citations and second-hand summaries.

We are no better informed on the Middle Stoa, represented by Panaetius of Rhodes (185–09 BC), who toned down the more rigid aspects of Stoic ethics, and Posidonius of Apamea (135–50) who, like Aristotle, had an encyclopaedic mind and exerted an influence on the philosophy and the sciences of his times that is hard to measure. With these two men, Stoicism truly penetrated the Roman world: Panaetius was an esteemed adviser to Scipio the Younger and Posidonius had Cicero among his audience.

Stoicism is nowadays synonymous with fortitude and austerity. This definition is not a misconception, but it is undoubtedly incomplete. To the Stoics, morality (which consists of 'living according to nature') is inseparable from physics (knowledge of the nature of human beings and the universe) and logic (which deals with both reasoning and language and allows human beings to attain the truth). This close connection between the parts of the system is illustrated by a series of comparisons. The Stoics, writes Diogenes Laertius in his *Life of Zeno*,

> compare philosophy to a living being: the bones and the nerves are logic, the flesh, ethics, and the soul, physics. They also compare it to an egg: the shell is logic, the white is ethics and the yolk at the centre is physics. They also compare it to a garden: the hedge around it is logic, the fruits, ethics and the earth and trees are physics. (VII, 40)

This unity between the various parts of philosophy is explained by the *logos*, identified with Zeus and universal reason, and the central role it plays in governing the universe – the notion of Providence is at the centre of Stoic cosmology. It also makes knowledge possible: it is because people have been given *logos* that they can acquire adequate knowledge. Lastly, *logos* lies at the heart of a system of ethics which strives to harmonise human will with the order of the world and wisdom with politics – unlike the Epicurean, the Stoic engages in action and takes part in public affairs. This mixture of rationalism and realism explains the extraordinary impact of Stoicism during the Hellenistic period, in both the Greek and the Roman worlds.

Historians and geographers

As far as we can tell from the extant titles, fragments or summaries – aside from Strabo's *Geography* no complete work has survived – the geographical literature of the time, like Hellenistic philosophy, combined concrete fact adaptations with abstract speculation.

A series of travel accounts and compilations, which we know of solely through adaptations or, worse still, their detractors, revived the Ionian tradition of enquiry. These were the *Periplus* (circumnavigation) of Pytheas of Massalia (*c.* 322–313 BC), who made a voyage up the Atlantic coast to the mysterious island of Thule; the chronicle of Alexander's admiral Nearchus, who explored the coast from the Indus to the Euphrates; and the *Indica* of Megasthenes (*c.* 350–290 BC), who travelled throughout the Mauryan empire. Later, the treatise *On the Red Sea* by Agatharchides of Cnidus (*c.* 215 to after 145 BC) gathered the results of explorations of this region undertaken at the request of the Ptolemies. Early in the first century, Artemidorus of Ephesus combined compilation with autopsy and used the traditional structure of the travel narrative (from West to East) to describe the whole of the inhabited world in his *Geography*.

The genre of the *periegesis*, which describes a site or region mixing mythology with history, and geography, like a travel guide, developed during this period. We shall mention two names: Polemon of Ilium and Demetrius of Scepsis, both authors of a *periegesis* of the Troad.

During the Hellenistic period, 'theoretical' geography reached its apogee with Eratosthenes (*c.* 276–202 BC) who relied on geometry, astronomy and physics to present a rational view of the world. A great scholar and head of the library of Alexandria, he wrote a treatise on the size of the Earth in which he calculated the length of the meridian, and a *Geography* in three books, which was sharply criticised by the astronomer Hipparchus in the second century BC in a treatise known from Strabo. Scientific geography also flourished with such scholars as the Stoic Posidonius (135–50 BC), who proposed a rational explanation for the tides in his treatise *On the Ocean*.

In both content and method, the *Geography* of Strabo of Amaseia (64 BC–AD 23) represents Hellenistic geography at its height. It combines theoretical discussion and concrete description, autopsy and compilation. The *Prolegomena* (Books I and II) discuss general geography and criticise the theses of Strabo's predecessors. Books III to XVII describe the inhabited world from West to East, region by region; starting with Spain, Gaul and Brittany, moving on to Italy and Greece and then to Asia Minor, the Orient, India, and finishing with Libya and Africa. Yet this work, which 'has a direct bearing upon statesmanship' (I, 1, 16) and was written for 'those holding important positions' (I, 1, 23), already belongs to the Roman world since Strabo, a Greek who was born in the Pontus (a region which fell under Roman influence after the defeat of Mithridates) spent a long time in Rome and used Greek erudition for the benefit of the Empire and its rulers.

Hellenistic history, like classical history, was closely linked to geography. It was, in fact, often written by the same men

(Eratosthenes, Posidonius and Strabo were also famous for their historical works), with the same methods (autopsy and compilation), and the same aims (Polybius' *History* is as political as Strabo's *Geography*). Unfortunately, historical works from the Hellenistic period have suffered greatly from the hazards of transmission (no text is preserved in its entirety).

History during the Hellenistic period catered to all tastes and audiences. Scientific minds could delight in chronologies with the *Chronographies* of Eratosthenes, which were continued by the *Chronicles* attributed to Apollodorus of Athens (*c.* 180–110). Those fond of amusing stories could read genealogies. The simply curious were offered local histories, covering migration, the founding of cities and kinship ties between peoples. These were focused on both the traditional centres and fringes of the Greek world. The Barbarians were not neglected, as demonstrated by Manetho's *History of Egypt* and Berossus' *History of Babylon*.

The *History of Sicily* from its origins to the eve of the first Punic war, written by Timaeus of Tauromenium (356–260), is of special importance. A Sicilian exiled in Athens, this historian was the first to recognise the importance of Rome in his history. Unfortunately, his work is usually known through the distorting lens of Polybius' criticism.

Historians also continued to write contemporary histories which encompassed the whole of Greek affairs, yet their spirit was a far cry from that of Thucydides. Their *Hellenica* appeal to the emotions and aim at the pleasure of the moment by 'trying to seize the reader's attention by means of extraordinary scenes' (Polybius, 3, 56). This 'tragic' history, sharply criticised by Polybius, is exemplified in the third century by Duris of Samos, who covers the period from 370 to 280 BC, and his successor, Phylarchus of Athens, who relates the events from 272 to 220 BC.

A great number of histories of Alexander, written by his close aides, emerge alongside the histories of Greece. We shall limit ourselves here to only three names: Callisthenes (370–327 BC), whose name was famous enough to be used as a pseudonym by the author of the *Alexander Romance* (a work of fiction only known in its later versions); Cleitarchus, who is best remembered for sensationalistic scenes, and Ptolemy, who became king of Egypt and seems to have been the most factual of them all.

All these works have been eclipsed by the universal histories of Polybius and Diodorus of Sicily.

The *History* of Polybius of Megalopolis (208–126 BC), like that of Thucydides, discusses the most important political and military event of its time (in Greek *pragmata* means 'affairs', hence the name 'pragmatic history'), the conquest of practically all the inhabited world by the Romans in less than fifty-three years. This topic was an obvious choice for a young aristocrat from the Peloponnese who was brought to Rome as a hostage after the defeat of Perseus at Pydna (167 BC). There he mingled with Roman high society, even participating in the siege of Carthage beside Scipio Aemilianus. He returned to Greece after the sacking of Corinth in 146 BC.

In the forty books of his *History*, of which only one-third remain, he retraces the first Punic war to explain the political situation in Rome in 220 BC, on the eve of the second Punic war (I and II). He then relates the events that led up to the battle of Pydna (III–XXIX), the capture of Carthage and the sacking of Corinth (XXX–XL) in chronological sequence (each book covers a period from one to four years).

Again, like Thucydides, his history is intended to be useful rather than to provide immediate pleasure. It claims to profit thoughtful minds by revealing 'why what was done or spoken led to failure or success' (XXII, 25, b), subordinating narration to 'demonstration' (in Greek, *apodeixis*, which explains why Polybius' history is also described as apodeictic). Not content with simply describing the expansion of Rome, which some of his contemporaries attributed to chance or destiny, Polybius explains and justifies it in his sixth book in terms of the particular qualities of the Roman constitution, which combines the advantages of monarchy, oligarchy and democracy while avoiding their drawbacks.

We should not minimise the originality of Polybius both morally and intellectually. Recognising the all-embracing power of Fortune, he proposed to teach man to 'bear the vicissitudes of fate bravely' (I, 1) – in other words, he invites the Greeks to submit to the Romans, whose power he deems irresistible. Through the organisation of his narrative he tries to 'bring before his readers, under one synoptical view, the operations by which [Fortune] has accomplished her general purpose' (I, 4). As conceived by Polybius, the unity of the universal history is the result, not of the author's arbitrary choice, but of the course of history, which has 'guided almost all the affairs of the world in one direction and forced them to incline towards one and the same end' (I, 4). Such a conviction undoubtedly accounts for the influence of a work that was subsequently continued by Posidonius and Strabo and imitated by Livy.

The *Universal History* of Diodorus of Sicily (first century BC) bears little resemblance to that of Polybius. Like the work of

Nicolaus of Damascus, it is based on compilation, hence its name, the *Library of History*. It is an attempt to blend the histories of various states into a single narrative like the work of Ephorus (causing serious organisational problems for the chronology since the different calendars did not coincide), but Diodorus' history exceeds that of Ephorus in its breadth. It goes back to events prior to the Trojan War (while Ephorus begins with the return of the Heraclidae) and encompasses both Greeks and barbarians.

The extant books (I–V and XI–XXII) and extracts transmitted by the Byzantines provide a sufficiently accurate picture of this work, which originally comprised forty books. Books I–VI give an account of mythical times and begin with Egypt, 'the country where mythology places the origin of the gods' (I, 9, 6). Books VII–XVII relate the 'universal history of events from the Trojan War to the death of Alexander' (I, 4, 6). In the last twenty-three books Diodorus enumerates 'all subsequent events down to the beginning of the war between the Romans and the Celts' (ibid.) or rather until the defeat of the last republican troops at Thapsus (III, 38, 2).

This book compiled from other books cannot be reduced to a simple collage of bits and pieces from here and there. Diodorus claims to exercise critical judgement. If he follows earlier historians in his account of Ethiopia, it is, he says, 'after inquiring carefully of them about each matter and testing the stories of historians, that we have composed our account so as to go with the opinions on which they most fully agree' (III, 11, 3). Even when he imitates closely the descriptions of Herodotus, he does not hesitate to introduce contemporary ideas into his narrative and transform into 'noble savages' the peoples whom Herodotus portrayed in a clearly negative light.

As it stands, this work, composed in both Alexandria and Rome, addressed to both educated Greeks and Romans, attests in its way to the continuity between the Hellenistic and Roman periods.

Part 4

THE ROMAN EMPIRE
From Compromise to Mutation

9

THE EMPIRE
FROM AUGUSTUS TO
CONSTANTINE

The age of compromise

After Octavian's victory at Actium (31 BC), Egypt became a Roman province. This annexation ended a process of conquest that had begun nearly two centuries before with the creation of the province of Macedonia. Henceforth the whole of the Hellenistic world was under Roman domination. This progressive political annexation, which respected the former structure of the city states, did not lead, however, to the acculturation of the Greeks. On the contrary, the Romans became Hellenised. Until at least the third century AD, the Roman Empire was bilingual: Latin was the political and legal language and Greek the language of culture. This explains why cultivated Romans, who received, for the most part, a rhetorical education in Greek, were proud of their knowledge of Greek language and literature. The Greeks, however, even when they had become Roman citizens and been appointed to important positions in the Empire, were almost embarrassed by their bilingualism, a necessity which they justified on practical grounds. They remained essentially ignorant of Latin literature, whereas the number of Romans who wrote in Greek was immeasurable.

All this explains the vitality of Greek literature during the Imperial period. It was patronised by the sovereign as it had been during the Hellenistic period: just as Ptolemy had created the Museum, so the Antonines created the chairs of rhetoric and philosophy in Athens. Its authors received imperial favours: Plutarch and Appian became procurators, and Arrian was appointed consul and governor of Cappadocia 'because of his eminent culture' (Photius, *cod*. 58). The influence of Greek literature continued to spread in both the East and West: the kingdom of Commagene,

home of Lucian, one of the period's greatest writers, was not hel-
lenised until after its integration into the empire (72 BC). Cadiz and
Arles produced 'Greek' sophists (Favorinus) and philosophers
(Moderatus). Rome, which benefited from the decline of Alexandria
became, like Athens and the rich cities of Asia Minor, a seat of
Hellenism and a centre for Hellenisation: it was in Rome that the
Numidian King Juba II received the education that made him a
Greek historian.

Like the literature of the Hellenistic period, Imperial literature
appealed to a cultured elite which, though geographically dispersed
(the Roman Empire extended from the Iberian peninsula to the
Euphrates), was nevertheless remarkably homogeneous due to
the prevalence of an education based on the classics and on rhetoric.
This classicism bore no resemblance to Hellenistic preciosity. The
writers of the Imperial period did not cultivate rare allusions, but
always refer to the best known texts which were the common
heritage of the cultivated elite. To translate their experience and
describe the present in terms understood by all, they imitated
the great models, used the same rhetorical topoi and resorted to a
deliberately archaic language, influenced by the Attic prose-writers
of the fifth and fourth centuries. Should we interpret this constant
reference to the past as a denial of the present? Probably not, since
the same men who ceaselessly evoke Greece at the height of classical culture also praise the Roman peace that ended the age-old
struggles among the city states and guaranteed social order. These
writers identified with Rome (most of them had already received
Roman citizenship even before the edict of Caracalla that abolished
the distinction between citizens and subjects within the Empire in
AD 212) and played an active role in the administration of the
Empire. The constant reference to the past and its great men was
first and foremost the means by which the cultivated class cemented
its unity and affirmed its identity through a language which was
their common heritage.

We are able to sketch a fairly accurate picture of the literary
production of the Imperial era because of the relatively large number
of extant texts, at least in prose. The art of poetry, in the first three
centuries of the common era, was largely neglected and supplanted
by poetic prose. For once, we cannot blame the hazards of textual
transmission, but must agree with Plutarch that 'as currencies,
poetry, music and song were no longer in circulation' (*Moralia*,
406b). There were, of course, some exceptions: The Anthology
Palatine inscriptions and papyri attest to the vitality of the epigram.

In the second century AD, the poems on fishing (*Halieutica*) and hunting (*Cynegetica*) attributed to Oppian and the *Description of the World* of Dionysius 'Periegetes' continued the Alexandrian tradition of didactic poetry in dactylic hexameters.

As a rule, the conferences of sophists replaced the recitations of rhapsodes. Hymns in prose – here we must mention Aelius Aristides – took over from hymns in verse. Dio of Prusa's *Euboicus* and Longus, *Daphnis and Chloe* returned to themes once addressed by Theocritus. Lucian's *Dialogues of the Gods* transposed the genre of 'the miniature epic' (*epyllion*) created by the Alexandrian poets into prose.

Since we cannot cover all the prose-writers of the period, let us first survey the critical works that laid the foundations of classical culture and then focus on two authors who embody Imperial literature, Plutarch and Lucian. We shall also outline the evolution of rhetoric, which supplanted all the other genres during this period, and the birth of the novel. Finally, we shall examine the history and philosophy produced during the Empire before concluding with the birth of Greek Christian literature during the second century.

Classicism

The Imperial period, which witnessed a return to classicism and imitation of the great models, was the golden age of prescriptive criticism. For every genre, the Hellenistic 'canons' were still authoritative and qualities to be imitated and faults to be avoided, were compiled for each author.

Dionysius of Halicarnassus, a Greek rhetor who settled in Rome in about 30 BC and thanked, in the Preface to his *On the Ancient Orators* 'those in power in Rome itself ... who are very well-educated people of good taste' (which, for a Greek, means, in no uncertain terms, that they are defenders of Hellenism), championed the cause of a return to the 'Attic Muse' and to ancient rhetoric, shamefully supplanted by 'a Muse from some ghastly hole in Asia' and bombastic Hellenistic rhetoric. Thus he exemplifies this ideal by analysing the masters of Attic prose from an essentially stylistic point of view. First among them, Dionysius placed Demosthenes, who combined the best elements of his predecessors and favoured a 'middle' style half-way between the plain and the grand.

The bulk of Dionysius' extant critical work concerns orators (his treatises *On the Ancient Orators, On Demosthenes* and *On Dinarchus* and his *First Letter to Ammaeus* on Demosthenes), Thucydides (*On*

Thucydides and the *Second Letter to Ammaeus*), and Plato (*Letter to Cheius Pompius*). Yet *On the Disposition of Words* and *On Imitation*, of which only fragments and a summary are extant, show us that he was also interested in poetry.

The treatise *On the Sublime*, long attributed to Longinus, a sophist of the third century, was probably the work of a contemporary of Dionysius of Halicarnassus. It reflects the same didactic concerns, but its aesthetic choices are different: it comes down firmly in favour of the sublime, which 'tears everything up like a whirlwind' (1, 4), teaches the reader to distinguish it from turgidity, and illustrates the qualities which contribute to it with examples from poets.

Despite their differences, these two works are both equally indebted to stylistic theories elaborated during the Hellenistic period. Our knowledge of these theories is largely derived from a treatise, *On Style*, wrongly attributed to a student of Aristotle, Demetrius of Phalerum, and difficult to date (possibly the first century BC). In this work, 'Demetrius' distinguished four styles (the 'plain', the 'elegant', the 'forceful' and the 'grand') and four deformed versions of these styles analysing their components. During the second century, the treatise of Hermogenes of Tarsus, *On Types of Style*, defines the virtues which lend grandeur to a style, starting from an analysis of Demosthenes as the exemplar of all types. Hermogenes deems such an analysis to be indispensable for orators since, in his view, excellence can only be achieved through imitating the style of the Ancients.

This interest in the literature of the past is present in the works of Plutarch (AD 40–120) and Lucian (born *c.* AD 120), two authors who played a unique role in the literary production of the time because of the importance and diversity of their work.

Plutarch and Lucian

Plutarch is known primarily as the author of the forty-four *Parallel Lives* (renamed the *The Lives of the Noble Grecians and Romans* by his most famous English translator, Thomas North), a set of biographies which pairs a Greek with a Roman and usually finishes with a comparison of the two. In addition, he also wrote biographies of the Caesars (only the *Lives* of *Galba* and *Otho* are extant) and isolated *Lives* (*Artaxerxes* and *Aratos*). Furthermore, Plutarch is the author of about eighty treatises, usually referred to by their Latin name, *Moralia* (moral works – a name that does not convey their extraordinary diversity. In fact, they not only address moral issues but are also concerned with philosophy, religion, politics, literature, history, science and even dietetics.

The work of Lucian is certainly less abundant (eighty-six works, often quite short, are attributed to him, but they are not all authentic). It is, however, more varied: Lucian wrote poetry (epigrams, a parody in verse) and composed, aside from the dialogues upon which his reputation is based, declamations, speeches, praises, letters, pamphlets, and even two biographies. Both are unclassifiable and do not belong to a well-defined genre. Plutarch, who alerts his reader to the differences that separate biography from history, is not quite a historian and does not adhere closely to the dogma of a philosophical school. Lucian was not recognised by either the rhetors or the philosophers as a member of their group. He was accused of having betrayed rhetoric and incurred the hostility of all the philosophical schools.

Both authors deride the excesses of the Atticists of their time. Plutarch mocks 'a style that is pure Attic and surely plain' (*Moralia*, 42d), while Lucian attacks the writers who 'talk to us from a thousand years ago' (*Lexiphanes*, 20). They are, however, the most representative writers of the literature of the Imperial period, embodying the two sides of this culture. They are different in everything: time (Lucian was born in the year of Plutarch's death), place (Plutarch of Chaeronea was a Greek from the mainland and Lucian of Samosata 'a Syrian born on the banks of the Euphrates'), social background (the former belonged to the elite, was respected by consuls, and honoured by the emperors Trajan and Hadrian, while the latter freely admits to being an upstart who owed everything to culture and ended up as a member of the staff of the prefect of Egypt), and their relation to literary tradition.

Plutarch parades his high regard for a tradition which, in fact, he did not hesitate to remodel. He warrants his literary choices by turning to the great authors of the past: if he writes 'table talk' it is because 'Plato, Xenophon, Aristotle . . . all considered the recording of conversations held at table a task worth some effort' (*Moralia*, 612d). However, such a claim does not prevent him from renewing the genre of the symposium: whereas Plato and Xenophon focused on one subject, Plutarch switches from one topic to another in his *Tabletalk*. Plutarch also searched the past for models of life that the present was unable to supply: the great men whose biographies he relates in his *Parallel Lives* provided him with an image of virtue and allowed him to 'free himself from any ignoble, base or vicious impressions, contracted from the contagion of ill company that one may be unavoidably engaged in' (*Life of Timoleon*, 1, 5). Yet, in order for these examples to become immediately useful to his contemporaries, he made them embody the values of his own time (his Pericles becomes a model for kindness and justice) without regard for historical accuracy. The past of Plutarch is a past rewritten in the present tense.

Lucian plays a more subtle game with tradition. He treats the great texts with delightful irreverence: in *A Professor of Public Speaking*, he summarises the Prologue of the *Theogony* in one phrase: 'Hesiod was given a leaf or two from Helicon, and at once he became a poet instead of a shepherd' (4). Yet he is the first to recognise, in the *Fisherman*, that he is constantly plundering these texts and that his work is a collage of passages borrowed from the great philosophers of the past. Even when he seeks inspiration in the present for models of vice (*Alexander the False Prophet*) and virtue (the Philosopher *Demonax*), his portraits are filled with echoes of the past: the biography of Alexander the false prophet parodies the biographies of Alexander the Great (Lucian explicitly cites Arrian, but he could just as well have referred to Plutarch).

These authors also had two diametrically opposed conceptions of literature and its role. Plutarch felt that the writer should favour usefulness over 'beauty of style' and that pleasure is merely a seasoning to help in the digestion of a moral lesson. This is why he denounces the malignity of Herodotus and claims the superiority of Menander over Aristophanes: the former is appreciated by cultivated men and quoted during banquets, while the latter flatters the taste of debauched revellers and slanderers. On the other hand, Lucian, who was a great admirer of Aristophanes, emphasises entertainment and readily confesses that he does not offer anything consistent to his readers; like the Prometheus of Hesiod, who kept the meat for men and offered only bones concealed in fat to the gods, he tricks his readers and offers them comic jests under philosophic solemnity' (*You're a Prometheus in words*, 7). Plutarch engages in a polemical debate with the Stoics because his view of the world is inconsistent with theirs. Lucian only attacks them because his interlocutor, Hermotimus, is a die-hard Stoic, but, as he says himself (*Hermotimus*, 85), he has no personal grievance against them.

In fact, Plutarch is a moralist and the tradition was correct in giving the title of *Precepts* to three of his treatises. In the *Moralia*, as in the *Lives*, he ceaselessly preaches an optimistic moral philosophy neither loose nor austere, to those around him and, more widely, to the elite to which he belongs. He professes to be able to tame passions without destroying them and wants to teach men how to see the bright side of things, 'to assign to each event a place in which what suits us shall help us most and what is unwanted shall do least harm' (*Moralia*, 467a–b). This wisdom claims to be Platonic, but Plutarch's Plato is revised and corrected in order to become 'kind and accommodating to civil life', as Montaigne cleverly notes. For Plutarch, unlike Plato, is a man of compromise in both political and religious matters.

In politics, he tries to reconcile the demands of the Roman Empire with the desire for Greek autonomy by advocating a harmony between the city states that would reduce the interventions of the Romans as much as possible, and he behaves accordingly. He is himself an example of good-spirited resignation: of course the liberty of the city states depends entirely on the goodwill of the Romans, but if they enjoyed more freedom 'perhaps it would not be better for them' (*Moralia*, 824c).

In religious matters, Plutarch, who was both a philosopher and a priest of Apollo at Delphi, denounces superstition and atheism, and tries to reconcile tradition and reason: reading myths allegorically, he attributes a symbolic value to ritual, depicts life in the beyond in such a way as to inspire a conversion to virtue and tirelessly defends the oracles.

It is the lively and concrete character of these lessons that gives them their impact, for Plutarch believes in the effectiveness of images, myths and, above all, examples. If he became the biographer of great men in the *Parallel Lives*, it was because 'acts of virtue also produce an emulation and an eagerness in the minds of the readers that may lead them to imitation' (*Life of Pericles*, 1, 4). He therefore emphasises their virtues and glosses over their vices. His portraits are artfully airbrushed to flatter their model. He eliminates villains as much as he can, only retaining one or two pairs for pedagogical purposes: they serve as foils and prevent a boring uniformity. The same concern perhaps explains his choice of presenting the portraits in pairs. Furthermore, the use of two examples taken from two different cultural contexts allows Plutarch to extract the essence of virtue with more clarity.

Lucian is an ordinary man 'completely unpractised in that acme of the virtues that the cream of men display' (*Apology*, 15). His moral standards can be summarised as 'laughing at most things and taking nothing seriously' (*Menippus*, 21). If he teaches virtue it is first and foremost through the spectacle of vice. In this respect he resembles one of his characters, the philosopher Nigrinus, who has chosen to reside in the most corrupt city, Rome, because 'one has cause to admire philosophy when one beholds so much folly'

(*Nigrinus*, 20). He is a satirist who claims to be 'a bluff-hater, cheat-hater, liar-hater, vanity-hater' (*Fisherman*, 20). His caustic irony spares neither the powerful nor the dead, nor even the gods. When he accepts an official position, he is well aware that he is selling out, but pleads his case by reminding his reader that 'no one does anything without pay' (*Apology*, 13) and that all men, beginning with the Emperor and the highest dignitaries, are 'mercenaries' (ibid). He mocks the dead and gives an unflattering image of the afterlife. He derides the gods by taking their myths and images literally (an approach which is diametrically opposed to the allegorical interpretation of Plutarch). Yet all this is but a game: Lucian is neither a militant atheist nor an 'enemy of Roman order'.

These two works differ not only in their aim but also in their form. Plutarch takes on history and philosophy, while Lucian contents himself with the minor genres and elementary exercises in rhetoric. Both wrote dialogues, but each gives the genre a distinctive slant. The dialogues of Plutarch retain the dignity of the philosophical dialogue; they are 'respectable', speculating 'upon the gods, nature and the cycle of the universe, treading the air high up above the clouds' (*Double Indictment*, 33). Lucian, on the other hand, as Dialogue complains, 'broke [his] wings . . . took away from [him] the respectable tragic mask that I had, and put another upon [him] that is comic, satyr-like, and almost ridiculous' (ibid).

Even when Plutarch and Lucian seem to switch roles, a difference in tone remains. Plutarch is serious even in his jokes: when he endows an animal with speech in the *Gryllus* (Gryllus is on one of the companions of Odysseus who is transformed into a pig by Circe), it is to attack the Stoics who deny animals reason and intelligence. The *Cock* of Lucian, which also portrays a speaking animal, is a whimsical and gratuitous farce which playfully accumulates references to literature and philosophical allusions, since the cock is one of the avatars of Pythagoras.

By the same token, Lucian teases his reader even when he is – or pretends to be – serious: the 'message' of the philosopher Nigrinus is preceded by a meticulous exordium respectful of the rules of rhetoric and followed by a hyperbolic eulogy whose irony casts doubt upon the sincerity of Lucian's 'conversion'.

Rhetoric

Neither Plutarch nor Lucian are included in the *Lives of the Sophists* written and compiled by Philostratus at the beginning of the third century. In this work, Philostratus dates the emergence of what he calls the 'Second Sophistic' with Aeschines, in the fourth century BC, and Nicetas of Smyrna, in the first century AD, and is then only concerned with the star orators of the first two centuries of the common era. He is, along with Dio of Prusa (*c.* AD 40–110, nicknamed Chrysostom 'golden mouth' for his eloquence), Aelius Aristides (117–189) and, to a lesser degree, Maximus of Tyre (end of the second century AD), our main source on the rhetoric of the period.

This label with its reference to the past and to the first sophists in particular was quite in keeping with the taste of the time. The analogies between the two movements are, however, superficial. Like the great sophists in Periclean Athens,[1] the sophists of Philostratus were successful orators and travelled frequently. Yet this name draws attention away from the change of setting and, more importantly, the change of purpose in rhetoric.

We shall start by considering the change of setting. The 'divas' of the second sophistic were travelling in a wider world, throughout all the lands of the Roman Empire at its height. Their tours took them to Rome and Alexandria (Aelius Aristides and Dio both went to these cities), to Athens and the richer cities of Asia Minor such as Smyrna, Ephesus and Pergamum. These men no longer displayed their talents in the homes of private individuals as had the sophists of the fifth century (Plato's *Protagoras*, for example, is set in the home of Callias), but gave their recitals in theatres, where they addressed the entire population, or in specially designed auditoriums, as richly decorated as Italian opera houses (Lucian provides us with a luscious description of such a room in *The Hall*). These were spectacular performances that even emperors did not miss: when Marcus Aurelius passed through Smyrna he asked to meet the local star, Aelius Aristides, and attended a declamatory performance. These shows probably started with an introduction (*prolalia*), which was intended to dazzle the listeners with its ingenuity, then continued with a declamation (*meletē*), which often borrowed its theme from the glorious past of the Greeks. As Lucian pointed out, the trick was to 'cap everything with references to Marathon and Cynegirus, without which you cannot succeed at all. Let Athos be continually crossed in ships and the Hellespont on foot; let the sun be shadowed by the arrows of the Medes, Xerxes flee the field and Leonidas receive admiration' (Lucian, *Professor of Rhetoric*, 18). In these performances, costumes and the musicality of the voice were as important as the text: even if the spectators did not understand

Greek, Philostratus tells us in a passage on Adrianus of Tyre: 'they listened to him as to a sweet-voiced nightingale, struck with admiration for his smooth tongue, his well-modulated and flexible voice, and his rhythms, whether in prose or when he sang in recitative' (II, 10).

The role of the sophists also changed. The development of the first sophistic was a purely Greek phenomenon, linked to the development of democracy in Athens. The second sophistic embodies, more than any other genre, the historical compromise between Greek culture and Roman power. This explains why some have stressed its historical importance,[2] while others have underlined its contribution to literature.[3]

Greece and Rome were now given equal praise as the work of Aelius Aristides demonstrates. His *Panathenaic Oration* celebrates, together with Athens, the universality of the Greek language and culture which had become the 'common' possession of all the inhabitants of the Empire: 'for all the cities and all the races of mankind turned to you and your form of life . . . emulation of your wisdom and way of life has spread over every land' (324). His oration *To Rome* recalls that the Empire, which has allowed all the elites of the peoples it has subjected to participate in its power has made the name Roman a 'common' title by the granting of Roman citizenship.

The sophists, who were almost always members of the elite, naturally came to play the role of mediator between the central authorities and their native Greek cities, voicing the latter's needs: after the earthquake that destroyed Smyrna in 178, Aelius Aristides wrote a letter to Marcus Aurelius that drew tears from the emperor and obtained from him substantial monetary aid. Wherever they went the sophists sought to resolve conflicts with local governors: for example, Dio of Prusa in his speech to Tarsus (*Discourse* 34). They also criticised the cities for vain quarrels over precedence, and preached concord and obedience to the will of Rome: Dio thus tried to resolve the differences between Nicomedia and Nicea (*Discourse* 38) and Prusa and Apamea (*Discourses* 40 and 41), while Aelius Aristides did the same for Ephesus, Pergamum and Smyrna (*Discourse* 23). Finally, they also worked to reconcile conflicting groups within the cities by threatening Roman intervention (Dio's *Discourse* 39 *On Concord in Nicea following the Cessation of Faction* and Aelius Aristides' *Discourse* 24, *To the Rhodians, On Concord*).

The sophists also dedicated themselves to the defence and display of Greek culture. They encouraged the Greeks to remain faithful to their traditions and warned them against possible deviations.

Dio, in his *Alexandrian Oration* (32), denounces the excessive enthusiasm of the Alexandrians for modern music and chariot races. Aelius Aristides addresses similar warnings to the inhabitants of Smyrna (*Discourse* 29) and to the Spartans (in a speech known through its refutation by Libanius).

They constantly celebrated the glorious past of Greece in declamations that borrowed subject matter from Homer and, more frequently, from Greek history and the great era of the city states, from Solon to Chaeronea (with a preference for the Persian wars and the fourth century). Examples abound; we shall limit ourselves to Aelius Aristides. His speech, *On the Embassy*, is a rewrite of the speech addressed to Achilles by the envoys of Agamemnon in the ninth book of the *Iliad*, and his *Sicilian Speeches* portray two orators at the time of the Sicilian expedition, who speak alternately, one exhorting the Athenians to send the reinforcements requested by Nicias, the other seeking to dissuade them.

These orators also kept alive the memory of classical authors. Not only did they cite them, they also wrote pastiches of their work, compiled and compared them, and simply praised them. Dio wrote praises of Homer and Socrates (*Discourses* 53 and 54). He compares the *Philoctetes* plays of the three great tragedians in his *Discourse* 52, which is strongly inspired by Aristophanes' *Frogs* in its critical approach, and thereby increases our understanding of the originality of Sophocles' play, the only one of the three that has survived. At the end of the second century, the *Letters* of Alciphron, like those of Aelian, re-create the world of New Comedy. Aelian was also the author of collections of excerpts and anecdotes, *On the Characteristics of Animals* and *Varia Historia* ('*Miscellany*'). The value of these two works for us lies mainly in the information they provide on lost works and the citations they preserve. The same can be said of Aelian's contemporary, Athenaeus of Naucratis, who used the convenient setting of a banquet given by a rich Roman consul for distinguished intellectuals (the physician Galen and the renowned jurist Ulpian are among the guests) to display his erudition on table manners and gastronomy. This dinner of wise men (*Deipnosophistai* in Greek) is in fact one of the major sources for our knowledge of Middle and New Comedy.

The orators of the second sophistic even tried to reconcile classical authors to create a homogeneous tradition. After praising Homer (*Discourse* 53) and Socrates (*Discourse* 54), Dio tries to reconcile his admiration for these two men and demonstrate 'that Socrates is in truth a pupil of Homer . . . first and foremost he resembles him in his character . . . and furthermore they were both devoted to the same things and spoke about the same things . . . human virtue and vice . . . and they were most effective at making similes and comparisons' (*Discourse* 55, 7–9). Similarly, Maximus of Tyre attempts to bridge the gap between Plato and Homer.

Even when the sophists were discussing the present and giving out advice on current events, they continued to refer to the past. Their speeches are written in a resolutely archaic style which echoes the great models: Dio's oration *To the Rhodians* recalls Demosthenes' *Against Leptines*, while the *Panathenaic Oration* of Aelius Aristides constantly refers back to Isocrates' *Panathenaic Oration*. They often hid behind the great names of the past to advance their own views: when Dio delivered his speech on kingship before Trajan, he used Alexander (*Discourse* 2) and Diogenes (*Discourse* 4) as mouthpieces. Even when he addresses the emperor directly, he begins with historical anecdotes that put the present into perspective: in *Discourse* 1 he takes on the persona of Timotheus, Alexander's favourite flautist and, in *Discourse* 3, he contrasts his positive judgement of Trajan with Socrates' view of the Persian king.

We should not be fooled by these disguises. When Aelius Aristides, in his discourse *To Plato, In Defence of the Four* (*Discourse* 3) defends rhetoric and the four great Athenian politicians against Plato's attacks in the *Gorgias*, he is not simply indulging in an academic exercise; he is also speaking about the status of rhetoric in the Roman empire and his assault on Plato is an attack against the philosophers of his own time. For rhetoric was in fact in direct competition with philosophy, claiming that 'orators are qualified to deliberate and their profession is competent to make man good' (Dio, *Discourse* 13), and to make useful speeches and exhort the young and others; (Aelius Aristides, *On the Four*, 404 Dindorf), an aim which was precisely that of philosophy. The dialogues and speeches dedicated to philosophical themes, such as beauty (21) and fortune (61), and moral themes, such as grief (17) and virtue (69), constitute a large part of the work of Dio of Prusa, a writer who has been difficult to classify. For Philostratus he is 'a philosopher particularly gifted in rhetoric', but for Synesius, who wrote a treatise on him in the fifth century, he is a rhetor who converted to philosophy after his exile (he was banished from Italy to Bithynia by Domitian). The same difficulty arises in the case of Maximus of Tyre, for his forty-one 'lectures' include Platonic developments (10: *Is knowledge reminiscence?*), moral treatises (14: *What distinguishes friends from flatterers?*), and purely rhetorical pieces such as 23 and

24, which alternately present two opposing theses on the comparative utility of the soldier and the farmer).

The orator who competed with the philosopher also took on the role of poet to 'add brilliance to ceremonies and honour the gods' (Aelius Aristides, *Discourse* 46, 404 Dindorf). Aelius Aristides composed anniversary speeches and funeral orations as well as praises of the cities through which he travelled. Dio celebrated the Olympian Zeus as represented by the sculptor Phidias (*Discourse* 13). Finally, there were also prose hymns in praise of the gods, such as those composed by Aelius Aristides in honour of Zeus, Sarapis, Asclepius, etc. Like the Homeric hymns, these consisted of an invocation to the god, a mythical narrative (or an enumeration of the god's powers) and a final prayer.

The five *Sacred Discourses* (only the first lines of the sixth are extant) of Aelius Aristides were also a celebration of divine might. Yet to exalt the power of Asclepius, Aelius undertook to recount 'the favours and miracles which the saviour has bestowed upon [him] to this day' (I, 1). Rhetorical praise then gives way to a personal journal which is 'the first and only religious autobiography which the pagan world has left us'.[4] Yet this autobiography is subordinated to aretalogy: if Aelius Aristides relates his illnesses at length, it is the better to convey the extraordinary powers of the healing god Asclepius; if he reports incidents scattered throughout his career as rhetor, it is because the god is the source of his talent and has led him back to the art of oratory. Finally, if he relates the stories of his nights and dreams, it is because the divinity manifests himself to him in his sleep. This strange work, combining 'all kinds of cures, dialogues, prolonged speeches, a great variety of visions, all kinds of predictions and oracles concerning all manner of things' (II, 8), still fascinates readers who are completely ignorant of the world of the second sophistic to which it belonged.

The novel

It is also to the age of the second sophistic that we owe, if not the birth, at least the development of a genre which was destined to flourish: the novel. There is no Greek equivalent for this word, nor for the word 'romance', first coined during the Middle Ages because these fictions were written in one of the vernacular languages as opposed to Latin. During its long history, the Greek novel remained an anonymous genre defined primarily by its content, a love-story, and by analogies with other genres: it was sometimes called '*drama*', which invites a comparison with theatre, sometimes 'myth' (*muthos*) or 'fiction' (*plasma*), to contrast it with history, and was often referred to by the vague term of 'narrative' (*diēgēsis*).

The five 'love-stories' that have been preserved, Chariton's *Chaereas and Callirhoe*, Xenophon of Ephesus' *Ephesian* story, Achilles Tatius' *Leucippe and Clitophon*, Longus' *Daphnis and Chloe*, and Heliodorus' *Ethiopian Story*, were probably written over a span of two centuries (first to third centuries AD). *Chaereas and Callirhoe* is now unanimously considered to be the oldest (some scholars even date this novel to the first century BC). Then comes the *Ephesian* story, which dates from the middle of the second century. Both *Leucippe and Clitophon* and *Daphnis and Chloe* were written at the end of the second century. Finally, the date of the *Ethiopian Story* is still disputed: some scholars would like to place it in the middle of the third century, whereas others prefer the fourth century. To complete our image of the genre, we should also add works that we know only from fragments of papyri which date back to the first or second century AD (*Ninus and Semiramis*, *Metiochos and Parthenope*, Lollianus' *Phoenician Story*) or Byzantine summaries (Iamblichus' *Babylonian Story*).

Much attention has been given to the question of the origins of the Greek novel, but without much success. To explain their originality, scholars have looked for foreign origins: in 1671, Daniel Huet, in his *Treatise on the Origins of the Novel*, maintained that 'the invention was due to Orientals, I mean to Egyptians, to Arabs, to Persians and to Syrians' (*sic*). Since then Egyptian origins have been very popular and indeed, more recently, Babylonian ones. Scholars have most frequently taken the view that the novel derived from earlier genres: they successively favoured the epic (like the *Odyssey*, the Greek novels are storm-filled travel narratives), history (the Greek novels often have a historical setting: Callirhoe is the daughter of Hermocrates who was the soul of the Syracusean resistance during the Sicilian expedition to which Thucydides dedicated two books of his *History*), ethnography (titles like the *Ephesian* story (*Ephesiaca*) and an *Ethiopian Story* (*Ethiopica*) encourage a connection with such works as the *Indica* of Megasthenes or the *Persica* of Ctesias, Hellenistic poetry (Longus' *Daphnis and Chloe* translates into prose the universe of Theocritus), New Comedy (the plots of the Greek novels are often modelled on those of Menander), tragedy (the story of Cnemon in the *Ethiopian Story* is an adaptation of the *Hippolytus*) and of course rhetoric. In short, all possible connections have been made, which is not surprising since the novel is an open genre. This is why a scholar such as B. E. Perry refused to address the issue of the origins of the novel by saying, 'the first romance was deliberately planned and written by an individual author, its inventor. He conceived it on a Tuesday afternoon in July or some other day or month or year'.[5]

Biographical indications do not shed much light on the works because very little is known about the authors of the Greek novels. Chariton of Aphrodisias (in Caria) and Heliodorus of Emesa (in Syria) are the only ones to name themselves in their novels, the former in his poem and the latter at the end of his work, but these names could well be linked to the place given to charm (*charis*) or the cult of the Sun (*Helios*) in these novels. The name of the novelist Xenophon sounds like a pen-name borrowed from the author of the *Cyropaedia*. For others, biographical indications are suspiciously linked to the content of their work: Achilles Tatius is from Alexandria where part of his novel takes place, and Longus, like his two heroes, is from Lesbos. The legend which makes Achilles Tatius and Heliodorus bishops seems to have been invented to appease the conscience of the Byzantine reader who relished their work.

We should start with the facts, in other words with the texts. All the Greek novels, from the shortest (the *Ephesian* story in five books) to the longest (the *Ethiopian Story* in ten books), narrate a love-story from start to finish (the marriage of the lovers or the reunion of a husband and wife who were separated shortly after their wedding.

Aside from *Daphnis and Chloe*, which holds a special place within the genre, all novels follow a similar format: a young man and a young girl, both members of illustrious families, fall in love at first sight. However, they are separated and then reunited after a perilous journey involving numerous hardships which do not change the heroes in any way (they remain beautiful and faithful to their love). The lovers then return to their starting point (the city or country which is home to at least one of them). The heroine of Xenophon of Ephesus makes a summary of her adventures which provides a good account of the content of the Greek Novel:

> Husband and master, she said, I have found you again, after all my wanderings over land and sea, escaping robbers' threats, pirates' plots and pimps' insults, chains, trenches, fetters, poisons, and tombs. I have reached you, Habrocomes, lord of my heart, the same as when I left you in Tyre for Syria. No one persuaded me to go astray. (V, 14)

The novels betray a desire for escape both in time and space. Some draw the reader into a world that belongs to a distant past: Chariton sets his story after the Sicilian expedition (413 BC); and during the Egyptian revolt against the Persian king (371–345 BC); Heliodorus at the time when Egypt was still under Persian rule. Others place their heroes in an undefined time (only the titles of certain magistrates hint that the novels of Xenophon and Achilles Tatius take place during Roman times). The heroes' travels lead the reader through a large geographical space. The world of the Greek novel encompasses Byzantium and Thrace to the North, southern Italy and Sicily to the West (however, Rome is never mentioned), the land from Asia Minor to Babylon in the East, and, to the South, Egypt and Ethiopia.

All the novels portray isolated individuals in an 'open' society. Collective events are meaningful only insofar as they affect the destiny of the heroes. Thus, in Achilles Tatius' novel, the war that breaks out between Byzantium and Thrace is a means to build up the plot (Leucippe is sent to Tyre where she meets Clitophon), while the victory of the Byzantines, which leads the father of the heroine to Ephesus, creates the possibility of a happy end.

Religion plays an increasingly important role in the novels as the genre develops. The gods are important to Chariton's plot: the action is instigated by Eros, governed by Fortune (*Tukhē*) and resolved by Aphrodite. However, these gods are only personified abstractions: Eros and Aphrodite represent love and *Tukhē* symbolises the unforeseen turns and courses of circumstance. The *Ethiopian Story*, however, whose author boasts of belonging to the clan of Descendants of the Sun, is steeped in the religiosity of late antiquity. The protagonists first encounter one another at Delphi, the city of Apollo, during a religious procession; they get married in Ethiopia, which is the land of the Sun, and their union makes them priests, one devoted to the Sun and the other to the Moon; furthermore, the three paternal figures who play a role in the life of the heroine (she is an abandoned child) are all priests: the head of the Ethiopian Gymnosophists who leads Chariclea to Egypt, the priest of Apollo who adopts her in Delphi, and the Egyptian priest, Calasiris, who helps her to leave Delphi and watches over her until his death in Memphis.

Certain scholars have taken their interpretation of the importance of religion in the novels one step further and consider the genre to be essentially religious. Some see it as a secularised version of the founding legend of the mysteries of Isis[6]. Others make it an instrument of propaganda for various mystery cults[7] (Isis for Xenophon of Ephesus and Achilles Tatius, Dionysius for Longus, the Sun for Heliodorus): the separations and wanderings of the protagonists would symbolise the trials of the soul in its quest for divinity, their weddings, the return of the soul to its celestial home and its union with god.

This thesis, which largely disregards the chronology of the novels (the oldest is the most secular), is based on allegorical interpretations which are often too subtle to be true. If we find a schema that involves trials and salvation in both novels and mystery cults, it may only be because they addressed the same audience and tried to satisfy the same spiritual needs. For they do this at different levels: the former appeals to the imagination, the latter to faith.

The Greek novel was indeed escapist literature. For a long time scholars consigned this frivolous genre, condemned in antiquity by serious thinkers such as Julian, to a second-rate readership consisting of young people, women, or all those who did not belong to the elite. In fact, the novel addressed the same public as the other genres, rich city-dwellers who could identify with the heroes because, like them, they belonged to the 'leisured class', and cultivated readers capable of understanding allusions and enjoying parodies. However, although these novels were all so many variations on a single theme, they were not all alike.

The least original work is probably that of Xenophon of Ephesus. It is however difficult to judge this author from what is, in all likelihood, only a summary of his work.

Chariton's *Chaereas and Callirhoe* is a historical novel in the full sense of the term. It is clear from the introduction ('I, Chariton of Aphrodisias, clerk to the attorney Athenagoras, am going to tell you a love-story that took place in Syracuse') that the author is modelling his style on that of a historian. Throughout the narrative he artfully intermingles fictional characters (the two heroes) and historical figures (Hermocrates of Syracuse, the king Artaxerxes) and uses History with a capital H to enhance his fiction: the glory of the victorious Athenians in the Persian war only helps to accentuate the prestige of Hermocrates, who was in turn victorious over them, and that of his daughter. It is also a psychological novel which describes, with a subtlety worthy of Jane Austen, the birth of love in the hearts of the two heroes and the conflict of passion and reason in the mind of Dionysius 'the wealthiest, noblest, and most cultured man in Ionia' (1, 12, 8).

The baroque and multi-faceted novel of Achilles Tatius provides a sharp contrast with the simplicity of Chariton's work. Its construction is complex: it opens with a scene in which the hero meets the novelist, and the story is told by the hero himself and not by an omniscient narrator. Digressions on various subjects (descriptions of paintings, extraordinary plants and animals; mythological narratives; psychological and physiological observations) interrupt the narrative. The author thereby delays the conclusion of his story and creates suspense. He can also impart a somewhat ironic detachment to his reader: it is hard to share the emotions of Leucippe as she is discovered by her mother in bed with Clitophon when the author goes to such pains to dissect the mixture of grief, shame and anger felt by the heroine. Indeed, irony is omnipresent in this novel, which challenges the conventions of the genre (the heroine remains a virgin only in spite of herself and the hero is unfaithful on at least one occasion).

The *Ethiopian Story*, which delighted the young Racine and inspired Verdi's *Aïda*, owes its durable success to the complexity of its construction: the narrative that carries the heroes from Delphi to Ethiopia begins *in mediis rebus* with an enigmatic scene: 'a mass of newly slain bodies, some of them quite dead, others half alive and still twitching . . . the miserable remnants of festivities . . . and a creature of indescribable beauty gazing steadily at a young man at her feet' (1, 1–2), which is explained only after a long flashback (the narrative of Calasiris (II, 24–V, 33) takes up more than three books). The conclusion of the tale is artfully drawn out: by the end of Book VIII, the heroine has met up with the man who is her biological father, but the recognition only takes place in Book X after a series of episodes (the most famous being the siege of Syene to which Book IX is entirely devoted) whose sole purpose is to further delay the awaited denouement.

Daphnis and Chloe is a love story that does not ship its heroes off to faraway lands: it takes place entirely on Lesbos. Yet a change of scenery is assured by transferring the action from the city to the country, which provides 'an exotic pleasure' for an urban audience, and by the cycles of seasons that constitute the temporal background for the amorous adventures of the two protagonists. This work of deceptive simplicity is a tribute both to Sappho (the choice of Lesbos is significant) and to Theocritus (it gives the same contrasted image of the countryside as the bucolic *Idylls*: on the one hand, oafish, greedy peasants and harsh toil, on the other the two divinely beautiful protagonists and gardens which are havens of delight). The novel establishes a subtle and sophisticated play between nature and culture: nature seems at times artificial (the trees 'stood around them like a man-made wall'; (4, 2)) while artifice re-creates nature (the farmers 'set aside the grapes with the best bloom on them and grafted them on the shoots, so that even the people coming from the city could delight in the image of the harvest' (4, 5)). The contrast between the naivety of the heroes and the intellectualism of the narrator also contributes to the enduring popularity of *Daphnis and Chloe*.

History

The ancients readily contrasted the novel with history, probable fiction with true narration. Nevertheless, a large part of the Greek history written during the Imperial period belongs, like the novel, to escapist literature. It is concerned not with the present, but with the mythical past of Greece and the monuments that bear witness to its ancient grandeur.

Apollodorus' *Bibliotheca* (*Library of Greek Mythology*), which dates from the second century (or the end of the first century), collects the traditional legends of Greece, carefully excluding Roman adaptations of Greek myths, such as the legend of Aeneas.

Pausanias' *Periēgēsis Hellados* (*Description of Greece*), the bible of modern archaeologists, also looks back wistfully upon the past. This rough work, without prologue or epilogue, is written in a language that is deliberately Atticised, although its author was most probably born in Lydia during the second century. This travel guide in ten books, which leads its reader through Attica, central Greece and the Peloponnese, covers only 'the most memorable sights' and 'the most venerable traditions'; in other words, those monuments and tales that bear witness to the grandeur of Greece during the archaic and classical periods and the magnificence of the kings of the Hellenistic period, excluding all events that took place after 150 BC. As J. Pouilloux says in his preface to *Pausanias, Description de l'Attique*,[8] 'the Greece of Pausanias is that of the tombs, the deserted sanctuaries, the museum-cities.'

However, the Greek-speaking historians did not limit themselves to Greece: they also wrote the history of Rome. In the first century, Dionysius of Halicarnassus and Flavius Josephus undertook to write such a history in order to encourage a reconciliation between the Romans and those whom they had conquered. Their successors completely identified with the Empire. Some celebrated the conquests of Rome (Appian) and the prosperity of the Imperial period (Dio Cassius) in works that embrace the whole of Roman history; others, such as Herodian, exalted the victories of the emperors of their time.

Dionysius of Halicarnassus' *Roman Antiquities* completes the work of Polybius (Dionysius ends his history where Polybius begins, at the beginning of the first Punic war) by presenting to the Greeks, who were almost entirely ignorant of early Roman history, the story of the birth of Rome and 'the most ancient legends, which previous historians have omitted (1, 8, 1). Yet, in this ambitious work, Dionysius, who does not separate the history of events from the history of institutions and customs, often sacrifices truth to rhetorical conventions and only retains the facts that serve his purpose. He intends to celebrate a hegemony that 'has far surpassed all those that are recorded from earlier times, not only in the extent of the dominion and in the splendour of its achievements . . . but also in the length of time during which it has endured down to our day' (1, 2, 1). He also wanted to help bring Romans and Greeks together by proving the Greek origins of the Romans, so that the Romans might cease to suffer from an 'inferiority complex' in relation to Greek culture, judged superior, and so that the Greeks 'may not feel indignation at their present subjection, which is grounded in reason' (1, 5, 2) and would willingly submit to those who were, after all, Greeks like themselves.

The work of Dionysius, which relies on oral tradition and mostly on 'histories written by approved Roman authors' (1, 7, 3) comprised twenty books (only Books I–X and most of Book XI are extant). The first four recount the foundation of the city and the reign of its kings. Those that follow retrace the history of the Republic year by year, combining the Greek and Roman chronologies as Diodorus did.

Dionysius was imitated by the Jewish historian, Flavius Josephus, who traced, in his *Jewish Antiquities* (also in twenty books), 'the origins of the Jews, the fortunes that befell them, the great lawgiver under whom they were trained in piety and the exercise of other virtues, and all those wars waged by them through long ages before this last in which they were involuntarily engaged against the Romans' (1, 6) in order to remove all the reasons the other peoples might have to hate them, thereby contributing to the reconciliation of the two peoples.

The first ten books of the *Jewish Antiquities* cover the history of the Jewish nation from its beginnings to the death of Judas

Maccabeus. The narrative slows down as it approaches the present: the life of Herod the Great spans nearly four books while the last three books relate the history of Judea, now a Roman province, until the final explosion during the second year of Nero's reign.

This renegade, who defected to the Romans in AD 67, had previously written a *Jewish War* in which he recounted the insurrection of Judea in AD 66 for Greek and Roman readers. This event, in which he actively participated, was, in his eyes, 'the greatest, not only of the wars of our own time, but, so far as accounts have reached us, almost of all that ever broke out between cities and nations' (1, 1). In seven books, in keeping with the purest tradition of Greek historiography (Josephus, like Herodotus, claims to immortalise great deeds, and, like Thucydides, combines narrative and speech), he tries to remind the victors of their adversaries' valour, to console those whom they have vanquished and to deter others who may be tempted to revolt' (3,108).

During the second century, the Egyptian Appian (born *c.* 96), a high-ranking Imperial official, also undertook the task of writing a history of Rome, using the works of his predecessors as his main source. However, he renewed the genre by emphasising the quality of life during the Imperial period: 'in the long reign of peace and security everything has moved towards a lasting prosperity' (Preface, 7) and by adopting an original plan: Appian chose to write the history of the Roman conquests people by people, thus using the Greek tradition of regional history for the benefit of Rome.

Only books VI–VIII, part of Book IX, and books XI–XVII of the original twenty-four volumes of Appian's history have survived. Yet the extant text provides enough information on Appian's method for us to note that he did not completely break with the tradition of annalistic history. The first three books related all the deeds accomplished by the Romans in Italy up until the Samnite wars. Books IV–XII listed the peoples (the Celts in Book IV), countries (Sicily in Book V), and individuals (Hannibal in Book VII and Mithridates in Book XII) with whom Rome successively came into conflict. The following five books covered the civil wars and were organised 'in relation to the main protagonists' (Preface, 14). The final three books returned to the region-by-region plan and described the conquests of the Empire up until the reign of Antoninus Pius.

After Appian, Dio Cassius (AD 160–235), a Greek from Bithynia who was a senator and consul, collected everything that concerned the Romans 'from the time for which he has collected the most trustworthy stories, for as long as fortune will allow' (LXXII, 23, 5), in other words, until the death of Elagabalus in AD 222, and presented them in eighty books (only books XXXIV–LX survive in full) according to an annalistic plan. This history, which sharply distinguishes between the Republic and the Empire, is for the most part the conscientious compilation of a man who has read 'pretty nearly everything on the subject that has been written by anyone' (1, 2) and does not hesitate to exercise critical judgement (he only relates 'what he has seen fit to select' (ibid.)). However, after the death of Marcus Aurelius, his history is based upon personal observation. Dio thus revives the Greek tradition of autopsy and contemporary history.

Besides these vast syntheses, there were legions of contemporary histories of the emperors and their campaigns. They were extremely popular, especially during the second century, and Lucian mocks them at length in his essay on history. His remarks were quite accurate if we look at the work of the Syrian, Herodian, who, in the third century, wrote an eight-book history of Marcus Aurelius' successors up until the accession to the throne of Gordian III (AD 180–238). This history, despite its claim to compete with the work of Thucydides both in the importance of its subject and the rigour of its method, is mostly reminiscent of the tragic history of the Hellenistic period in its taste for rhetoric and its use of sensationalist scenes.

The works of Arrian of Nicomedia (c. AD 85–175), who was consul and governor of Cappadocia, exemplify many aspects of historical writings during the Empire. This high official does not separate Roman politics from Greek culture. In his *Circumnavigation of the Black Sea*, a report to the emperor Hadrian of a personal tour of inspection of the Black Sea, he displays a marked interest in works of art and antiquities. He also wrote a history, now lost, of Trajan's campaigns against the Parthians. He often celebrated the past of Greece. The eight-book history dedicated to his native province, Bithynia, from mythical times to its integration into the empire, is lost. His history of the successors of Alexander suffered the same fate, but the history of Alexander, for which he was widely acclaimed, has survived. Noticing that 'no prose history, no epic poem was written' (1, 12) about this hero, who had accomplished deeds unequalled among the Greeks and barbarians, he decided to become the new Homer for this new Achilles, but a Homer in prose. As in his treatise on hunting (*Cynegeticus*), he took Xenophon as his model and wrote, like him, an *Anabasis* in seven books in which he exalts the conquests of Alexander (and by the same token of the Roman empire they foreshadow) using Ptolemy and Aristobulus, the two companions of Alexander he deemed most trustworthy. He used an artificial diction copied from the Attic of Xenophon and 'a plain style, yet not deprived of grandeur' (Photius, Cod, 92, 72b). To this history he added a complementary treatise on India (*Indica*), which imitated Herodotus and was written in Ionian dialect, in which he described the country and narrated the journey of Alexander's fleet (under the command of Nearchus) from the mouth of the River Indus to the Persian Gulf.

However, Arrian was not exclusively a historian. Following the example of Xenophon, he also regarded himself as a philosopher: in his *Memorabilia*, Xenophon had written down the memories he had of the words and actions of Socrates. Arrian tried to transcribe, 'word for word, as best as [he] could', the *Discourses* of his master, the Stoic philosopher, Epictetus. He also published a *Manual* (*Encheiridian*) that summarised his key teachings according to a methodical plan and in a style that was dry and precise. This *Manual* was to be regarded as the Stoic buviary for many years.

Pagan philosophy: between moral theory and exegesis

Arrian's *Discourses* (in Greek *Diatribai*) provide the best portrait of Epictetus (born *c.* AD 55), a former slave who taught philosophy in Nicopolis (a little town in Epirus), after being banished from Rome by the emperor Domitian, the arch-enemy of philosophy.

In this work, written in the vernacular without rhetorical adornments (the *Discourses* are only notes taken during the lectures that relate the conversations between Epictetus and his students), in which Arrian claims to have completely withdrawn behind his model, Epictetus appears as 'clearly aiming at nothing else but to incite the minds of his hearers to the best things' (Preface, 5). Like the founders of Stoicism, he makes his philosophical aim the 'good life'. He places more importance than his predecessors on concrete training, the 'exercise' (in Greek *askesis*), which no exegesis of philosophical texts could replace. This statement holds true for the three parts of philosophy, logic, physics and ethics. For Epictetus, alert reasoning is the only true logic, for 'what is to prevent a man having the eloquence of Demosthenes and yet being unhappy, and what is to prevent him from analyzing syllogisms like Chrysippus, and yet being wretched, from sorrowing, envying, in a word, from being

disturbed and miserable? Absolutely nothing' (II, 23, 4). Physics
(in other words, knowledge of the system of the world) allows
man to put events in their proper place in the universal order of
nature. Ethics is a therapy for the passions, thanks to which man
will obtain inner freedom (the notion of freedom lies at the core
of the system of thought of this former slave) and live 'free of
pain, fear and upset' (IV.3.8) once he has given up on all that does
not depend on him. Ethics also requires that all fulfil their oblig-
ations towards the community of humans: man is a soldier in
a campaign who during his life, must obey orders with discipline
and submission. These lessons of Epictetus are, in theory, meant
for all; in fact, however, they address men like Arrian (in other
words, members of the Greek-speaking elite who have powerful
friends in Rome). With a series of examples taken from life in Rome
and the world of the court, Epictetus teaches them the vanity of
ambition and independence in the face of a fate which often depends
on the emperor's whim.

The *Meditations* of the emperor Marcus Aurelius (AD 121–180),
like the *Discourses* of Epictetus, have a practical aim. These 'speeches
to himself', as they are called in our manuscripts, are self-addressed
exhortations to lead a philosophical life. This work is often presented
as a personal diary in which the emperor poured out his feelings,
but it is more accurate to speak of 'spiritual exercises'[9] practised in
accordance with 'the very method practised by Epictetus', when
reading these 'short and elemental axioms'. As said by Marcus
Aurelius 'when set before thee, [these axioms] will at once rid thee
of troubles and send thee away without discontent; (IV, 1). These
sentences are heavily dependent upon a rhetoric which values conci-
sion and incisiveness.[10] Marcus Aurelius summarises, for his personal
use, the essential points of Stoicism. To teach himself magnanimity,
he measures the human world against the whole universe: Europe
and Asia are but 'corners of the universe': the present is but 'a point
in eternity' (VI, 36). He demystifies luxury: 'this purple-edged
robe is nothing but sheep's wool steeped in the blood of a shell-
fish' (VI, 13). He denounces the vanity of human achievements: 'all
that we prize so highly in our lives is empty and corrupt and paltry'
(V, 33, 2). He exhorts himself to virtue: 'every hour make up your
mind sturdily as a Roman and as a man to do what you have in
hand' (II, 5), and shields himself in advance against the ills that
could befall him: 'say to yourself at daybreak: I shall come across
the busybody, the thankless and the overbearing' (II, 1). Finally,
he applies himself to the task of accepting with joy and piety all

that belongs to the order of a cosmos governed by Providence (his work opens with a series of prayers giving thanks and listing all that he owes to both men and gods).

With such stoics as Epictetus and Marcus Aurelius, philosophy turns towards action and becomes prescription. However, it also returns to the texts of the past and their exegesis. Our modern era, obsessed with originality, often tends to neglect philosophers such as Plotinus who modestly present their work as 'interpretations (exegeses), relying on Plato's own writings for evidence that these views are ancient' (*Enneads*, 5, 1, 8) even if they also claim not to forfeit their critical judgement ('Now we must believe that some of the blessed philosophers of ancient times have found the truth; but it is proper to investigate which of them have really hit the mark, and by what guiding principles we can ourselves attain a certitude' (*Enneads*, 3, 7, 1). Yet this contempt would be unjustified, for it would stem from a complete ignorance of the creative processes at work during the Imperial period. These are always based on imitation and rewriting: the exegete uses the text which he pretends to explain, develops the allusions it contains, overcomes the contradictions it presents through interpretation, and creates an organic whole from elements borrowed from Pythagoras, Plato, Aristotle, and even the Stoics.

No two works, different as they may be, demonstrate this better than those of Philo (20 BC to AD 41), who was a distinguished member of the large Jewish community of Alexandria (he represented this community in an embassy sent to Caligula), and of Plotinus (204–270), who settled in Rome to teach having long been the student of Ammonius in Alexandria.

The work of Philo is essentially (thirty-one treatises out of the thirty-eight that are extant) a running commentary of the Pentateuch along with developments on biblical themes. It belongs to a tradition inaugurated during the Hellenistic period by the *Septuagint* (the Greek translation of the Hebrew bible): 'at the expense of important (and inevitable) shifts in meaning that have distorted both the content of the myths and the values' of Judaism, 'and the content of the Greek tradition',[11] it transposes the biblical message into terms borrowed largely from Platonism (Pythagorean and Stoic elements are also present). None could have been better qualified for this task than Philo, a liberal theologian who was admired by the Christians both for 'the extent and quality of the labour he bestowed on the theological learning of his race' and his 'position in philosophy and the liberal studies of the heathen world') Eusebius, *Ecclesiastical History*, II, 4, 2–3).

Whom was this work intended to address? The Greeks, in order to introduce Jewish law in terms which they could accept? The Hellenised Jews of Alexandria, in order to restore their faith with arguments adapted to their Greek culture? This question has been much debated. It is however certain that this conciliation of the bible and philosophy, made possible by a systematic use of allegorical exegesis developed by the Stoics, in no way sacrifices Judaism for Hellenism: in the *De Congressu*, the status of Agar, the servant of Sarah, symbolises the subordination of culture (the Greek *paideia*) to true knowledge (the knowledge of the sacred: in other words, the Jewish religion).

In the *Enneads* (a collection of treatises which owes its name to Porphyry who edited the works of his master and organised them into six books of nine essays (in Greek *ennea*)), Plotinus also presents his work as an exposition of Platonic thought.

However, the Plato of Plotinus is both enriched and mutilated: enriched because 'his writings are full of concealed Stoic and Peripatetic doctrines' (*Life*, 14) as his biographer Porphyry tells us; but also mutilated because the political dimension has been removed. The contemplation that was to allow the philosopher to govern the city according to reason in the *Republic* has become an aim in and of itself in Plotinus: 'if [the sage] judges political activities to be unworthy of him, let him remain up there, if he can' (VI, 9, 7).

His Plato is also rethought. Plotinus, in fact, posits, beyond even the Intellect, the absolute transcendence of the One, and constructs an extremely hierarchical system with the One, from which all the realities proceed, at the very summit, followed by the Intellect, which is an imitation and reflection of the One, then the Soul, which begotten by the intellect and can therefore only be inferior to its father. The philosophical process that leads the soul towards true being in Plato is replaced by a mystical longing for a complete identification with the Divine, so that the soul is no longer aware of the existence of the body and forgets that it was ever incarnated.

Finally, his Plato is rewritten. When Plotinus again takes up Platonic myths, as he often does, he adds an allegorical exegesis which gives them new meaning. In the *Symposium*, Plato made *Eros*, Love, the son of *Poros*, Plenty and *Penia*, Poverty. In Plotinus, *Penia* is identified with matter which is also 'in every way in need' (III,5,9), *Poros* is the *Logos* (Reason), 'son of the Intellect' (III, 5, 9), and *Eros*, who unites the natures of both parents, is a

'*Logos*, but an impure *Logos* since he has in himself an indefinite, irrational, unbounded impulse' (III, 5, 7). Similarly, when Plotinus borrows an image, he transforms it and gives it a more immediate and sensual character: while the sun in the *Republic* lit up the forms and those who looked at them, the sun in the *Enneads* irradiates the landscape and those who wander through it and blends them into oneness: 'as often men, when they go up into high places where the earth has a red-gold colour, are filled with that colour and made like that upon which they walked' (V, 8, 10).

Philo and Plotinus are the two most original exegetes of Middle- and Neo-Platonism. However, they do not represent all the aspects of philosophical thought of the first three centuries of the common era. The Imperial period, to which Athenaeus, Aelian, Sextus Empiricus, Diogenes Laertius, Galen and Artemidorus all belong, was also the time of miscellanies and encyclopaedias of every kind.

The *Deipnosophists* (literally 'the Sophists at dinner' of Athenaeus of Naucratis (*c.* AD 200), which narrates a 'dinner' (Books I–X) followed by a symposium (Books XI–XV) is truly a gastronomic encyclopaedia which displays an extraordinary erudition about all matters of food, drink and table manners. It delighted its Renaissance readers and provides us with an invaluable collection of excerpts drawn from a vast number of authors, especially comic poets.

The works of Aelian (*c.* 170–235), a freeman born in Praenesta, a small town in Latium, also belong to the genre of miscellany. His *Miscellaneous History* in fourteen books as well as his treatise *On the Nature of Animals* in seventeen books put side by side anecdotes about extraordinary behaviours of animals and great men of the past, all written in the purest Attic diction.

The work of Sextus Empiricus (second half of the second century) is an apology for scepticism, which catalogues in fourteen books all the forms of knowledge the better to destroy them. His three books of *Pyrrhonian Hypotyposes* (literally 'Sketches') criticize the dogmatic philosophers, whereas the six books of *Against the Professors* launch a fierce attack against all those who claim to possess knowledge and are confident they can transmit it, namely grammarians, rhetoricians, mathematicians and so on.

Even more ambitious is the aim of the *Lives and Opinions of Eminent Philosophers*, probably written during the middle of the third century by a certain Diogenes Laertius, about whom next to nothing is known. This work, which combines, as its title indicates, biography and doxography, is a systematic history of philosophy from its origins, which Diogenes claims to be purely Greek.

Diogenes begins with the 'wise men' who were not seven, but eleven (I); he then turns to the Ionian tradition derived from Thales and Anaximander (II, 1–4) and traces its evolution through the various schools. First, he successively discusses Socrates and the Socratics (II, 5–17), Plato (III) and the leaders of the Academy up to Clitomachus (IV), Aristotle (V, 1) and the Peripatetics (V, 2–6). He then goes back in time to trace the development of another branch of the heirs of Socrates, one that stems from Antisthenes (VI, 1), with, on the one hand, the Cynics from Diogenes to Menedemus (VI, 2–9) and, on the other, the Stoics from Zeno to Chrysippus (VII, 1–7). He then contrasts the Ionians with the Italians who proceed from Pythagoras (VIII, 1), and prior to him, from the 'wise man' Pherecydes. Their biographies occupy the eight chapters of Book VIII, while books IX and X are dedicated to isolated philosophers from Heraclitus to Epicurus.

The sections devoted to each philosopher vary considerably in length (Plato and Epicurus each occupy an entire book, while Clitomachus is dealt with in a paragraph). They are nearly all organised according to the plan that P. Moraux has successfully analysed for Aristotle:[12] first comes a biography (1–11), then the text of the philosopher's will (11–16), a collection of his 'sayings' (17–21), a list of his works (21–27) and an overview of his doctrine (28–34). The sections end with a list of namesakes (35). On the whole, they provide the modern reader with a large amount of citations and summaries of lost works (hence their value) and present a strange mixture of precise erudition and fabulous tales. Diogenes Laertius does not hesitate to adjust the lives of the philosophers to their theories. For example, he makes Diogenes the Cynic, who advocated a return to nature, die of indigestion after eating a raw octopus.

The voluminous body of work of the 'physician-philosopher' Galen of Pergamum (129–200) (more than 19,000 pages in the Kühn edition without including the treatises that have only been preserved in a Latin, Hebrew or Arab version) plays a role in the history of literature because it deals not only with medicine, but also with philosophy (Galen claimed in a treatise that 'the best physician is also a philosopher' and wrote an *Introduction to Dialectics* and a treatise *On Demonstration*, of which only fragments have survived), and philology (he was interested, for example, in the vocabulary of the comic poets). His work addressed those who were simply curious, such as the Roman consul Flavius Boethius who, 'more than any of his contemporaries', was filled with a violent love of the science of anatomy, the cultivated people to whom he endeavours to reveal the mysteries of nature and the order of Providence, and fellow physicians whom he helps in the practice of their art. These eclectic writings, which combine theory and practice belong to various genres.

Galen wrote monographs (for example, his *Treatise on the Passions of the Soul*) as well as broad syntheses on a given topic that draw on the theories of various medical sects and assess their value (such as the three pharmacological treatises, in which he analyses first simple then compound drugs, classified by type or by the parts of the body where they were applied). He also produced commentaries (to help his contemporaries understand a difficult work, Galen undertook a commentary of the whole of Hippocrates' work, annotating and assessing all the previous existing commentaries).

Artemidorus of Daldis, a contemporary of Galen, also combined personal experience (Artemidorus is a professional dream interpreter) and compilation ('there is no book on dreams that I do not have', he writes in his preface) to which he adds a knowledge of oral tradition ('For a great many years I had exchanges with the soothsayers in the public squares'). His *Oneirocritica* (*Interpretation of Dreams*), in five books, provide a clear and methodical account of the beliefs of the time in the field of oneiromancy. Like the work of Galen, it addresses both specialists and a wider public. Others such as Marcus Aurelius, Aelius Aristides and Lucian, also attest to the popular interest in dreams during this period.

This interest is only one sign among many of the rise of the irrational and the desire to experience union with God and transcend individual limitations. With the Neoplatonists Porphyry of Tyre (AD 232–301) and Iamblichus of Chalcis (AD 250–326) philosophy becomes a search for the divine and a religious experience.

Porphyry is best known for his *Introduction* (in Greek *Eisagoge*) to the five fundamental concepts of Aristotle's philosophy and his two commentaries on Aristotle's *Categories* (only the shorter of the two, organised as a series of questions and answers, survives complete). He also wrote commentaries on Plato (fragments of his works on the *Timaeus* and the *Parmenides* have survived).

Furthermore, he proposed a series of elaborate allegorical interpretations of the eleven lines of the *Odyssey* containing the description of a cave dedicated to the Nymphs (XIII, 102–12). Without excluding a literal meaning (he claims that if geographers such as Strabo cannot find a cave similar to the one which Homer describes on Ithaca, it is probably because the terrain has changed since Homeric times), Porphyry offers apparently contradictory interpretations of the Homeric text, for the cave symbolises successively the world of the senses, since it is rocky, obscure and humid (5) and the intelligible essence, since it is invisible, permanent and immobile (9). But as suggested by Pépin, this may be a calculated pluralism.[13]

Porphyry was also deeply interested in religious issues. He believed in a Philosophy from Oracles and explained the symbolical meaning of divine attributes in his treatise *On Statues*. He preached vegetarianism in his treatise *On Abstinence*. In his *Life of Plotinus*, he not only celebrated this eminent philosopher, who was on the best of terms with the Roman aristocracy of his time and was 'venerated by the emperor Gallienus and his wife Salonina' (12), he also depicted him as a spiritual guide who led an ascetic life, a 'demonic' man who was interested in astrology, had the gift of second sight, could catch magicians in their own trap, and ascend towards divinity. His biography of Pythagoras, which is largely concerned with the Pythagorean doctrines and their origins, placed more emphasis than had Diogenes Laertius' account on the supernatural powers of a man who was said to understand the language of animals.

Nevertheless, Porphyry remained critical of miracles and theurgists who claim direct contact with the divine, even though he was the first Neoplatonist to cite the Chaldaean Oracles (these theological oracles, which probably originated in Syria during the reign of Marcus Aurelius, reported the revelations of a medium, Julian the Chaldaean, who had spoken to the soul of Plato) in his treatise *On the Soul*. He fought against superstition, attacking the Christians in a fifteen-book treatise, now lost, and was involved in a lively polemic against Egyptian wisdom in his *Letter to Anebo*.

His student, Iamblichus, who also produced commentaries on Plato and Aristotle (now lost), was not so scrupulous. Under the pseudonym Abammon, he opposed his master and tried, in his treatise *On the Mysteries of Egypt*, which is a response to the *Letter to Anebo*, to defend theurgy and promote the union of the human soul with the divine 'through the religious accomplishment of ineffable actions that pass understanding' (II, 11). His biography of Pythagoras, which was probably the first book of a large synthesis of the Neoplatonic doctrines (only the *Exhortation to Philosophy* (*Protrepikos logos*), which seeks to convert its readers to the Pythagorean way of life, and three treatises on numbers, are extant), emphasised the miracles accomplished by this 'divine man' more than Porphyry's had.

These biographies of philosophers, which are as entertaining and extraordinary as the *Lives* of the Saints, point to a profound transformation in the philosophical ideal: the philosopher was no longer merely an accomplished individual. He was now a 'holy man' endowed with supernatural powers.[14] This new ideal was embodied by Apollonius of Tyana. His highly unreliable biography written by the rhetor Philostratus is a masterpiece of pagan hagiography as well as a manifesto of Hellenism.

In this work, which dates from the beginning of the third century, Philostratus claims to provide his readers with an 'exact view' of the controversial character of Apollonius, who lived during the first century AD, by using both oral sources and written documents (the memoirs of the Assyrian Damis which may just be a convenient invention). In reality, he preaches the Pythagorean creed in a narrative that leads its hero – and its readers – through the inhabited world of the time, from Gibraltar to India and Ethiopia. For Apollonius is a transposition of Pythagoras into the Roman Empire of the first century. A strict vegetarian, he condemns bloody sacrifices. He is also endowed with supernatural powers, understanding the language of animals and preventing earthquakes. This holy man, whom some pagans heralded as the rival of Christ, also received the martyr's crown: arrested by order of Domitian, he was led before the emperor and narrowly escaped death by mysteriously disappearing.

Classical culture and Christianity: the birth of Greek Christian literature

It is tempting to establish a parallel between the biographies of philosophers and the Gospels, which relate the life and the words of Jesus, and, even more so, to compare them to the *Acts of the Apostles*, a skilful propaganda for Christian belief that accounts for conversion and inner religious experience through dramatic narratives. However, these works, addressed primarily to Christians with secondary concerns for literature, represent a cultural event outside of the Greek tradition.

The same observation can be made of the *Epistles of the Apostles*, whether they be apocryphal or canonical, and of apocalyptic literature that uses a genre invented by the Jews to promote the Christian faith. We shall also exclude the *Epistles of the Apostolic Fathers*: these Christians, who wrote during the first century or at the beginning of the second century and are said to have had direct contact with the Apostles (hence their name), also exclusively addressed the early church for the edification of its members.

It was only when Christians were recruited from among men who had assimilated the Greek culture of their time, when they began to address an educated public to justify and expound their religion, and when they attempted to defeat the pagan philosophers on their own ground by presenting Christianity as a philosophy, that a literature that is both Greek and Christian was born.

This integration of Christian faith and Greek culture started at the beginning of the second century with the apologists. These Christians were certainly cultivated men. The earliest apologist, Aristides, who lived during the reign of Hadrian, presents himself as an Athenian philosopher, and Justin (who died c. 162–168) acknowledges having been a member of all the philosophical schools before converting to Christianity. These men not only addressed their fellow Christians, but also composed, according to the rules of classical rhetoric, 'apologies', that is, fictitious forensic defences addressing the authorities (Justin, for example, wrote two apologies, one for the emperor Antoninus Pius and his two adopted sons, Marcus Aurelius and Lucius Verus, the other for the Roman senate) or, like Tatian's, *Oration to Greeks*, a violent attack on 'Greek', that is, pagan, culture. They wrote letters to high-ranking pagans (*Epistle to Diognetus*). They conversed in dialogues with Hellenised Jews (such as Papiscus and a certain Tryphon who was, according to Eusebius, 'the most famous Hebrew of his time' (*Ecclesiastical History*, IV, 18, 6). The most important among the apologists, Justin, was the first to attempt a reconciliation between Christian religion and Greek philosophy: in both his two petitions and in his dialogue with Tryphon, he does not merely refute pagan calumnies, but admits that philosophical schools have, on some points, foreshadowed Christian truth, since all rational beings have a share in Logos, who is Christ.

However, 'It is Clement of Alexandria who marks the decisive turning point from which the straight road of Christian Hellenism extends'.[15] As a philosopher who had travelled throughout the Roman world before settling in Alexandria (towards the end of his life he left Egypt for Jerusalem, where he died in AD 211–215), he knew both the Scriptures and the classics and drew extensively on Greek culture to win the members of the elite over to Christianity. His *Protreptic*, which is addressed to 'Greeks' (in other words, to non-converts), belongs to the genre of exhortations which philosophers (such as Aristotle and Iamblichus) addressed to possible disciples to ignite a radical transformation in their beliefs and 'turn them towards' (that is, the meaning of the Greek verb *protrepein*) philosophy. His *Stromateis* 'Patchwork') belong to the genre of miscellanies illustrated by Aulus Gellius' *Attic Nights* or Aelian's *Varia Historia*. His *Hypotyposes* (literally 'Sketches') which we know only from a summary of Photius bear a title reminiscent of pagan philosophical treatises such as the *Pyrrhonian Hypotyposes* of Sextus Empiricus and resemble scholia in their aim (they consisted mainly of notes on passages from Genesis and the Psalms). Yet Clement borrows not only the literary genres of Hellenism, but also ideas which might apply to Christianity, and, in a manner reminiscent of Philo, causes them to undergo a thorough transformation. In a treatise intended to instruct new converts and called the *Tutor* (the name paidogogos) designating the slave who takes care of children and is in charge of their basic education, reveals that this work is only propaedeutic), Clement transforms the Greek ideal of moderation and harmony by integrating it into a Christian perspective. The eight books of the *Stromateis* probably most clearly betray this desire for a reconciliation of Christian faith with Greek philosophy which, like the Old Testament, can help 'bring souls to God' (1, 5, 28). 'In it Clement weaves together not only elements taken from the Holy Scriptures, but also elements from the Greeks, when it seems to him that they have said something useful' (Eusebius, *Ecclesiastical History* IV, 13, 4).

Origen (AD 185–254) also lived in Alexandria for an extended period of time. It was there that he taught first grammar and then philosophy, before settling in Caesarea, Palestine. Following the example of Clement of Alexandria, he tried to 'take from the philosophy of the Greeks itself . . . a preparatory teaching for Christianity' (*Letter to Gregory*, 1). Moreover, he also wrote a *Protrepic*, which was an exhortation to martyrdom, and *Stromateis*, now lost. However, he was primarily an exegete (in this respect he resembles Plotinus who was perhaps a student of Ammonius like himself). The bulk of his work, which was voluminous, is dedicated to editing and commenting on the scriptures.

Two thousand – perhaps even six thousand – treatises are attributed to Origen (though he did not write them down himself; but dictated them to copyists who took turns by his side). Only a few of these have survived (Sometimes in Greek, but more often in Latin translation. He was responsible for the first critical edition of the Old Testament, the famous *Hexapla* which displayed, in six (in Greek *hex*) parallel columns, the Hebrew text, the Hebrew text transliterated into Greek letters, and four Greek translations (among them the *Septuagint*). He is also the author of commentaries which vary in form. They are at times simply 'scholia' (brief notes in the margins of particularly difficult passages). There are also 'homilies', sermons intended for Christian congregations which explained passages of the Bible, elucidated the literal meaning and then extricated the spiritual or 'mystical' meaning (twenty such homilies on Jeremiah have survived in the original Greek). Finally, there are 'treatises' which address a more cultivated public, applying to the scriptures rules perfected by Hellenistic philologists and methods of allegorical interpretation consistently used by Stoics for the exegesis of myths and poetry and then by Philo in his interpretation of the Pentateuch (eight books of a Greek commentary on the *Gospel of John* have survived).

Origen is also famous for his apologetic writings. The most important of these, preserved in the original Greek, is *Against Celsus*, an eight-book, point-by-point refutation of the *True Discourse* of this philosopher. It addresses those who have no experience of faith in Christ or those who, as the Apostle says, 'are weak in their faith' (Preface 8).

We would also mention his treatise, *First Principles*, which presents structural affinities with the contemporary philosophical treatises and is regarded as the first synthesis of ecclesiastical doctrine, had this work not been preserved, for the most part, only in its Latin translation.

Between them, Clement and Origen represent the two possible forms of a reconciliation between Christianity and Hellenism: the first was primarily sensitive to the seductive power which literature could confer on sermons while the second was interested in the technical resources which philosophical argumentation could offer to theology.

10

LATE ANTIQUITY
The age of mutation

In AD 312, Constantine, who had converted to Christianity, defeated
Maxentius in a battle near the Mulvian bridge. In AD 529, Justinian
closed down the school of Athens. These two symbolic dates conve-
niently mark the beginning and end of an era. Yet we should not
be fooled by this simplicity. 'The Making of late Antiquity'[1], to
quote the title of P. Brown's famous book, begins at the end
of Marcus Aurelius' reign with the crisis of the third century.
Furthermore, Hellenism did not die out in AD 529: the Platonic
philosophers who left the empire for the court of the Persian king
recrossed the border a few years later, the teaching of the classics
remained in the hands of the 'Hellenes' in sixth-century Alexandria
and the poetry of the time, which was giving out its last sparks,
was essentially pagan.

Late antiquity represents a genuine mutation. 'A new spirit per-
meates every field from the most material and external forms of
everyday life to the most hidden structures of collective mentalities.'[2]

Firstly, political changes. The reforms of Diocletian (AD 286–305)
and Constantine truly mark the end of the *polis*. Under the High
Empire, city-states with their own laws and local elites still flourished. The restored Roman Empire of the Tetrarchs and Constantine
was a centralised monarchy: power was concentrated in the hands of
the emperor, and leading citizens were increasingly attracted by
the court and Constantinople, the 'new Rome'. It was also more
unified economically (by fiscal and currency reforms), administra-
tively (with a bureaucracy reorganised and modelled after the army)
and judicially (under the rule of Theodosius II and Justinian, new
codifications restated the whole of Roman law).

Society was also transformed. Late antiquity was 'an age of ambition'[3] in which soldiers, lawyers and imperial secretaries, sometimes
of humble origin, could climb the social ladder and become high

154

officials and even consuls or praetorian prefects. However, it led to a society that was strictly hierarchical and, with the institutionalisation of hereditary offices, tended to be divided into castes.

Finally there was a religious mutation. Salvation and direct contact with the divine became priorities. The 'friends of God', whether Christian saints or their pagan equivalent, 'holy men', played an increasingly important role in this society, and the emperor, whose source of power was divine, also partook of divine transcendence. A change in the balance of power between Christians and pagans also occurred. After the conversion of Constantine, Christianity was endorsed by the state and paganism was outlawed by the edict of Theodosius I in AD 392.

The relationship between Greek culture and the Christian religion was inevitably affected by these changes. As Christianity spread among the elite, it absorbed pagan *paideia*. The emperor Theodosius II, a fervent Christian, created a chair of Greek rhetoric in Constantinople. Christians occupied the chairs of rhetoric and philosophy in Athens and Alexandria. Furthermore, Julian's law forbidding Christians from teaching Greek literature is perhaps the clue that best reveals their presence in the educational system during the fourth century.

At about the same time, the first signs of a shift in the linguistic equilibrium appear. During the High Empire, Latin had been the language of power and Greek the language of culture. The shift of the political centre of gravity of the empire towards the east favoured the progress of Latin which began to challenge the position of Greek as the language of culture. Theodosius II created chairs of Latin grammar and rhetoric in Constantinople. Papyri from Egypt prove that schoolchildren read Virgil and translated his poems into Greek. The works of the last Greek poets, in which the influence of Virgil and Ovid can sometimes be discerned, also attest to the progress of Latin culture in Greek parts of the empire. Certain writers, such as the historian Ammianus Marcellinus and the poet Claudian, whose mother-tongue was Greek, even chose to write in Latin. Finally, the 'importance of the changes that occurred in the Orient ... can be measured by the amount of protest they provoked among communities where traditional Hellenism still thrived.'[4] In fourth-century Antioch, the rhetor Libanius complained that an increasingly large number of young Greeks chose to study law and Latin in Beirut and Rome instead of dedicating themselves to the study of Greek literature.

The combination of this new spirit and inherited traditional forms accounts for the originality of late Greek literature, be it Christian or pagan. If it appears rigid or conservative, this is only a façade. Beneath the smooth surface of traditional literary genres, citations and imitation of the classics, transformations, innovations and breaks with the past constantly emerge.

The poetry of late antiquity: between plagiarism and transfiguration

Poetry, which had almost disappeared during the High Empire, underwent a renaissance during the fourth and fifth centuries. Re-creating the splendours of the Hellenistic period, it was again Egypt that became the centre of poetry. In AD 405, in his *Lives of the Sophists*, Eunapius wrote of the Egyptians' 'insane infatuation' (493) with poetry. All the poets of the time, with the exception of Quintus of Smyrna, were born and educated in Egypt. They came not only from Alexandria but from the Thebais, particularly from the district of Panopolis. This poetry continued to borrow its forms, metres, and even its language from the great models of the past. It was therefore learned, or worse, academic (authors such as Tryphiodorus, Musaeus and Palladas were professors of literature) and was intended to be read, not performed. However, at its best, the poetry of late antiquity transfigures these models by breathing new spirituality into them.

As in the Hellenistic period, the poets composed encomia, epithalamia, and epics in hexameter which celebrated the exploits of sovereigns. However, these works did not outlive the contemporary events which they described. All that remain are fragments from papyri and titles such as the *Isaurica* of Christodorus, which celebrated in six books the victory of Anastasius over the Isaurians in AD 497.

However, the mythological epics were continually read and recopied. The fourteen books of Quintus of Smyrna's *Posthomerica*, the *Orphic Argonautica*, Nonnus' *Dionysiaca* in forty-eight books, the poems of Tryphiodorus (the *Sack of Troy*), of Colluthus (the *Abduction of Helen*) and Musaeus (*Hero and Leander*) have all survived and allow us to measure the combined influence of Homer and the Alexandrian poets on the late Empire.

Most of these epics were composed between the fourth (and perhaps the third, for Quintus) and sixth centuries. Their authors borrow their subject matter from the Trojan cycle and, quite literally, try to compete with Homer in poems that can be either half as long (Quintus) or twice as long (Nonnus) as their Homeric counterparts. The influence of the Alexandrian poets, whose works were paraphrased in iambic trimeters around AD 500 to make them more accessible, is, however, equally significant: the *Orphic Argonautica*, which makes Orpheus both the narrator of the expedition and a central figure in the plot, are greatly indebted to Apollonius of Rhodes. Musaeus' poem (sixth century), which relates the story of a lover who drowns as he is crossing a strait to meet his beloved, is a 'miniature epic' in the style of Callimachus' *Hecale*. During the Renaissance, this poem enjoyed a success that was perhaps not proportionate to its quality. For the poet Marlowe it was 'the finest love poem in the world'.

The author of the *Posthomerica* was a certain Quintus, about whom we know very little. His origins are uncertain. He claims to come from Smyrna, which, among all the 'homelands' attributed to Homer, was, during the Imperial period, the most illustrious. But this assertion was doubtless a means of highlighting the similarities between himself and his famous model. His dates are equally uncertain (some place him in the third century, others in the fourth).

The *Posthomerica* is antiquarian and academic in its very aim. It tries to fill the gap between the *Iliad* and the *Odyssey* and covers, in fourteen books, the period from the death of Hector to the departure of the Acheans from Troy, a period known from prose summaries of the lost poems of the cycle (the *Aethiopis*, the *Little Iliad* and the *Iliupersis*, 'Sack of Troy') by 'Apollodorus' and Proclus.

A series of episodes built around a heroic figure relates the arrivals and deaths of Penthesilea, the queen of the Amazons (I) and Memnon (II), the death and funeral of Achilles (III) along with the funeral games held in his honour (IV), the awarding of the arms of Achilles to Odysseus and the suicide of Ajax (V), the battles that take place at the gates of Ilium while two embassies set forth to fetch Neoptolemus and Philoctetes (VI–IX), the death of Paris (X), the battles in which Aeneas distinguishes himself (XI), and finally (XII), the construction of the wooden horse, the sacking of the city, the departure of the fleet, the storm that disperses it and the destruction of the wall built by the Acheans.

Quintus remorselessly plagiarises his great model. At first reading, his work seems to be a vast compilation. He borrows verses, similes, typical scenes (embassies, battles, funerals, storms, etc.), and even entire episodes: the funeral games in honour of Achilles are modelled after those held in honour of Patrocles in Book XXIII of the *Iliad*. However, Quintus also echoes the Greek poetic tradition from Hesiod to the Alexandrian poets: in Book XII, when he relates how he received the gift of poetry from the Muses, Quintus is inspired by the Prologue of the *Theogony*. He even cites Latin poets (scholars have found allusions to the *Aeneid* and the *Metamorphoses*). He drops the formulaic style which only made sense within the context of oral poetry, avoiding repetition, dismantling the formulas and creating free variations. He amasses Homeric comparisons and sometimes outdoes them. However, at his best, Quintus successfully creates a new aesthetic: the combat between Achilles and Penthesilea echoes the fights of Achilles and Ajax, but the personality of the adversary, a woman whose beauty Quintus describes in detail, introduces a mixture of eroticism and horror which is entirely foreign to the spirit of the Homeric epic.

The *Dionysiaca* of Nonnus of Panopolis (probably composed between the years AD 450–470) is entirely different in its aim from the *Posthomerica*. Clearly divided into two groups of twenty-four books, each introduced by a prelude and an invocation of the Muse, this poem is a praise of the god Dionysus. It follows rhetorical principles, and more specifically, those delineated by Menander the Rhetor in his outline for the praise of sovereigns. Nonnus first describes the homeland and mortal ancestors of Dionysus: the story of Cadmus and his children (I–V). He also includes, in Book VI, the myth of the first Dionysus, Zagreus, of whom Bacchus is the reincarnation. He then narrates the birth (VII–VIII) and the childhood (IX–XII) of the god. The remaining books of the poem deal with the exploits of Dionysus, his expedition against the Indians (XII–XL) and his triumphant return, his union with Aura which produced Iacchus, the third Dionysus, and his apotheosis (XLI–XLVIII)

Like the *Posthomerica*, this poem, written in hexameters and equal in length to the *Iliad* and the *Odyssey*, is deliberately in the Homeric tradition. However, Nonnus transforms the Homeric hexameter; he adheres to the strict rules followed by Callimachus, but makes allowances for contemporary pronunciation, which substituted stress accent for tonal accent and made little distinction between long and short vowels. He also transforms the epic into an open form, capable of including other genres, such as hymns, epigrams, 'descriptions' (*ekphraseis*) and praises of cities, as well as astronomy, local history and theology.

Nonnus also shares with Quintus a taste for redundancy. At times he repeats verses and even entire episodes: Dionysus successively marries two nymphs, Nicaea in Book XVI and Aura in Book XLVIII. He also makes a rule of 'diversity' (*poikilia*) and justifies this aesthetic with the changeable and diverse nature of the god on whom he models his poem ('If, as a snake, he slithers his undulating tail along, I shall sing of the divine combat in which ivy-crowned thyrsus destroyed the hairy hordes of Giants with their snake-like hair. If he becomes a lion, shaking the bristling mane on his neck, I shall cry "evohe!" for Bacchus' (I, 16–20).

However, by reversing the reasoning, we may as well say that he only chose such a subject because it lent itself to a baroque aesthetic of colourful and intricately woven verses. This elaborate art, in which excessive ornamentation often obscures the main design, is the literary equivalent of the 'invasion of interlacing' in the plastic arts: 'From the third or fourth century onwards, this motif, which had hitherto played only a minor role in the framing edges . . . sometimes becomes the principal motif of the decor.'[5]

The inspiration of the *Dionysiaca* was in tune with the mentality of the 'Age of Spirituality'.[6] Nonnus sometimes explicitly resorts to allegorical exegesis: in the theomachy of Book XXXVI Hera personifies air, Apollo fire, and Poseidon water. The triumph of cosmic order over the forces of disorder is one of the leitmotifs of a work suffused with religious inspiration.

After reading the *Dionysiaca* it is tempting to see Nonnus as one of the last apostles of paganism. Yet the reality was perhaps more complex. We have evidence that Nonnus was the author of a poem in hexameters paraphrasing the Gospel of Saint John. These two aspects of the poet can be reconciled without necessarily doubting the existence of an impermeable division between pagan religiosity and the Christian religion, by viewing Nonnus (as has often been the case) as either a convert or an apostate. Why not simply admit that a Christian poet could have written the *Dionysiaca* and applied the same epithets to Athena and the Virgin Mary? This would in no way be surprising since Nonnus was the product of an era in which allegorical reading was the norm, where a mosaic could represent Christ and Bellerophon arm in arm killing the Chimera, and Orpheus charming the animals was transformed into a Christian symbol.

Such an interpenetration of pagan spirituality and Christian faith is also visible in hymns. The fourth and fifth centuries were marked by a revival of liturgical hymns in verse. Seven (or perhaps eight hymns composed by the Neoplatonic philosopher Proclus (AD 412–485), as well as a collection of Orphic hymns (a collection of prayers for a religious community in Asia Minor) were undoubtedly pagan, whereas the contemporary hymns of Synesius of Cyrene (born *c.* AD 370) were Christian. However, they both have the same format: an invocation of the divinity followed by a prayer. They are both inspired by the classical literary tradition and filled with echoes of Pindar, Anacreon and Sappho. They use similar terms to celebrate a divinity who is 'dazzling light' (Synesius, I, 155) and 'makes a pure light shine in his face' (Proclus, VII, 31), and both express desire for purity and yearn for the beyond.

To finish this sketch of poetry in late antiquity, we must also mention the continued vogue for the epigram. This genre, so popular in Alexandria, was widely adopted throughout the Greek-speaking world, as demonstrated by the publication (*c.* AD 567–568) of the *Cycle*, a collection of recent epigrams by Agathias (born *c.* AD 532). Like the hymn, the epigram was a vehicle for the expression of both *The Pagan Reaction*[7] and the Christian faith. The two authors of the period best represented in the *Palatine anthology* are the pagan poet, Palladas (born *c.* AD 319) and the Christian Gregory of Nazianzus (330–390): the former attacked the 'solitary ones' (the etymological meaning of 'monks') who gathered together in their thousands (AP, XI, 292) and described with bitter irony the 'conversion' of the Olympian gods as their statues were transferred to churches, thus escaping destruction, and the sad fate of the last pagans, who were now like living dead; the latter endeavoured to fight the pagans with their own weapons and composed funerary epigrams which display all the clichés of the genre (he laments the fact that Eros has not lit the flames of marriage for a young man who died unwed). The epigrams of Agathias and his friend and contemporary Paul the Silentiary are even more typical of the time. With Agathias the epigram, like the epic of Nonnus (who greatly influenced Agathias' work), becomes more prolix (sometimes twenty verses in length) and opens up to other genres. Though it borrows themes from such Alexandrian poets as Leonidas of Tarentum and Antipater of Sidon, it also echoes the rhetorical tradition and imitates Latin poets, sometimes quite markedly so. The Christian faith of Paul the Silentiary, author of a famous description of Agia Sophia, did not prevent him from composing erotic epigrams which contain the most sensual verses of the *Cycle*.

History and biography: rupture and confrontation

It is tempting to contrast the synthesis of old and new that was occurring in poetry with the new departures in the field of history.

On the one hand we find the emergence of a genre that was new both in its subject and its methods, Eusebius' *Ecclesiastical History*, while Zosimus' *New History* faithfully follows classical models.

Eusebius of Caesarea (AD 254–340), counsellor of the emperor Constantine, was in fact aware of 'advancing down a path little trod before him' (1, 1, 4) when he set himself the task of writing an ecclesiastical history which combined elements of political history and doxography without belonging to either of these genres. This new history presents itself as the history of the Christian nation and its struggles against persecution from the time of the founding of the church (which happily coincides with Augustus and the founding of the Roman empire (4, 26, 7)), to its triumph, with Constantine's victory over Maxentius (AD 324). It narrates the church's exploits, 'all the great things that are said to have been accomplished in the course of ecclesiastical history' and enumerates its heroes, 'all the people who have so excellently presided over the conduct of the most illustrious dioceses' (I, 1, 1). Yet this nation is unlike other nations. It has a transcendental origin and its adversaries are incarnations of the Devil.

The work is also a history of the doctrinal controversies that opposed orthodox and heretic thinkers, 'those in each generation who, in word or deed, have been the ambassadors of the divine word' and 'those, who, moved by an unfortunate desire for innovation, have been led into the most extreme forms of error (I, 1, 1). Yet, again, the presence or absence of a divine authority creates a radical assymetry between the two camps.

The overall plan is clear. Book I, which is 'a sort of introduction' (II, 1) is devoted to Christ. The history of the Church really starts in Book II, which covers the period from the Ascension of Christ to the Jewish wars. It is then clearly divided into two parts: the narrative of past events until the end of the third century (books III–VII), and then contemporary history with the persecutions of Diocletian, Galerius (VIII), and Maximian (IX) and the triumph of the Church (X). Eusebius gives it a chronological framework which links the succession of bishops in the most important dioceses to that of the emperors.

Eusebius' history differs from all previous Greek histories in both inspiration and method. Written by an inspired author, who relies on divine help, it reveals the constant presence of God in the course of human history. Based on the permanence of an orthodoxy personified by the succession of bishops, it presupposes a revelation and concludes with a victory that is the 'fruit of piety' (X, 9).

Furthermore, 'Eusebius introduces a new type of historical discussion, characterised by the importance given to the most distant past, the central position of doctrinal controversies and the profusion of documents used.'[8]

The genre created by Eusebius did not perish with him. We have evidence of three more ecclesiastical histories written in the first half of the fifth century, by Socrates, Sozomen, and Theodoret of Cyrrhus.

Unlike the Christian Eusebius, who proudly heralds the novelty of his enterprise, the pagan Zosimus, about whom we know little other than the fact he was a fiscal lawyer in Constantinople, wanted his *New History*, which he composed between the years AD 507 and 518, to be the counterpart of Polybius' history. The latter had related 'how the Romans acquired their empire in a short time'. Zosimus, for his part, sets out to relate 'how they quickly destroyed it through their insane presumption' (I, 57, 2).

For the Greek Zosimus, history obviously begins with the Trojan War. He rapidly covers the events prior to the reign of Augustus (I, 1–5) and devotes six books to the period from 31 BC to AD 410. His narrative becomes progressively more detailed as he nears the present: Book II covers fifty years (AD 305–354); Book V, fifteen years (AD 395–409); Book VI, a little under two years (AD 409–410).

Just as Polybius reflected on the causes of the rise of Rome, so Zosimus reflects on the causes of its decline and his response often parallels that of his model. Polybius emphasised the quality of the institutions which allowed Rome successfully to reach universal domination. Zosimus attributes Roman decadence to the institution of monarchy for as long as the aristocracy remained in power they continued to expand their empire year on year' (I, 5, 2)

However, this history is only apparently true to tradition, and genuinely deserves its title. For Zosimus invented 'the End of the Ancient World', a theme which was destined for a long and brilliant future among historians.[9] His religious outlook brought him closer to Eusebius and Augustine than to Polybius. Like them, he saw the hand of God in the historical events and linked misfortune to impiety: if 'the Roman empire gradually became weaker', if 'it became a receptacle of barbarians', it is because 'sacrificial rites were ended in Rome and the ancestral traditions neglected' (IV, 59, 3) in the reign of Theodosius. He also believes in supernatural signs: lightning, earthquakes, dreams and oracles foreshadowing the ills to come. Thus, although he lays the blame for the decline of Rome on the advent of Christianity, Zosimus is not the first philosopher of the Enlightenment and is far from being the precursor of Gibbon, the great English historian of the eighteenth century. Like his adversaries, he puts his faith in God and defends religion. His work is a *Historia adversus Christianos* (History against the Christians), a counterpart to the *Historiae adversus Paganos* (Histories against the Pagans) which were compiled in Latin by the Christian Orosius at the beginning of the fifth century and demonstrated that paganism had been the bane of mankind.

The boundary between history and biography in late antiquity is not always easy to spot as demonstrated by Book VI of Eusebius' *Ecclesiastical History*, which relates the life of Origen. This importance given to biography by a historian is not surprising for a time which has seen 'the rise of the holy man'.[10] In fact all the biographies written in late antiquity, which could take many forms (narratives, but also letters or speeches), be they pagan or Christian, were religious works aimed at the conversion or edification of their audience. They therefore relate, for the most part, the lives of holy men and saints. The exception, the *Reflections on the Life of Constantine* by Eusebius, perhaps best proves the rule. For Eusebius does not pay much attention to his military exploits and his reorganisation of the government and retains from the life . . . of 'this model of piety' only those actions which contributed to the development of Christianity and which could serve as models for religious instruction.

Thus his aim was similar to that of the Bishop of Alexandria, Athanasius (AD 295–373), who wrote around the year AD 357 a *Life of Saint Anthony* in order to 'teach the monks what their lives should be' and convince pagans of the superiority of Christ.

This biography, based on firsthand accounts (Athanasius reminds the reader that he was acquainted with the saint) which claims to adhere scrupulously to the facts, is an elaborate praise of the hermit and his monastic life (Gregory of Nazianzus even states that it is 'a rule of monastic life in the form of a narrative' (PG 35, 1088a): all the acts of Anthony attest to the strength of his faith and the near divine mastery he had over his body. Anthony's long speech to monks at the heart of the work (16–43) eloquently conveys the ideal of physical dissociation from the world. It celebrates a new kind of hero, the saint who 'wins supernatural victories over terrible and resourceful enemies, the evil demons' (21).

This aspect of the work perhaps explains its popularity in a time obsessed with the invisible. *The Life of Saint Anthony* was the bestseller of Christian literature; it was translated into Latin, Syriac, Coptic, Ethiopian, Georgian and Aramaic. Through the centuries it continued to inspire the hellish hallucinations of Bosch and Bruegel and moved Flaubert to write his *Temptation of Saint Anthony*.

Gregory of Nyssa presents another model of Christian perfection in his biographies of Gregory the Thaumaturge and his own sister Macrina. The Life of Macrina comes in the form of a letter which is written in simple and unaffected language and relates to a single miracle. In his panegericus of Gregory the Thaumaturge, presented as a speech and filled with a multitude of tales of exorcism and fights with demons, Gregory of Nyssa pulls out all the stops in rhetoric to extol the man who was 'the Moses of his time' (901c).

With his *Contemplation on the Life of Moses*, Gregory sought inspiration in the works of Philo to add a new spin on biography which he justifies in these terms: 'Since it is impossible to imitate the admirable arts of the Saints in a material way, it is necessary to reassess those things that are amenable to such treatment in such a way as to move from an historical to a spiritual meaning' (340c). In this illustration of perfection of virtue (the subtitle of the work), the various episodes of Moses' life are only of secondary importance. The biographer can even skip over the events he deems less suited to his aim. What is important is allegorical interpretation. Told by Gregory, the life of Moses 'shows . . . how it is possible to bring the soul to the peaceful harbour of virtue' (304a).

With more literary flourish, Christian biographers of the fourth century built upon the heritage of the edificatory works of the third century, such as the Acts of the Apostles, the passions, and the lives of the martyrs. They continued to bear witness to the power of the divinity and the salvation which it could bestow upon man. Pagan biographies of the same period, whether written by Eunapius (*Lives of the Sophists*), Marinus (*Life of Proclus*), or Damascius (*Life of Isidorus*), continued the neoplatonic tradition of the third century by relating the lives of philosophers who reached a divine state of wisdom. They differed only in their increased obsession with the supernatural and miracles.

A comparison of the *Lives of the Sophists* by Eunapius of Sardis (AD 348–414) with the work by Philostratus from which it takes its name and which it continues, is very revealing in this respect. In the first half of the third century, the rhetorician Philostratus had artfully constructed a series of biographies to capture the power and radiance of Greek oratory during the Roman period. He had taken great pains accurately to characterise the eloquence of those men he proposed as models. Eunapius was a hierophant who started by 'prostrating himself before the gates of the truth' (Preface, 455). His biographies, spanning the two centuries from Plotinus to Chrysanthius, a sophist contemporary with the emperor Julian, portray thaumaturges rather than orators: the 'divine' Iamblichus 'who has the ear of the gods' (458) could make them appear at will and could make their statues come to life. Maximus of Ephesus, who was the spiritual guide of the emperor, Julian, could make the statue of Hecate smile and light the torches she held in her hands with his magical formulae. Eunapius' portrait of Sosipatra, the wife of the sophist Eustatius, is a pagan hagiography fit to rival the biography of Macrina.

The comparison of the life of the Neoplatonic philosopher Proclus (AD 412–485), written by his disciple Marinus in AD 486, with Porphyry's *Life of Plotinus*, is equally instructive. Porphyry's Plotinus already had 'something more than other men' (*Life*, 10). The Proclus of Marinus exudes a supernatural aura and is on equal footing with the Gods. He arrives in Athens 'accompanied by all the good demons who preside over literature and watch over philosophy' (10, 18). He constantly receives divine signs, can predict the future, and accomplishes miracles as wondrous as those of the saints: he heals the sick, controls rain, and averts earthquakes.

Rhetoric, mirror of the tensions in Hellenism

In rhetoric, respect for tradition and constant references to the great models of the past tended to attenuate differences and wrap change in a cloak of continuity. Yet there is a wide gap between Julian, Libanius and Themistius, who belonged to the same time, claimed the same Hellenic heritage, and knew each other well enough to correspond on a regular basis (letters from Julian to Libanius and Themistius as well as letters from Libanius to Julian and Themistius have survived). All three exemplify a different reaction to the mutations they witnessed or even caused.

The emperor Julian (AD 331–353) symbolises the tensions and contradictions of late Hellenism. As emperor, he claimed to embody the double heritage of Roman power and Greek culture and fancied himself as both king and philosopher. In reality however, he merely vacillated between these two roles. He was a great admirer of Marcus Aurelius and the golden age of the Antonine emperors, who tried to restore the autonomy of the Greek city states, but his interventionism only earned him the reputation of tyrant among the citizens

of Antioch, who loathed him. Though he received a Christian education (which is why he was named the Apostate by Christian authors),
Julian was a staunch champion of paganism who saw himself as the
restorer of Hellenism. However, he tried to transform it into a religion on the Christian model by endowing it with a coherent
theology and an organised clergy, recruited for the most part among
Neoplatonic philosophers. Though his admiration for Greek culture
was boundless, he condemned the Greeks of his time and often
compared their flaws with the virtues of the Celts and Germans.
Through force of circumstance, he was destined to become a man
of action, though he preferred dreams to reality and would gladly
have spent his time with books: he scorned the popular entertainment of the hippodrome, preferring to read the scene of the chariot
race in *Iliad* XXIII. He was the only emperor who was also a literary
man: he wrote letters, panegyrics, hymns and satires. His fasci-
nating, disconcerting work is full of contradictions, mingling official
pronouncements with confidences, acerbic irony with mystic
fervour, and has played no small part in the creation of the myth
of Julian.

Julian composed praises of the sovereigns Constantius (speeches
I and III) and his wife Eusebia (Speech II). Like a good student, he
applied the rules of rhetoric and celebrated the ancestors, education, great deeds and the eminent virtues of rulers. However, he
sometimes breaks with convention and speaks his own mind. The
philosopher lurks under the rhetor in Speech III. In his praise of
Constantius, he slips into a portrait of the ideal king. His tone can
be biting and, as he himself concedes his words 'drawn as though
by the downhill slope of a road, give themselves over to unbridled
denigration' (III, 85d). Personal anecdotes creep into his official
speeches: at the heart of his praise of Eusebia, Julian confides that
the generosity of the empress once allowed him to satisfy his passion
for reading.

His prose hymns addressed to the Mother of Gods (VIII) and to
Helios the King (XI) do more than simply reiterate the common-
places of divine praise. The Hymn to the Mother of Gods aims to
communicate a mystical experience and 'tells unspeakable truths
and . . . forbidden, ineffable secrets' (VII, 158d). Following the
tradition set by Iamblichus and the Neoplatonic philosophers, Julian
espoused allegorical interpretations of rites and myths. Attis, con-
sort of Cybele, thus becomes 'the immediate creator of the material
world' (VIII, 175a). The *Hymn to Helios the King* on 'the essence
of the God and his origins, capacities and efforts, both visible

and invisible' (XI, 132b) betrays the desire for a unification of the pagan pantheon under the aegis of a single god, who, like the Byzantine sovereign, gathers a multitude of gods into a unified whole around his individual essence' (XI, 151a). This hymn also reveals Julian's passion for the god's rays and ends with a prayer in which death and a preoccupation with the beyond overshadow terrestrial concerns: 'May he grant me', Julian asks of Helios the King, 'a virtuous life, more perfect wisdom and divine intelligence. May he also allow me to leave this life in all serenity, at the time fate chooses. May I then rise up to him and stay beside him forever' (XI, 151 b–c).

Yet, Julian the mystic possesses a satirical wit. In an ongoing polemic, he reviles the Cynics, who blaspheme against all gods (VII and IX), and the Christians even more (we know he wrote a speech *Against the Galileans*, which we know only through his reputation by Cyril of Alexandria). His *Symposium*, also entitled the *Saturnalia*, derides, with a verve that is at times worthy of Lucian, both the Roman Cesars and the Greek conqueror Alexander, attacks Constantine with unrelenting spite (he is prone to softness and debauchery and finally expiates his impiety, together with Jesus), and spares only Marcus Aurelius.

In his most personal and interesting work, the *Misopogon*, literally, the 'Beard Hater', Julian's satirical verve is also directed against himself. Disconcerting many a reader, this pamphlet, addressed to the citizens of Antioch which is why it is also called the *Antiochicus*, the Antiochian), mocks the person of the emperor. With stunning violence, Julian targets himself. Should we read this work as the expression of infantile rage, a pathetic attempt to win over the people of Antioch, or the confession of a man who is ill at ease with himself? The outrageousness of the criticism (Julian's beard is infested with vermin and long enough to be plaited into cables) and the fact that according to the Byzantine historian Malalas, it was posted in the public square; suggest parody. The emperor Julian would thus be turning on its head the imperial rescript which usually combines praise of a city with that of the emperor: with an irony worthy of Socrates, he seems to have written a deprecation of the emperor which turns against the Antiochians. By daring to taunt philosophy in the person of Julian, they are only revealing the depth of their own corruption.

It is tempting to compare Julian's attack on Antioch with the *Antiochicus* composed a few years earlier by Libanius in honour of his home town, and to contrast the aggressive and innovative

Hellenism of Julian with the nostalgic affection of this sophist for the Hellenic tradition.

For Libanius (AD 314–393) was aware that he represented a bygone era. A proud citizen of Antioch, he remained a staunch defender of the autonomy of the city state in an age of centralised government. He was a civilian in a world oppressed by the increasing weight of the army. He regretfully yearns for the golden age of paganism, the time when 'the sanctuaries were full of people making sacrifices' (2, 26), although, except for Julian's brief three-year reign, he experienced only a Christian empire. He taught Greek rhetoric at a time when 'people are fleeing the language of the Hellenes and setting sail for Italy' in order to learn Latin eloquence which 'procures power and money, whereas ours offers only itself' (1, 214).

For the most part, his abundant and varied work seems to signal a resurgence of the Second Sophistic in its language (Libanius was a purist who refused terms borrowed from the Latin and willingly resorted to archaic vocabulary and atticism, for which Byzantine scholars nicknamed him Demosthenes), and even more in its themes.

Like his great models, Dio of Prusa and Aelius Aristides, Libanius, who saw himself as the intermediary between the central power and the city states, was a prolific writer of political speeches. He tried to obstruct the extortionate demands of governors in a series of often violent pamphlets. In *For the Temples*, a plea for paganism, he defended the temples. He also denounced the monks, 'those black-robed blackguards, more voracious than elephants', who were destroying the temples and ruining the countryside (Speech 30, 8). He evoked the difficult issue of recruiting members for the municipal senate in Speech 49. He tried to gain Julian's indulgence towards the citizens of Antioch (Speech 15), but also reprimanded them (Speech 16). After the uprisings that shook the city in 387, he addressed Theodosius I to beg for his clemency (Speech 19) and thanked him (Speech 20) while preaching moderation to the special investigators sent by the emperor (Speeches 21 and 22), and reproaching those citizens who had fled the city in their thousands (Speech 23).

Like his models, he was a master of epideictic rhetoric. He composed a *Hymn to Artemis* (Speech 5) as a counterpart to Aelius Aristides' hymns. He also celebrated the pagan festival of the Kalends of January, which was a dangerously close rival to the Epiphany. In encomia, welcome speeches and funeral speeches, he successively celebrated the emperors Constantius and Constans, Gallus, Valens, and, more than any other, his beloved Julian, who had bravely attempted to restore paganism (he dedicated five speeches to him). He also praised a number of high officials, either on his own initiative or at a patron's bequest. Finally, he also celebrated cities: his praise of Antioch emulates Aelius Aristides' *Panathenaicus*, just as his *Lamentation on Nicomedia*, which was destroyed in an earthquake, echoes the monody composed by Aristides after the earthquake that ravaged Smyrna.

Like this author, he also composed declamations on mythological and historical subjects. His *Response of Achilles to Odysseus* is in fact a response to Aelius Aristides and his *Speech of the Embassy to Achilles*. His Attic declamations are the counterparts to the Sicilian speeches.

Unlike his role models, however, he was a teacher, with the status that implied. He addressed his students in end-of-year speeches (distant ancestors of prize-giving speeches), but turned them inside out by speaking on the refusal to make a speech. He also preached love of eloquence and literature and ceaselessly exhorted his pupils and ex-pupils to temperance, work and civic virtues.

But Libanius was not only a second-century man lost in the fourth century. His religiosity and the importance of intimate confidences in his work were characteristics of his time. Even in his ceremonial speeches, (for example, the lamentation on Julian or the *lamentation on Nicomedia*), personal feelings play an important role. He also expresses these in his letters (his correspondence, the second most voluminous after Cicero, numbers more than 1,500 letters). Finally, he also felt compelled to write his autobiography. Directly inspired by Isocrates' *Antidosis*, it focuses on the public rather than the private man (confidences are rare and tend to concern his health rather than his emotional life). However, through the rhetorical structure of a debate on fortune (Was Libanius happy or unhappy?), he betrays his belief in an all-powerful divine power.

Libanius sees divine providence everywhere: if Fortune has kept him away from his beloved Nicomedia 'it was because she knew of the impending catastrophe' (1, 78). He believes in premonitory dreams and cosmic signs (such as the earthquake that marked Julian's death). He is aware of the powers of magicians and relates the circumstances by which he fell prey to their manoeuvres. Like his contemporaries, he awaits divine remedies for all ills. This is why the speech in which he deplores present misfortune and longs for the happy time of the pagan empire before Constantine ends with a prayer: 'What is there left to do? Pray to the gods to give a helping hand to the sanctuaries, the farmers, the soldiers, the curia and the Greek language.'

Themistius (AD 317–388) bears little resemblance to Libanius. This philosopher, who was born into an academic family, soon left his native province and moved to the capital. He eventually gave up teaching and accepted a position as prefect of Constantinople.

His paraphrases of the *Analytics* and *Physics* of Aristotle bear witness to the activity of 'this zealous amateur of philosophy' (Photius *cod.* 74), but he is best known for his rhetorical works: thirty-two complete speeches, which provide precious material on the political and intellectual life of the fourth century.

Themistius differs even more radically from Julian in his philosophical opinions and political sympathies. His speeches 21 to 29 on the relationship between philosophy and rhetoric and the definition of true philosophy reveal his attempt to bridge the gap between philosophy and action. He attacks philosophers who, following Plotinus, want to confine philosophy to contemplation and are content to 'mumble to a group of young people in a corner (22, 265b) and protests against the esotericism of Neoplatonism, demanding the right to 'bring the teachings of philosophy into broad daylight' (22, 265c).

In the official speeches, delivered, for example, before the senate of Constantinople or in Antioch, in which he congratulates the emperors Constantius, Jovian, Valens, Gratian and Theodosius (with the notable absence of Julian) for a victory or peace treaty, celebrates anniversaries and consular nominations or expresses thanks for a favour, he deploys arguments for a politics of tolerance, which would respect all the different religions: Greek paganism, Syriac Christianity and Egyptian theurgy. 'Just think', he says to the emperor Jovian, (5, 70a) 'that the master of the universe also takes pleasure in such diversity'. He advocates the assimilation of the barbarians. Finally, he reaffirms the ecumenical vocation of the empire and the absolute rule of the emperor, who is the 'living law'.

Yet these new ideas are expressed in stereotypical rhetoric and formulas borrowed from tradition. In Speech XXVII his invectives against neoplatonic philosophers echo the themes developed by Dio Chrysostom in his Speech XXXII, *To the Alexandrians*, and in a classic case of bad faith, uses Platonic expressions to defend arguments that are not theirs[11]. The assimilation of the barbarians is presented as a return to a policy that has proved effective in the past. His developments on the universality of the empire are expressed in terms borrowed from the cosmopolitanism of the Stoics, while they are in fact inspired by Christian ecumenism. Even his defence of innovation makes use of traditional arguments and exploits the authority of Aristotle (Speech 26). It is then necessary to examine more closely the form of his borrowings and the manner in which he refashions traditional themes to grasp the originality of his thought. When Themistius uses the Platonic image of a chorus singing in unison to symbolise the harmony of the state, he places a conductor centre stage, thereby implying that harmony among citizens depends on the actions of the head of state.

To complete our overview of fourth-century rhetoric, we must mention the rhetor Himerius (AD 310–380), one of the stars of eloquence in Athens best known for his brilliant style. Like Libanius, he composed declamations on historical themes (for example, a speech by Themistocles against the Persian king) and a series of ceremonial speeches celebrating such things as departures, arrivals, marriages and anniversaries. Placing himself under the patronage of the Muses, he created a poetic prose, rich in mythological allusions. He is heralded by some as the Pindar of the fourth century, though is perhaps rather its Quintus.

Synesius of Cyrene (AD 370–412) was a man of a different generation and milieu. He was born a Christian and died a bishop. Yet this aristocrat, who represented his province before the emperor, was as well-versed in philosophy as Themistius (Hypatia was his true initiator into the mystical celebrations of philosophy' (*Ep.* 137) in Alexandria) and as passionate about Greek culture as Libanius. Like Themistius and Libanius, he imitated the great masters of the Second Sophistic, modelling his speech on kingship to Arcadius on Dio's speech to Trajan, replying to Dio's *Praise of Baldness* with his *Praise of Hair*, and by naming his speech in defence of Greek culture *Dio*. Like them, he also participated in debates over current issues and used myths to promote his political opinions, for example assimilating Aurelian to Osiris and his adversary to Typhon in his *Egyptian Tales*. Finally, like them, his work is more personal (much of his voluminous correspondence is still extant) and reveals a strong interest in supernatural phenomena (he wrote a philosophical treatise on the causes and interpretations of dreams).

Neoplatonism: philosophy as theology

Synesius, who considered himself to be both a Neoplatonist and a Christian, represents a species that thrived at the end of the fourth century. But although, as we shall see, Christians were quick to draw on Platonism, the Neoplatonist philosophers of the fourth and fifth centuries were faithful heirs of Porphyry and Iamblichus who placed greater emphasis on the religious dimension of their search, for them the quest for God was the sole aim of philosophy.

On this point, attempts have been made to contrast the Athenian school and its leaders, from Plutarch to Simplicius, including Syrianus, Proclus, Isidorus, Zenodotus and Damascius, with the Alexandrian School, made famous by Theon and his daughter Hypatia, Hermias, Ammonius and Olympiodorus. The former are described as mystical Platonists and militant pagans, the latter as Aristotelians, more given to compromise and more welcoming to Christians. Such a contrast is undoubtedly illusory however.[12] There were close ties between the two schools and it was possible to move easily between them. Syrianus and Isidorus came to Athens from Alexandria, while Hierocles, Hermias and Ammonius studied in Athens. A close comparison of the seven commentaries preserved in Aristotle's *Categories* would seem to establish that there was no significant difference between the Athenian and Alexandrian attitudes.

For these philosophers, philosophical study was a religious activity and their works frequently open and close with prayers. Proclus begins his *Parmenides*, by saying: 'I pray to all the gods and goddesses to guide my mind towards the subject I propose to deal with', while Simplicius concludes his commentary on Aristotle's *On Heaven*, as follows: "I offer you these words, oh Lord, maker of the whole Universe and simple bodies, as hymns to you and to the realities that you have made.'

The soul's conversion towards the divine was to happen gradually as a result of reading a series of texts and commentaries arranged in a strictly hierarchical order, as P. Hadot has recently shown.[13] First came moral works such as Epictetus' *Manual* (Simplicius' commentary has been preserved) and Pythagoras' *Golden Verses* (with a commentary by Hierocles), then the works of Aristotle or minor mysteries (for example, Simplicius' commentaries on *On Heaven*, the *Physics* and the *Categories*) and finally the great mysteries, the works of Plato, starting with the first *Alcibiades* and concluding with *Timaeus* and *Parmenides*. For, as Proclus repeatedly states, 'according to the divine Iamblichus, all of Plato's philosophy is incorporated in these two dialogues'. The former contains all of the natural science and the latter 'teaches all the divine categories' and 'sheds the perfect and complete light of theology'.

The fact that the reading of these texts played such a central role in the philosophical process explains why commentary occupied a prime place in philosophical production. The greatest of these, the Platonic commentaries of Proclus and the Aristotelian commentaries of Simplicius, required a vast amount of historical documentation. At the beginning of his commentary on the *Parmenides*, Proclus thus enumerates all the exegetes, from Plotinus to his teacher Syrianus, who 'have developed most holy explanations of divine principles'. Such commentaries also required a great deal of systematisation. The commentators sought to bring all the elements of the work in question within the scope of a single 'aim' (Greek *skopos*) (this is particularly apparent in Proclus' commentaries), retaining in the tradition the interpretation that best synthesised the partial truths of earlier interpretations.[14]

We have all of Proclus' commentaries on the *Timaeus*, the *Parmenides* and the first *Alcibiades*, as well as a series of essays on *The Republic*, Simplicius' commentaries on Aristotle's treatises *On Heaven*, *Physics*, the *Categories* and *The Soul* (although the authenticity of the latter is disputed), and a commentary on Epictetus' *Manual*. To these can be added the commentaries of Hermias, Ammonius, Olympiodorus and Damascius on some dialogues of Plato and Aristotle.

In addition, these philosophers have left us works that open with a problem which they then attempt to solve through a play of question and answer in the manner of Plato's dialogues, such as Damascius' *Questions and Answers on the Principles*. They also wrote treatises. Some of these deal with precise problems, such as providence (Proclus' *Three Studies*), while others are more systematic and provide a rational organisation of the doctrine as a whole, presented in the form of a series of propositions following each other logically, in the manner of Euclid's *Elements*. Two major works by Proclus are arranged according to this format: *Elements of Physics*, which builds a theory of movement on the basis of books VI and VIII of Aristotle's *Physics*, and *Elements of Theology*, which brings together all the universal propositions of Platonic metaphysics. These treatises develop *more geometrico* and are the distant ancestors of Spinoza's *Ethics*.

Finally, we should note Proclus' *Platonic Theology*, 'an original systematic work in which the author was not confined by any established literary genre'.[15] This discourse on divinity and the gods successively considers the divine attributes, the levels of the divine hierarchy and the individual gods located within the world (encosmic gods) and outside it (hypercosmic gods).

The Plato of Neoplatonism was carefully 'filtered' – even more so than that of Plotinus – through an entire tradition, to emerge transformed: at once mutilated and expanded. He had become no more than a theologian, but his theology now incorporated all of Greek thought on the divine since earliest times, and that of the Barbarians as well.

Plato had become 'the guide of the true mysteries . . . and the high priest of integral and immobile apparitions', as Proclus puts it in his *Platonic Theology* (1, 1, 6). His work provided revelations concerning the origins of a divine world whose pyramidal hierarchy copied that of the Byzantine empire. At the bottom of this ladder were the heroes, then came the intelligible gods, the good demons, the angelic choir, the gods who presided over the world. At the top were the supra-celestial and intellective gods. Reading Plato became a spiritual exercise, a prayer, enabling the reader to 'leave behind all that comes after the One and to establish contact with the unutterable, the beyond of everything that exists', as Proclus says at the start of his *Platonic Theology* (1, 3, 16).

At the same time Plato's writings had been enriched by a number of additional elements. His philosophy now included that of Aristotle, following a subtle reconciliation which did not shrink from bending the meaning of the texts: 'when Aristotle opposes Plato it is necessary to look not only at the letter of the text . . . but also to take the meaning into consideration and to seek out their agreement', wrote Simplicius in his commentary on the *Categories*. Plato's doctrines had to be brought into harmony with Homer's poems, from which 'he seems to have borrowed them', if we are to believe Proclus. In fact, the sixth dissertation of Proclus commentary on the *Republic* is entirely devoted to the 'objections of Plato in the *Republic* to Homer and the art of poetry' and its sole aim is to establish an agreement between the poet, interpreted allegorically, and the philosopher (to appreciate this *tour de force* one need only consider the virulence of Plato's attacks on the poets). Finally, it had to be demonstrated that Plato's teaching converges with that of Orpheus, Pythagoras and the Chaldaean oracles. The great merit of Proclus was, according to his biographer Marinus, that he succeeded in reconciling 'Greek theology (Plato) with that of the Barbarians (the Chaldaean oracles) and that which is hidden in the fictions of myth (the Orphic poems)'.

Christianity was excluded from this synthesis; however, in an empire that had adopted Christianity as a state religion, the time was no longer right for open polemic, at least from the 'Hellenes'.

The Neoplatonists' contempt for their enemies manifested itself in a series of allusions in coded language. Thus, in Proclus' work, Christians are assimilated to 'neighbours who abandon sobriety' or, worse, 'typhonic winds' causing tempests. The sole, but important, exception is of course the emperor Julian's *Against the Galilaeans*. This work is revealing in two respects: it proves that only a man with power could now openly attack Christianity and that only someone brought up among Christians could be sufficiently interested in their doctrine to criticise it precisely.

Patristics: the conversion of Hellenism

On the other hand, Christian apologists, who felt protected by the authorities, could sometimes be heard loud and clear, but their works reflected, almost despite themselves, the penetration of Christianity by the Greek *paideia* in the fourth century.[16] Thus the two treatises by Athanasius (295–373), Bishop of Alexandria, which combine a regular refutation of paganism (*Against the Hellenes*) with a defence and illustration of the Christian faith (*On the Incarnation of the Word*) are very precisely aimed at both popular polytheism and the pantheism of the philosophers. However, Athanasius' work was not typical of the time. It was chiefly in the second half of the century, after Julian's attempt to restore both Greek culture and religion, that an increasing number of works of polemic writings were produced. Yet these sometimes very violent attacks on Julian and the Neoplatonists who had inspired him, notably Porphyry, came largely from cultivated Christians, scandalised that anyone should dare to deny them the teachings of philosophy and rhetoric. Their critiques sometimes overstepped the bounds of reality, since they often attacked Julian for having sought to deny Christians all access to culture, thereby demonstrating that for Christians too, culture was inseparable from the Greek *paideia*.

Christian polemic against Julian is well documented: besides Gregory of Nazianzus' *Invectives against Julian* (discourses 4 and 5), written less than a year after the emperor's death, John Chrysostom's treatise of 384 celebrating the posthumous defeat of Julian by the martyr Babylas (to which should be added the same author's demonstration of Christ's divinity for the Jews and Greeks, written around the same time), and the ten books in which Cyril of Alexandria refutes, point by point, Book I of Julian's *Against the Galilaeans* around the year 433 (preserved fragments indicate that the original work was much longer), there were also a series of works which have been lost, including the refutation of Porphyry in thirty books and the discourse *On Truth* by Apollinarius of Laodicea (310–390?). All in all, however, there were not very many of these treatises (after the fourth century the Christians first took on the enemy within, who were the heretics, and the number of treatises and discourses against the Arians was far greater than that against the pagans) and their production seems to have come to an end in the first half of the fifth century. Cyril of Alexandria's *Apology Against Julian*, which was, with Theodoret of Cyrrhus' *Cure of Pagan Maladies* (423 at the latest), the last treatise of apologetics, is earlier than 441. They could not hide the fact that a literature was developing which was both Greek and Christian and reached its zenith in Asia Minor with Eusebius of Cesarea (263–339), the Cappadocian Fathers Gregory of Nazianzus (329–390), Basil of Caesarea (330–379) and Gregory of Nyssa (355–394) and the fathers of the Antiochene School, John Chrysostom (334?–407), Theodore of Mopsuestia (died around 428) and Theodoret of Cyrrhus (393–466).

All these people belonged to the elite. They had all studied rhetoric and sometimes philosophy, both in their home cities and in prestigious centres such as Antioch, Constantinople or Athens. Some of them had been taught by the stars of the profession: in Athens Basil of Caesarea and Gregory of Nazianzus were students of the sophists Himerius and Prohaeresius, while John Chrysostom and Theodore of Mopsuestia followed the lessons of Libanius in Antioch. They were, it is said, brilliant students: one legend, no doubt spread by the Christians, even tells how Libanius on his deathbed acknowledged that only John Chrysostom was worthy to succeed him. Some (such as Gregory of Nazianzus and Basil of Cesarea) were even professionals themselves, at least for a time. They were on friendly terms with pagans in their milieu: Gregory of Nazianzus wrote to Themistius to recommend a friend and he sent an epigram to Libanius. The very existence of apocryphal correspondence between Libanius and Basil, in which the Sophist clearly admits to being defeated by his interlocutor's eloquence, shows to what extent it was normal in this period for a cultivated bishop to exchange letters with a famous pagan teacher.

Yet, despite such education, the synthesis between Hellenism and Christianity was far from being a natural thing even for those who were its creators. Before examining some practical examples of how patristics restructured genres and themes borrowed from Hellenism, it is worth considering how the problem was posed and settled in theory. This is a partial point of view and will doubtless seem reductive; however, we have deliberately chosen to look at Hellenism and what was borrowed from it, leaving others to emphasise the 'originality of patristics'[17] and show how its different genres were born of the primordial needs of Christian communities[18]. For the fourth century was the period when the Christians most clearly considered the question of the utility of Greek literature and the school in which it was taught. Their answers, however, were somewhat contradictory.

The first contradiction was between words and deeds. Unlike the Jews, Christians were quick to opt for the Greek school and John Chrysostom's calls to parents to send theirs sons to the monks from the age of 10 in order to arm them against the seductions of pagan culture found few echoes among Christians in the higher social strata in Antioch or elsewhere. Yet these same Christians constantly distanced themselves from the pagan culture they had received. After undergoing a solid training in rhetoric, Basil regrets having 'wasted a lost of time in the service of vanity' (Letter 223, 2) and Gregory of Nyssa echoes his words when he denounces the sterility of 'profane education which constantly conceives but never gives birth' (*Life of Moses*, 2, 11).

There was also a contradiction between the content and form of the response. For the rejection of Hellenism was often expressed in terms directly borrowed from Greek culture. When, in Letter 4, Gregory of Nazianzus expresses his indignation that Basil should have 'preferred the title of rhetor to that of Christian', he borrows an image from Hesiod to describe Basil's abandonment of the holy books, saying, 'You have placed them above the hearth, in the smoke, like the tiller and hoe in winter'.

Conversely, the Christians are reticent when it comes to acknowledging their love of pagan literature and its utility. When Gregory of Nazianzus confesses, 'I felt a great love of literature when my cheeks were still beardless', he at once adds, 'I sought to make the bastard [in other words Greek] literature serve legitimate literature [in other words the Scriptures]' (*On His Life*, 112–14). Basil of Cesarea's treatise, which claims to give directions for the use of pagan literature in the education of young Christians, *To the Young, on the Way to Profit from Hellenic Literature*, opens with a warning: 'I have come to advise you not to abandon the helm of your thoughts, once and for all, to these men [the Hellenes], as one might with a ship (1, 24–6).

For a Christian who lives in hope of the afterlife, there is only one truly useful text to read, and that is Holy Writ, which leads to real virtue. From profane literature one can glean only 'a shadowy outline of virtue' (10, 2–3). Thus Greek literature can only be instructive at a lower, secondary level. It is a propaedeutic: 'While waiting for age to allow us to understand the depth of the Holy Scriptures, we undertake our first exercises in other books which are not entirely different from them' (2, 27–9); it offers a preliminary initiation before the great mysteries, a training in preparation for the real fight. The only true reference point remains the Scriptures. This is no doubt why Basil, in what is only an apparent paradox, takes his example from the Old Testament and successively quotes Moses, 'who bent his mind to the knowledge of Egypt', and Daniel, who 'learned, it is said, the wisdom of the Chaldeans' (3, 12–18) to justify preliminary study of the sciences 'of the outside'.

Not content with the complete subordination of Greek literature to the Scriptures, the Christians maintained that they alone were able to gain real profit from it. For Basil, the Christians were like bees, who are able to make honey from flowers (pagan literature), while the others (the pagans) can only take useless pleasure in their scent and colour. Other writers went further still: in itself, says Gregory of Nazianzus, pagan literature is a poison; but, 'just as we can make medicines using snakes, so we can draw from [profane literature] certain principles of enquiry and thought' (*Praise of Basil*, 11, 3).

Yet, here again, it is impossible to separate these loftily proclaimed principles from their context. We should not forget that Basil's strategy in the *Letter to the Young* is copied from that of Plato in the *Republic*. He takes a selective approach to profane literature, retaining only that which is useful for the teaching of virtue. Plato had also made such a choice, taking from the poets only that which was compatible with philosophy. Further still, Basil resembles the Neoplatonists when he succeeds in reintegrating 'almost all of Homer' (5, 27–8), 'recycling' him by means of an allegorical reading. When Homer shows Odysseus escaping from the shipwreck and arriving naked on the shores of the Phaeacians, 'this is a way of shouting to us: "Men, you must cultivate a virtue that will survive shipwrecks"' (5, 39–40). The style is equally significant. Basil borrows from Plato the image of the eye of the soul, which must first 'look at shadows or mirrors' (2, 29–31). He also borrows one of Homer's metaphors to invite the young to resist the charms of poetry: 'You need to avoid these examples by blocking your ears as they say Ulysses did against the Sirens' song' (4, 8–11).

A brief glance at some works of patristic literature will enable us to show that Basil's approach was indeed in accord with his time and that Christians did not shrink from either the rhetoric or the philosophy of the pagans. Basil himself admits that rhetoric is not useless: it gives the truths of the faith an appearance which is not without charm and provides them with a kind of 'packaging'. The homilies put Christ's message across to terms suited to the taste of the times, as is provided by the Christian Isidore of Pelusium's eulogy of John Chrysostom's masterpiece, the thirty-one homilies on the Romans: 'I think,' he wrote in Letter 5, 'that if the divine Paul had wanted to present his own writings in the Attic language, he would have spoken no differently from this celebrated master, so remarkable is his interpretation by its content, beauty of form and exactitude of express.' Neither rhetorical clichés nor mythological expression were rejected by the writers of the homilies. Gregory of Nazianzus developed the classical theme of the description (*ecphrasis*) of spring in the homily he delivered the Sunday after Easter (44), as can be seen by comparing it with Libanius. Gregory displayed his knowledge of pagan feasts even as he vigorously attacked them in his homily on the Epiphany (such references are so common in his work that at the beginning of the sixth century a collection of scholia, the mythological scholia of pseudo-Nonnus, was compiled to explain them). The same is true for the eulogies of the saints. These panegyrics almost ritually open with a repudiation of oratorical amplifications and a refusal to 'bow to the rules of the eulogies' (Basil, *Praise of the Forty Martyrs*, 509a). Yet they fit perfectly into the categories of epide-ictic eloquence and follow exactly the rhetorical schemas for the eulogy, although some *topoi* which do not sit easily with the spirit of religion (for example, impressive lineage or physical beauty) are notable only by their absence. They use and abuse mythological comparisons and witticisms. Thus, in his *Eulogy of Basil*, Gregory of Nazianzus compares the friendship that bound him to the saint with that of Orestes and Pylades (44) and, in his *Funeral Oration for Gorgonia,* he rejects those things 'that make the elegance of language' to praise a woman 'who knew nothing of coquetry and turned this lack of beauty into beauty' (792c).

Even more is borrowed from philosophy, which is not surprising when one realises that 'Christianity was presented by an entire section of the Christian tradition as a philosophy' indeed as the only 'complete' philosophy.[19]

Like any philosophy, this 'philosophy according to Christ' was centred on a founding text and made reading into a spiritual exercise. It thus gave prime importance to exegesis, which allows the soul to rise towards the divine, and went so far as to borrow Hellenistic culture's exegetic method. If tradition is to be believed, Aristarchus said that one should 'interpret Homer by Homer'. The Neoplatonists also used Plato to interpret Plato and the Christians used the Bible to interpret the Bible.

Compared to this similarity of approach, the other forms of borrowing are ultimately not very important; but it would be easy to prove that the Christians adopted almost all the literary forms and all the *topoi* of ancient philosophy.

We shall consider the literary forms first. Thus, in the fourth and fifth centuries, one finds many commentaries (no less than ten commentaries on the Psalms were produced in this period) and scholia (for example, Evagrius' *Scholia*). Scholia are also found in combination with commentary – as illustrated in the preceding century by Clement of Alexandria's *Stromateis* – in the thirteen books of the 'Polishings' (in Greek, *Glaphyrai*) in which Cyril of Alexandria interprets selected passages of the Pentateuch. Theodoret of Cyrrhus also produced a commentary on the Pentateuch and the Books of Joshua, Judges and Ruth, organised into question and answer form, exactly like that of the Neoplatonist Damascius. One can also find systematic theological treatises whose aim and structure are similar to Proclus' *Platonic Theology*, while Gregory of Nyssa's *Catechism* is presented as a full account of Christian doctrine destined for 'teachers who need systematic instruction'. Even the Platonic dialogues were imitated: shortly after the death of their brother Basil, Gregory of Nyssa and his sister Macrina, who was also dying, came together in the dialogue *on the Soul and the Resurrection*, a Christian transposition of the *Phaedo*, as is the *Dialogue on the Life of Saint John Chrysostom* by Palladius (363–431).

Like the philosophers, the Christians found echoes of their gospel in all the other texts. The former found Platonic doctrines in the work of Homer, the latter demonstrated the convergence between pagan philosophy and the Bible. Thus Basil, in Letter 9, cites Plato's words: 'One should only become attached to the body if one uses it as an aid to philosophy', adding, 'this precept conforms, unless I am mistaken, to that of Paul, who warns us not to care for the body in order to feed its lusts'. The frescoes of the Byzantine monasteries of Mount Athos, which transform Socrates, Pythagoras and even Hypatia (despite the fact that she was lynched by the Christians of Alexandria) into prophets of Christianity, are manifestations of the same logic.

Finally, in its fight against heresy, Christian 'philosophy' used weapons developed in the controversies between the different philosophical schools. It turned its enemies into bad exegetes or, worse, rhetors.

When knowledge is nothing but textual exegesis, refutation always involves the demonstration that the text has been misinterpreted. Two examples recently analysed by P. Hoffmann[20] and G. Dorival[21] can be considered in parallel: the former analyses the commentary of Simplicius on Aristotle's categories and shows that one of the philosopher's main arguments against his adversary Philoponus was that he did not have the qualities of a good exegete. The latter examines Saint Basil's treatise *On the Holy Spirit* (written around 375) and established that Basil was able to condemn his adversary by showing up his incompetence as an exegete.

In the same way, it is easy to see the similarities between Gregory of Nyssa's attacks on Eunomius and the criticisms which Themistius addressed to the sophists. The former calls his adversary a castanet player, because he likes to put harmonious words together and uses a great many figures of style without concern for the meaning. The latter compared the rhetors to nightingales who know only how to warble. In both cases the same effort is made to reduce the other person's words to a simple noise, while the orator presents himself as a second Socrates who puts a concern with truth above the artifices of rhetoric.

There are also similarities in the *topoi*. For example, Plato had defined philosophy as practising for death, death being understood as the separation of the soul from the body. This theme of meditation was taken up time and again by Christianity. It could be considered in a way close to Stoicism, as in these words from a monk: 'since the beginning of our conversation we have come closer to death. Let us be vigilant while we still have the time.' But it was radically changed when it was combined with the explicitly Christian theme of partaking in Christ's death.[22]

Under such conditions it is understandable that the patristic literature of the fourth and fifth centuries has been judged in diametrically opposing ways: some (W. Jaeger)[23] have stressed the element of borrowing, while others (J. Daniélou)[24] have emphasised that of transformation. Pagan thought has been shown to be deformed and humiliated by Christian thinking and, at the same time and in total contrast, enslaved Greece has been revealed as succeeding once again in subjugating its conquerors. But by thinking in terms of a struggle, one fails to understand what happened. Patristics is the fruit of osmosis and its productions almost always refer back to two models. Borrowings from the Scriptures are the most obvious and the most loudly acknowledged. Borrowings from 'outside' authors are more discreet, but no less real; they can be seen as forming the conjunctive tissue of the texts. For patristic literature reflects a translation of Christian ideals into the Greek culture of the time. Such a translation is not always entirely faithful; yet the very fact that one can still ask what it was exactly that was betrayed proves the success of the undertaking. Should we speak of the Hellenisation of Christianity or the Christianisation of Hellenism? Should we consider Gregory of Nyssa – to take the most revealing example – as a Neoplatonist thinly disguised as a Christian or as a Christian who put Neoplatonism to work for the faith? The jury is still out.

In any case, it is in and thanks to this translation that Greek literature survived. If today we can still read Demosthenes and Plato it is perhaps because the Byzantines saw the Cappadocians as classics, because they ceaselessly copied the discourses of Gregory of Nazianzus (1,500 manuscripts) and commented on them (fourteen commentaries) and because they made him into a Christian Demosthenes and the equal of Plato.

NOTES

INTRODUCTION

1 We are aware that the choice of this date is open to debate. Some historians date the beginning of Byzantine history earlier, to the time when Rome was replaced by Constantinople as the capital of the Empire. Others maintain that the three centuries from Constantine to Justinian fall within the continuity of the Roman Empire and the real break occurs later, with the Islamic conquest in the seventh century.

2 R. Thomas, *Literacy and Orality in Ancient Greece* (Cambridge 1992) p. 3.

3 R. Pfeiffer, *History of Classical scholarship. From the Beginnings to the End of Hellenistic Age* (Oxford 1968) p. 102.

4 Irenaeus, *Against the Heretics* 3.21.2, quoted by Eusebius, *Ecclesiastical History* 5.8.11.

5 H.R. Jauss, *Towards an Aesthetic of Reception* (Brighton 1982).

6 *Palimpsestes. La littérature au second degré* (Paris 1982).

7 *The Rhetoric of Imitation* (Ithaca 1986).

8 'Longinus', *On the Sublime* 13.2 (trans. D.A. Russell, Oxford 1964).

9 Quintilian, *Education of an orator* X.1.54.

10 L.D. Reynolds and N.G. Wilson, *Scribes and Scholars. A Guide to the Transmission of Greek and Latin Literature*, second edn., (Oxford 1974), p. 8.

Part 1

1 HOMER AND THE EPIC AGE

1 *L'épithète traditionelle chez Homère* (Paris 1928). English translation in *The Making of Homeric Verse: The Collected Papers of Milman Parry* ed. A. Parry (Oxford 1971).

2 See W. Arend, *Die typischen Szenen bei Homer* (Berlin 1933).

3 M. Finley, *The World of Odysseus* (Harmondsworth 1979).

4 V. Bérard, *Les navigations d'Ulysse*, Paris 1927–1929.

5 J. de Romilly, *Homère* (Paris 1985). See also J. Chadwick, 'Homère: un menteur?' *Diogène* 1977: 10 ff.

6 See E. Auerbach, *Mimesis* English translation (Princeton 1953).

2 THE ARCHAIC PERIOD

1 See P. Veyne, *Roman Erotic Elegy* (Chicago 1988).
2 Translation by Frank J. Nisetich, *Pindar's Victory Songs* (Baltimore 1980).
3 Isocrates, XV, 268.
4 Cf. J. Burnet, *Early Greek Philosophy* (1908).
5 Cf. W. Jaeger, *Theology of early Greek Philosphers* (Oxford 1947).

Part 2

3 THEATRE

1 G. Murray, *Aeschylus, The Creator of Tragedy* (Oxford 1940).
2 B.M.W. Knox, *The Heroic Temper* (Berkeley 1964).
3 T. Zielinski, *Die Gliederung der Altattischen Komödie* (Leipzig 1985).
4 Cf. P. Mazon, *Essai sur la composition des comédies d'Aristophane* (Paris 1904).
5 Cf. V. Ehrenberg, *The People of Athens* (Oxford 1951).
6 Cf. J. Taillardat, *Les images d'Aristophane* (Paris 1965).

4 HISTORY

1 Cf. J. Pouilloux and F. Salviat, 'Lichas Lacedemonien, archonte à Thasos et le livre VIII de Thucydide', *CRAI*: 376–403 (1983).
2 On this type of constitutional history or *politeiai*, see J. Bordes, *Politeia dans la pensée grecque* . . . (Paris 1982).
3 Fragments of the lost historians have been edited in F. Jacoby, *Die Fragmente der Griechischen Historiker* (Berlin 1923–1958).

5 PHILOSOPHY

1 For a history of the attempts to do this, see E.N. Tigerstedt, *Interpreting Plato* (Upsala 1977).
2 See, in particular, K. Gaiser, *Protreptik und Paranese bei Platon* (Stuttgart 1959); T. Szlezk, *Reading Plato* (London 1999).
3 See the cameo of the bronze bust of Pseudo-Donatello analysed in A. Chastel, *Art et humanisme à Florence* (pp. 41–4).
4 On 'platonic transposition' see A. Diès, *Autour de Platon* (Paris 1927).
5 Cf. M.D. Richard, *L'Enseignement oral de Platon* (Paris 1986), from whom we have borrowed this expression.
6 See P. Hadot, 'Les divisions des parties de la philosophie dans l'antiquité', (Museum Helveticum 1979) p. 201.
7 For a philosophical commentary of this treatise, see V. Goldschmidt, *Temps physique et temps tragique chez Aristote* (Paris 1982), whose analyses we sum up here.

6 RHETORIC

1 Cf. N. Loraux, *The Invention of Athens* (Cambridge, MA 1986).
2 Cf. K. Dover, *Lysias and the Corpus Lysiacum* (Berkeley 1968).
3 Cf. M. Delaunois, *Le Plan rhetorique dans l'eloquence grecque d'Homère à Demosthène* (Brussels 1959).

Part 3

INTRODUCTION

1 Translated from H.I. Marrou, *Décadence Romaine ou Antiquité Tardive? IIIème-IVème siècles*, (Paris 1977) p. 44.
2 M. Foucault, *The Care of the Self. History of Sexuality* III (New York 1986).
3 *On the Fortune or the Virtues of Alexander* 329c.
4 G. Droysen, *Geschichte der Hellenismus* 1877.

7 POETRY

1 *Moralia* 347e.
2 See W. Kroll, Studien zum Verständnis der römischen Literatur (1924) p. 202–224.

9 FROM AUGUSTUS TO CONSTANTINE

1 J. de Romilly, *The Great Sophists in Periclean Athens*, trans. Janet Lloyd (Oxford 1992).
2 G. Bowerstock, *Greek Sophists in the Roman Empire* (Oxford 1969)
3 E.L. Bowie, 'The importance of Sophists', *Yale Classical Studies* 27 (1982): 29–59.
4 E.R. Dodds, *Pagans and Christians in an Age of Anxiety* (1979).
5 *Ancient Romances* (Berkeley 1967) p. 195.
6 K. Kerenyi, *Die Grieschiel-orientalische roman-literatur in religionsgeschichter beleuchtung* (Tübingen 1927).
7 R. Merkelback, *Roman und myslenium* (Munich 1962).
8 J. Pouilloux, *Pausanias, Description de l'Attique* (Paris 1983) p. 10.
9 See P. Hadot, *Exercises spirituels et philosophie antique* (Paris 1981: 119: 53), and *The inner citadel: the meditation of Marcus Aurelius* (Cambridge, MA 1998).
10 See M. Alexandre, 'Le travail de la sentence chez Marc Aurèle: philosophie et rhétorique', in *Formes brèves, La Licorne*, Vol. III (Poitiers 1979: 125–58).
11 P. Hadot's statement on all the cultures that came into contact with the Greek tradition from the fourth century BC onwards can be adapted to the work of Philo (cf. his inaugural lesson at the College de France, Paris 1983).
12 See 'La composition de la vie d'Aristote' (*REG*, 68, 1955).
13 See J. Pépin, 'Porphyre exégète d'Homère;, in *Porphyre*. Entretiens sur l'Antiquité Classique 12 (Geneva 1965).

14 See G. Fowden, 'The pagan holy man in large Antique society' (*JHS* 102, 1982), pp. 33–59.
15 H.I. Marrou's Introduction to Clement of Alexandria's pedagogue ('Sources chretiennes', 70, 1960) p. 68.

10 LATE ANTIQUITY

1 See P. Brown, *The Making of Late Antiquity* (Cambridge 1978)
2 See H.I. Marrou, *Decadence Romaine ou Antiquité Tardive?* (Paris 1977), p. 13.
3 See P. Brown, op. cit no. 1.
4 G. Dagron, 'Aux origines de la civilization byzantine: langue de culture et langue d'Etat' (*Revue historique*, 1969), pp 23–56.
5 See H.I. Marrou, *Decadence*, p. 163.
6 This is the title of the colloquium devoted to late Antiquity edited by K. Weitzmann (1980).
7 See P. de Labriolle, *La réaction paienne*, (Paris 1934).
8 See Momigliano.
9 See S. Mazzarino, *The End of the Ancient World* (1966).
10 See P. Brown, 'The rise and function of the holy man', reproduced in P. Brown, *Society and the Holy in Late Antiquity* (Berkeley 1982).
11 See L. Meridier, *Le philosophe Themistios devant l'opinion de ses contemporains* (Rennes 1906), pp. 12–14.
12 See I. Hadot, *Le problème du néo-platonisme alexandrin: Hieroclès et Simplicius* (Paris 1978).
13 See esp. his *Leçon inaugurale de la chaire d'histoire de la pensée hellénistique et romaine du Collège de France* (Paris 1983).
14 See e.g. P. Hoffmann, 'Categories et langage selon Simplicins', *Actes du Colloque international de Paris* (September to October 1985) devoted to Simplicius (Berlin 1987), pp. 61–90.
15 See Proclus, Theologie platonicienne, ed. H.D. Saffrey and I.G. Westerink (Paris 1968), p. ix.
16 See I. Sevcenko, 'A shadow outline of virtue; the classical heritage of Greek Christian Literature (second to seventh century) in age of spirituality: a symposium', ed. K Weitzmann (New York 1980), pp. 53–73.
17 The title of an illuminating paper from G. Dorival, published in *Congresso internacional* as 'Humanidades greco-latinas e civilizaçao do universal' (Coimbra 1988), pp. 383–420.
18 As did J. Fontaine in his 'que sais-je' on *La littérature latine chrétienne.*
19 See P. Hadot, 'Exercices spirituels antique et "philosophie chrétienne", in *Exercices spirituels et philosophie antique* (Paris 1981).
20 See P. Hoffmann, 'Sur quelques aspects de la polémique de Simplicius contra Jean Philopon', in *Actes du Colloque*, pp. 183–221.
21 See G. Dorival, *Congresso internacional.*
22 See P. Hadot, *Exercices spirituels*, p. 41.
23 See J. Daniélou, *Platonisme et theologie mystique* (Paris 1954) and *Le IVᵉ siecle* (Paris 1984).

BIBLIOGRAPHY

The following selection consists mostly of books written in or translated into English and does not include textual editions, commentaries and translations of the primary sources.

HISTORY OF LITERATURE

Ancient Writers: Greece and Rome, New York 1982
The Cambridge History of Classical Literature, I: Greek Literature edited by P.E. Easterling, B.M.W. Knox, Cambridge 1985
A. Dihle, *A History of Greek Literature from Homer to the Hellenistic Period*, London 1994
—— *Greek and Latin Literature of the Roman Empire*, London 1994
A. Lesky, *History of Greek Literature*, London 1966
S. Saïd, M. Trédé, A. Le Boulluec, *Histoire de la Littérature Grecque*, Paris 1997
Lo Spazio Lettterario della Grecia antica I-IV edited by G. Cambiano, L. Canfora, D. Lanza, Roma 1992–1995

WORKS OF REFERENCE

E. Benveniste, *Indo-European Language and Society*, New York 1973
The Cambridge History of Literary Criticism I: Classical Criticism edited by G. Kennedy, Cambridge 1989
F. Desbordes, *La Rhétorique Antique*, Paris 1996
E. R. Dodds, *The Greeks and the Irrational*, Berkeley 1966
C. Fornara, *The Nature of History in Ancient Greece and Rome*, Berkeley 1983
W.K.C. Guthrie, *A History of Greek Philosophy, I-IV*, Cambridge 1962–1981
W. Harris, *Ancient Literacy*, Cambridge, Mass. 1990
W. Jaeger, *Paideia: The Ideals of Greek Culture*, 3 vols. Oxford 1939–1945
H.I. Marrou, *A History of Education in Antiquity*, London 1990
A. Momigliano, *The Development of Greek Biography*, Cambridge, Mass. 1971

—— *The Classical Foundations of Modern Historiography*, Berkeley 1990
The Oxford Classical Dictionary edited by S. Hornblower, A. Sprawforth, Oxford 1996
Realencyclopädie der klassischen Altertumswissenschaft edited by Pauly, Wissowa *et al.*, Stuttgart 1893–1980
L.D. Reynolds, N. Wilson, *Scribes and Scholars: A Guide to the Transmission of Greek and Latin Literature*, Oxford 1974
D.A. Russell, *Criticism in Antiquity* 1981 (repr. Bristol 1995)
B. Snell, *The Discovery of the Mind*, Cambridge, Mass. 1953

PART 1: HOMER AND THE ARCHAIC PERIOD

General

H. Fränkel, *Early Greek Poetry and Philosophy*, London 1975

Homeric Poetry

M. Edwards, *Homer, Poet of the Iliad*, Baltimore 1987
M. I. Finley, *The World of Odysseus*, Harmondsworth 1978
J. Griffin, *Homer, "The Odyssey"*, Cambridge 1987
Homer: Tradition und Neuerung edited by J. Latacz, Darmstadt 1979
R. Janko, *Homer, Hesiod and the Hymns: Diachronic Developments in Epic Diction*, Cambridge 1982
G.S. Kirk, *The Songs of Homer*, Cambridge 1962
J. Latacz, *Homer, his Art and his World*, Princeton 1996
A. Lesky, *"Homeros" RE Suppl. Bd 11(687–846)*, 1968
The Making of Homeric Verse: the Collected Papers of Milman Parry edited by A. Parry, Oxford 1971
A New Companion to Homer edited by I. Morris & B. Powell, Leiden 1997
M. Silk, *Homer "The Iliad"*, Cambridge 1987

Hesiod

Hesiod edited by F. Heitsch, in "Wege der Forschung" 44, Darmstadt 1967
Hésiode et son Influence edited by O. Reverdin, in "Entretiens sur l'antiquité classique" 7, Geneva 1962
R. Lamberton, *Hesiod*, New Haven 1988
P. Pucci. *Hesiod and the Language of Poetry*, Baltimore 1977
F. Solmsen, *Hesiod and Aeschylus*, Ithaca 1949
J.P. Vernant, *Myth and Thought among the Greeks*, London 1980

Lyric Poetry

C.M. Bowra, *Greek Lyric Poetry*, Oxford 1961
D. Campbell, *The Golden Lyre: the Themes of Greek Lyric Poets*, London 1983
B. Gentili, *Poetry and Its Public in Ancient Greece*, Baltimore 1990

Iambic and Elegiac Poetry

Archiloque edited by J. Pouilloux, in "Entretiens sur l'antiquité classique" 10, Geneva 1964
C. Miralles, J. Portulas, *Archilochus and the Iambic Poetry*, Roma 1983
—— *The Poetry of Hipponax*, Roma 1988
Theognis of Megara: Poetry and the Polis edited by T.J. Figueira, G. Nagy, Baltimore 1985
M.L. West, *Studies in Greek Elegy and Iambus*, Berlin 1974.

Monody

A.P. Burnett, *Three Archaic Poets: Archilochus, Alcaeus and Sappho*, London 1983
G.M. Kirkwood, *Early Greek Monody*, Ithaca 1974
Reading Sappho: Contemporary Approaches edited by E. Greene, Berkeley 1996
U. von Wilamowitz-Moellendorf, *Sappho and Simonides*. Berlin 1913

Choral Lyric

C.M. Bowra, *Pindar*, Oxford 1964
E. Bundy, *Studia Pindarica*, Berkeley 1986
A.P. Burnett, *The Art of Bacchylides*, Cambridge, Mass. 1985
M. Lefkowitz, *The Victory Ode*, Park Ridge, NJ. 1976
G. Nagy, *Pindar's Homer: the Lyric Possession of the Epic Past*, Baltimore 1990
Pindare edited by A. Hurst, in "Entretiens sur l'antiquité classique" 31, Geneva 1985
Pindaros and Bacchylides edited by W.C. Calder, J. Stern "Wege der Forschung" 134, Darmstadt 1970

Presocratic Philosophy

J. Barnes, *The Presocratic Philosophers*, 2 vols, 2nd edn, London 1982
W. Jaeger, *The Theology of Early Greek Philosophers*, Oxford 1947
G.E.R. Lloyd, *Early Greek Science from Thales to Aristotle*, London 1970

PART 2: THE CLASSICAL AGE AND THE FLOWERING OF ATHENS

Introduction

The Sophists

G.B. Kerferd, *The Sophistic Movement*, Cambridge 1981
J. de Romilly, *The Great Sophists in Periclean Athens*, Oxford 1992

—— *Magic and Rhetoric in Ancient Greece*, Cambridge, Mass. 1970
Sophistik edited by C.J. Classen, in "Wege der Forschung"187, Darmstadt 1976
The Sophists and their Legacy edited by G. Kerferd, in "Hermes Einzelschriften" 44, 1981

Hippocratic Medicine

L. Edelstein, *Ancient Medicine: Selected Papers of L. Edelstein*, edited by O. & C.L. Temkin, Baltimore 1967
G.E.R. Lloyd, *Magic, Reason and Experience: Studies in the Origins and Development of Greek Science*, Cambridge 1979

Theatre

Generalia

E. Csapo, W.J. Slater, *The Context of Ancient Drama*, Ann Arbor 1995
J.R. Green, *Theatre in Ancient Greek Society*, London 1994

Tragedy

The Cambridge Companion to Greek Tragedy edited by P.E. Easterling, Cambridge 1997
S. Goldhill, *Reading Greek Tragedy*, Cambridge 1989
J. Herington, *Poetry into Drama: Early Tragedy and the Greek Poetic Tradition*, Berkeley 1985
J. Jones, *On Aristotle and Greek Tragedy*, London 1962
A. Lesky, *Greek Tragic Poetry*, London 1965
Oxford Readings in Greek Tragedy edited E. Segal, Oxford 1983
J. de Romilly, *L'évolution du Pathétique d'Eschyle à Euripide*, Paris 1961
S. Said, *La Faute Tragique*, Paris 1978
R. Seaford, *Ritual and Reciprocity: Homer and Tragedy in the Developing City-State*, Oxford 1994
O. Taplin, *Greek Tragedy in Action*, London 1978
J.P. Vernant, P. Vidal-Naquet, *Myth and Tragedy in Ancient Greece*, Cambridge 1988
G. Xanthakis-Karamanos, *Studies in Fourth-century Tragedy*, Athens 1980

Aeschylus

J. Herington, *Aeschylus*, Yale 1986
K. Reinhardt, *Aischylos als Regisseur und Theologe*, Bern 1949
O. Taplin, *The Stagecraft of Aeschylus*, Oxford 1977
R.P. Winnington-Ingram, *Studies in Aeschylus*, Cambridge 1983

Sophocles

B.M.W. Knox, *The Heroic Temper*, Berkeley 1964
K. Reinhardt, *Sophocles*, Oxford 1979
C. Segal, *Tragedy and Civilization: An Interpretation of Sophocles*, Cambridge, Mass. 1981
Sophocle edited by J. de Romilly, in "Entretiens sur l'antiquité classique" 29, Genève 1982
C. Whitman, *Sophocles: a Study in Heroic Humanism*, Cambridge, Mass. 1951
R.P. Winnington-Ingram, *Sophocles: an Interpretation*, Cambridge 1980

Euripides

D.J. Conacher, *Euripidean Drama: Myth, Theme and Structure*, Toronto 1967
Directions in Euripidean Criticism edited by P. Burian, Durham 1985
Euripide edited by J.C. Kamerbeek, in "Entretiens sur l'antiquité classique"6, Geneva 1958
Euripides: A Collection of Critical Essays edited by E. Segal, Englewood Cliffs 1968
K. Reinhardt, "Die Sinneskrise bei Euripides"1957 (reprinted in *Tradition und Geist*, Göttingen 1960)

Aristophanes

Aristophane edited by J.M. Bremer, E. Handley, in "Entretiens sur l'antiquité classique" 38, Geneva 1993
J.C. Carriere, *Le Carnaval et la Politique*, Paris 1979
K.J. Dover, *Aristophanic Comedy*, London 1972
Oxford Readings in Aristophanes edited by E. Segal, Oxford 1996
J. Taillardat, *Les Images d'Aristophane*, Paris 1965
C.H. Whitman, *Aristophanes and the Comic Hero*, Cambridge, Mass. 1964

History

General

K. Von Fritz, *Griechische Geschichtsschreibung*, Berlin 1977
A. Momigliano, *Studies in Historiography*, London 1966

Herodotus

C.W. Fornara, *Herodotus: An Interpretative Essay*, Oxford 1971
J. Gould, *Herodotus*, New York 1989
F. Hartog, *The Mirror of Herodotus*, Berkeley 1988

Herodot: eine Auswahl aus der Neueren Forschung edited by W. Marg, München 1962

Hérodote et les Peuples non Grecs edited by G. Nenci, Reverdin, in "Entretiens sur l'antiquité classique" 35, Geneva 1990

H. Immerwahr, *Form and Thought in Herodotus*, Cleveland 1966

J.L. Myres, *Herodotus: Father of History*, Oxford 1953

Thucydides

M. Cogan, *The Human Thing: the Speech and Principle of Thucydides' History*, Chicago 1981

W.R. Connor, *Thucydides*, Princeton 1984

J. Finley, *Thucydides*, Cambridge, Mass. 1942

S. Hornblower, *Thucydides*, London 1987

J. de Romilly, *Thucydides and the Athenian Inperialism*, Oxford 1963

—— *Histoire et Raison chez Thucydide*, Paris 1956

H.P. Stahl, *Thukydides: die Stellung des Menschen im Geschichtliches Prozess*, München 1966

Local Histories

F. Jacoby, *Atthis: The Local Chronicles of Athens*, Oxford 1949

Theopompus

W.R.Connor, *Theopompus and Fifth-Century Athens*, Washington D.C. 1968

Ephorus

G. Shepens, "Historiographical Problems in Ephorus" in *Historiographia antica*, Leuven 1977, 95 -118

Xenophon

J.K. Anderson, *Xenophon*, London 1977

H.R. Breitenbach, "Xenophon von Athen" *RE* IX (1569–2051) 1966

W.E. Higgins, *Xenophon the Athenian*, Albany 1977

S.W. Hirsch, *The Friendship of the Barbarians: Xenophon and the Persian Empire*, London 1985

D. Levine Gera, *Xenophon's Cyropedia: Style, Genre and Literary Technique*, Oxford 1993

Philosophy

Socrates

G. Vlastos, *Socrates: Ironist and Moral Philosopher*, Ithaca 1991

Plato

A. Dies, *Autour de Platon* 2 vols, Paris 1927
P. Friedländer, *Plato* 3 vols, Princeton 1958–1969
V. Goldschmidt, *Les Dialogues de Platon*, Paris 1971
—— *Platonisme et Pensée Contemporaine*, Paris 1970
R.H. Kraut (ed.), *The Cambridge Companion to Plato*, Cambridge 1992
R. Schaerer, *La Question Platonicienne*, Neuchâtel 1938
P. Shorey, *What Plato Said*, Chicago 1965

Aristotle

D.J. Allan, *The Philosophy of Aristotle*, London 1970
Articles on Aristotle edited by J. Barnes, M. Schofield & R. Sorabji, 4 vols, London 1975–1979
J. Barnes, *Aristotle*, Oxford 1982
The Cambridge Companion to Aristotle edited by J. Barnes, Cambridge 1996
H. Cherniss, *Aristotle's Criticism of Presocratic Philosophy*, Baltimore 1944
Essays on Aristotle's Ethics edited by A. Rorty, Berkeley 1980
Essays on Aristotle's Rhetoric edited by A. Rorty, Berkeley 1996
V. Goldschmidt, *Temps Tragique et Temps Physique chez Aristote*, Paris 1982
W. Jaeger, *Aristotle*, Oxford 1934
P. Moraux, *Aristote et les Problèmes de Méthode*, Louvain 1961
R. Weil, *Aristote et l'Histoire: Essai sur la Politique*, Paris 1960

Rhetoric

General

F. Blass, *Die Attische Beredsamkeit*, 4 vols, Leipzig 1887–1898 (reprinted Hildesheim 1979)
M. H. Hansen, *The Athenian Democracy in the Age of Demosthenes*, Oxford 1991
A.R.W. Harrison, *The Law of Athens*, 2 vols, Oxford 1971
R.C. Jebb, *The Attic Orators*, 2 vols, London 1893
G. Kennedy, *The Art of Persuasion in Greece*, Princeton 1963
H. Lausberg, *Handbuch der Literarischen Rhetorik: Eine Grundlegung der Literaturwissenschaft,* 2 vols, 3rd edn, Stuttgart 1990
O. Navarre, *La Rhétorique Grecque avant Aristote*, Paris 1900

Antiphon

B. Due, *Antiphon: A Study in Argumentation*, Copenhagen 1980
F. Solmsen, *Antiphons Studien: Untersuchung zur Entstehung der attischen Gerichtsrede*, Berlin 1931

Lysias

K.J. Dover, *Lysias and the Corpus Lysiacum*, Berkeley 1968

Isocrates

C. Eucken, *Isocrates*, Berlin 1983
Isokrates edited by F. Seck, in "Wege der Forschung" 351, Darmstadt 1978
Y.L. Too, *The Rhetoric of Identity in Isocrates: Text, Power, Pedagogy*, Cambridge 1995

Demosthenes

W. Jaeger, *Demosthenes: the Origin and Growth of his Policy*, Berkeley 1938
H. Montgomery, *The Way to Chaeroneia: Foreign Policy, Decision Making and Political Influence in Demosthenes' Speeches*, Oslo 1983
L. Pearson, *The Art of Demosthenes*, Meisenheim am Glan 1976

Aeschines

E.M. Harris, *Aeschines and Athenian Politics*, Oxford 1995
J.F. Kindstrand, *The Stylistic Evaluation of Aeschines*, Upsala 1982

PART 3: THE HELLENISTIC PERIOD

General

P. M. Fraser, *Hellenistic Alexandria*, 3 vols, Oxford 1972
R. Pfeiffer, *History of Classical Scholarship from the Beginning to the End of the Hellenistic Age*, Oxford 1968
F. Süsemihl, *Geschichte der Griechischen Literatur in der Alexandrinerzeit* 2 vols, Leipzig 1891–2 (reprinted Hildesheim 1965)

Menander and New Comedy

R. Hunter, *The New Comedy of Greece and Rome*, Cambridge 1985
D. Konstan, *Greek Comedy and Ideology*, Oxford 1995
Ménandre edited by E.G. Turner, in "Entretiens sur l'antiquité classique" 16, Geneva 1970

T.B.L. Webster, *An Introduction to Menander*, Manchester 1974

N. Zagagi, *The Comedy of Menander: Convention, Variation and Originality*, London 1994

Hellenistic Poetry

General

P. Bing, *The Well-Read Muse: Present and Past in Callimachus and the Hellenistic Poets*, in "Hypomnemata" 90, Göttingen 1990

G.O. Hutchinson, *Hellenistic Poetry*, Oxford 1988

U. von Wilamowitz-Moellendorf, *Die Hellenistische Dichtung in der Zeit des Kallimachos*, 2 vols, Berlin 1924

Callimachus

Callimachus edited by M.A. Harder, R.F. Regtuit, G.C. Wakker, in "Hellenistica Groningana" 1, Groningen 1993

A. Cameron, *Callimachus and his Critics*, Princeton 1995

Theocritus

R. Hunter, *Theocritus and the Archeology of Greek Poetry*, Cambridge 1996

T.G. Rosenmeyer, *The Green Cabinet: Theocritus and the European Pastoral*, Berkeley 1969

C. Segal, *Poetry and Myth in Ancient Pastoral*, Princeton 1981

Theocritus edited by M.A. Harder, R.F. Regtuit, G.C. Wakker, in "Hellenistica Groningana" 2, Groningen 1994

Apollonius Rhodius

C.R. Beye, *Epic and Romance in the Argonautica of Apollonius*, Carbondale-Edwardsville, Ill. 1982

M. Fusillo, *Il Tempo delle Argonautiche: Un' Analisi Del Racconto in Apollonio Rodio*, Rome 1985

R. Hunter, *The Argonautica of Apollonius: Literary Studies*, Cambridge 1993

A. Hurst, *Apollonios de Rhodes: Manière et Cohérence*, Rome 1967

Aratos

R. Hunter, *Written in the Stars: Poetry and Philosophy in the Phainomena of Aratos* in "Arachnion" 2, September 1995

J. Martin, *Histoire du Texte des Phénomènes d'Aratos*, Paris 1956

Nicander

H. White, *Studies in the Poetry of Nicander*, Amsterdam 1987

Herondas

G. Mastromarco, *The Public of Herondas*, Amsterdam 1984

Epigram

A.Cameron, *The Greek Anthology from Meleager to Planudes*, Oxford 1993
L'Epigramme grecque edited by A.E. Raubitschek in "Entretiens sur l'antiquité classique" 14, Geneva 1967
S.Taran, *The Art of Variation in Hellenistic Epigram*, Leiden 1979

Philosophy

General

Aspects de la philosophie hellénistique edited by H. Flashar, O. Gigon, in "Entretiens sur l'antiquité classique" 22, Geneva 1986
A.A. Long, *Hellenistic Philosophy: Stoics, Epicureans, Sceptics* 2 edn, London 1986

Academy

J. Dillon, *The Middle Platonists*, London 1977
J. Glucker, *Antiochus and the Late Academy*, Göttingen 1978

Lyceum

J.P.Lynch, *Aristotle's School*, Berkeley 1972
J. Moreau, *Aristote et son École*, Paris 1962

Cynics

The Cynics: The Cynic Movement in Antiquity and its Legacy edited by R. Bracht Branham, M.O. Goulet-Cazé, Berkeley 1996
D.R. Dudley, *A History of Cynicism*, London 1937

Sceptics

R.J. Hankison, *The Sceptics*, London 1995
Lo Setticismo antico edited by G Giannantoni 2 vols, Napoli 1981

Epicurus

C. Bailey, *The Greek Atomists and Epicurus*, New York 1928
J.M. Rist, *Epicurus: an Introduction*, Cambridge 1972
Suzhthsis, *Studi sull' Epicureismo Greco e Latino Offerti a M. Gigante*, 2 vols, Naples 1983

Stoics

V. Goldschmidt, *Le Système Stoïcien et l'Idée de Temps*, 4 edn, Paris 1979
The Stoics edited by J.M. Rist, Berkeley 1978
A.A. Long, *Stoic Studies*, Cambridge 1996
F.H. Sandbach, *The Stoics*, London 1975

Historians and Geographers

General

C. Jacob, *Géographie et Ethnographie en Grèce Ancienne*, Paris 1991
P. Pedech, *La Géographie des Grecs*, Paris 1976
Purposes of History: Studies in Greek Historiography from the 4th to the 2nd Century B.C edited by H. Verdin, G. Shepens & E. de Keyser, Leuven 1990

Strabo

G. Aujac, *Strabon et la Science de son Temps*, Paris 1966
C. Nicolet, *Space, Geography and Politics in the Early Roman Empire*, Ann Arbor 1991
Strabone: Contributi allo Studio della Personalita e dell'Opera edited by F. Prontera, 3 vols, Perugia 1984–1989

Minor Historians

L. Pearson, *The Lost Histories of Alexander the Great*, Cleveland 1960
—— *The Greek Historians of the West: Timaeus and his Predecessors*, Chico 1988
P. Pedech, *Trois Historiens Méconnus: Théopompe, Duris, Phylarque*, Paris 1989

Polybius

Polybe edited by E. Gabba, in "Entretiens sur l'Antiquité Classique" 20, Geneva 1974
K. Sacks, *Polybius on the Writing of History*, Berkeley 1981
F.W. Walbank, *Polybius*, Berkeley 1972

Diodorus of Sicily

K. Sacks, *Diodorus Siculus and the First Century*, Princeton 1990

PART 4: THE ROMAN EMPIRE

General

Aufstieg und Niedergang der Römischen Welt: Geschichte und Kultur Roms in Spiegel der Neueren Forschung edited by H. Temporini, W. Haase, Berlin 1972
Antonine Literature edited by D.A. Russell, Oxford 1990
E.L. Bowie, "The Greeks and their Past in the Second Sophistic" in *Studies in Ancient Society* edited by M. Finley, London 1974
A. Dihle, *Greek and Latin Literature of the Roman Empire*, London 1994
E.R. Dodds, *Pagan and Christians in an Age of Anxiety from Marcus Aurelius to Constantine*, Cambridge 1965
Later Greek Literature edited by J.J.Winkler, G. Williams, *Yale Classical Studies* 27, 1982
B.P. Reardon, *Courants littéraires Grecs des IIe et IIIe siècles après J.C.*, Paris 1971
The Greek Renaissance in the Roman Empire edited by S. Walker, A. Cameron, in "Bulletin of the Institute of Classical Studies Supplement" 55, 1989
S. Swain, *Hellenism and Empire: Language, Classicism and Power in the Greek World AD 50–250*, Oxford 1996

Poetry

E.L. Bowie, "Greek Poetry in the Antonine Age" in *Antonine Literature*, pp. 53–90

Classicism

S.F. Bonner, *The Literary Treatises of Dionysus of Halicarnassus*, Cambridge 1939
Le Classicisme à Rome aux Iers siècles avant et après J.C edited by H. Flashar, in "Entretiens sur l'Antiquité classique" 25 Geneva 1979
M. Patillon, *La Théorie du Discours chez Hermogène le Rhéteur. Essai sur les Structures Linguistiques de la Rhétorique Ancienne*, Paris 1988
D.A. Russell, *"Longinus", On the Sublime*, Oxford 1964
W. Schmid, *Der Atticismus in seinen Hauptvertretern von Dionysios von Halicarnassus bis auf dern zweiten Philostratus* 5 vols, 1887–1897 (reprinted Hildesheim 1964)
D.M. Schenkeveld, *Studies in Demetrius on Style*, Amsterdam 1964

Plutarch

Essays on Plutarch's Lives edited by B. Scardigli, Oxford 1995
D. Babut, *Plutarque et le Stoïcisme*, Paris 1969

C.P. Jones, *Plutarch and Rome*, Oxford 1971
D.A. Russell, *Plutarch*, London 1973
A.E. Wardman, *Plutarch's Lives*, London 1974
K. Ziegler, *Plutarchos von Chaironea*, Stuttgart 1964

Lucian

J. Bompaire, *Lucien Écrivain*, Paris 1958
R.B. Branham, *Unruly Eloquence: Lucian and the Comedy of Traditions*, Cambridge, Mass. 1989
C.P. Jones, *Culture and Society in Lucian*, Cambridge, Mass. 1986

Rhetoric

G. Anderson, *The Second Sophistic: A Cultural Phenomenon in the Roman Empire*, London 1993
Approaches to the Second Sophistic edited by G. Bowersock, Penn 1974
G. Bowersock, *Greek Sophists in the Roman Empire*, Oxford 1969
G. Kennedy, *The Art of Rhetoric in the Roman World*, Princeton 1972
L. Pernot, *La Rhétorique de l'Éloge dans le Monde Gréco-Romain*, 2 vols, Paris 1993
D.A. Russell, *Greek Declamations*, Cambridge 1983

Aristides

A. Boulanger, *Aelius Aristide et la Sophistique dans la Province de l'Asie au IIe siècle de notre ère*, Befar 126, Paris 1923

Dio Chrysostom

C.P. Jones, *The Roman World of Dio Chrysostom*, Cambridge, Mass. 1978

Philostratus

G. Anderson, *Philostratus: Biography and Belles Lettres in the Third Century AD*, London 1986

Novel

Greek Fiction: The Greek Novel in Context edited by J.R. Morgan, R. Stoneman, London 1994
T. Hägg, *The Novel in Antiquity*, Oxford 1983
N. Holzberg, *The Ancient Novel: an Introduction*, London 1995
The Novel in the Ancient World edited by G. Schmeling, Leiden 1996
B.E. Perry, *The Ancient Romances: a Literary-Historical Account of Their Origins*, Berkeley 1967

BIBLIOGRAPHY

B.P. Reardon, *The Form of Greek Romance*, Princeton 1991
E. Rohde, *Der Griechische Roman und seine Vorlaufer*, Leipzig 1914 (reprinted Hildesheim 1960)
The Search for the Ancient Novel edited by J. Tatum, Baltimore 1994

Chariton

G.L. Schmeling, *Chariton*, New York 1974

Xenophon of Ephesus

J.N. O' Sullivan, *Xenophon of Ephesus: his Compositional Technique and the Birth of the Novel*, Berlin 1995

Longus

R.L. Hunter, *A Study of Daphnis and Chloe*, Cambridge 1983

Heliodorus

G.N. Sandy, *Heliodorus*, Boston 1982

History

Pausanias

C. Habicht, *Pausanias' Guide to Ancient Greece*, Berkeley 1985
Pausanias Historien edited by J. Bingen, in "Entretiens sur l'antiquité classique" 41, Geneva 1996

Dionysus of Halicarnassus

E. Gabba, *Dionysius and the "history of Archaic Rome"*, Berkeley 1991

Josephus

L.H. Feldman, "Flavius Josephus Revisited: the Man, his Writings and his Influence" ANRW II 21.2, 1984
T. Rajak, *Josephus: the Historian and his Society*, London 1983

Appian

E. Gabba, *Appiano e la Storia delle Guerre Civili*, Firenze 1956

Cassius Dio

F. Millar, *A Study of Cassius Dio*, Oxford 1964

BIBLIOGRAPHY

Herodian

G. Alföldy, "Herodians Person", in *Ancient Society* 2, 1971

Arrian

P.A. Stadter, *Arrian of Nicomedia*, Chapel Hill 1980

Philosophy and encyclopedias

Epictetus

P.A. Brunt, "From Epictetus to Arrian", in *Athenaeum* 65, 1977

Marcus Aurelius

P. Hadot, *The Inner Citadel: the Meditations of Marcus Aurelius*, Cambridge, Mass. 1998
R.B. Rutherford, *The Meditations of Marcus Aurelius: A Study*, Oxford 1989

Philo

E. Brehier, *Les Idées Philosophiques et Religieuses de Philon d'Alexandrie*, Paris 1950
E.R. Goodenough, *An Introduction to Philo Judaeus*, Oxford 1962
F. Sandmel, *An Introduction to Philo Judaeus*, Oxford 1979

Plotinus

The Cambridge Companion to Plotinus edited by L.P. Gerson, Cambridge 1996
P. Hadot, *Plotinus or the Simplicity of Vision*, Chicago 1998

Diogenes Laertius

J. Meier, *Diogenes Laertius and his Hellenistic Background*, Wiesbaden 1978

Galen

Galen Problems and Prospects edited by V. Nutton, London 1981

Artemidorus

M. Foucault, *The History of Sexuality*, vol. III, New York 1988
G. W. Bowersock, *Fiction as History: Nero to Julian*, ch. IV, Berkeley 1994

Porphyry

Porphyre edited by H. Dörrie, in "Entretiens sur l'antiquité classique" 12, Geneva 1965

Iamblichus

De Jamblique à Proclos edited by H. Dörrie, in "Entretiens sur l'antiquité classique" 21, Geneva 1975
The Divine Jamblichus Philosospher and Man of Gods edited by H.J. Blumenthal, E.G. Clark, Bristol 1993

Classical Culture and Christian Literature

General

B. Altaner, A. Stuiber, *Patrologie: Leben, Schriften und Lehre der Kirchenväter*, 8th edn, Freiburg-Basel-Vienna 1978
H. Chadwick, *Early Christian Thought and the Classical Tradition*, Oxford 1966
A. Harnack, *Geschichte der Altchristlichen Literatur bis Eusebius*, 2 vols, Leipzig 1893–1896 (reprinted 1958)
J. Quasten, *Patrology*, Belmont, Mass. 1986

Apologists

L.W. Barnard, *Justin Martyr: His Life and Thought*, London 1967
R. Joly, *Christianisme et Philosophie: Etudes sur Justin et les Apologistes Grecs du Ie siècle,* Brussels 1973

Clemens of Alexandria

S.R.C. Lilla, *Clemens of Alexandria: A Study in Christian Platonism and Gnosticism*, Oxford 1971
E.F. Osborn, *The Philosophy of Clement of Alexandria*, Cambridge 1957

Origen

H. Crouzel, *Origen*, San Francisco 1989
Origenes edited by U. Berner, Darmstadt 1981

Late Antiquity

General

G.W. Bowersock, *Hellenism in Late Antiquity*, Ann Arbor 1971
P. Brown, *The Making of Late Antiquity*, Cambridge, Mass. 1978
Christianisme et Formes Littéraires de l'Antiquité Tardive edited by M. Fuhrmann, in "Entretiens sur l'antiquité classique" 23, Geneva 1977
P. Chuvin, *A Chronicle of the Last Pagans*, Cambridge, Mass. 1990
The Conflict between Paganism and Christianity in the Fourth Century edited by A. Momigliano, Oxford 1963

A. Festugiere, *Antioche Paienne et Chrétienne: Libanius, Chrysostome et les Moines de Syrie*, Paris 1959
R.A. Kaster, *Guardians of Language: The Grammarian and Society in Late Antiquity*, Berkeley 1988
J.H.W.G. Liebeschuetz, *Antioch: City and Imperial Administration in the Later Roman Empire*, Oxford 1972
A.D. Nock, *Conversion*, Oxford 1933

Poetry

General

Alan Cameron, "Wandering Poets: A Literary Movement in Byzantine Egypt" in *Historia* 14, 1965
N. Hopkinson, *An Imperial Anthology*, Cambridge 1994

Orphica

M.L. West, *The Orphic Poems*, Oxford 1983

Hero and Leander

G. Shott, *Hero and Leander bei Musaios and Ovid*, Diss. Köln 1957

Quintus of Smyrna

F. Vian, *Recherches sur les Posthomerica de Quintus de Smyrne*, Paris 1959

Nonnus of Panopolis

P. Chuvin, *Mythologie et Geographie Dionysiaques*, Clermont Ferrand 1991
Studies in the Dionysiaca of Nonnus edited by N. Hopkinson, "Proceedings of the Cambridge Philological Society Supplement," 17, 1994

History and biography

T.D. Barnes, *Constantine and Eusebius*, Cambridge, Mass. 1981
P. Cox, *Biography in Late Antiquity: A Quest for the Holy Man*, Berkeley 1983
A. Momigliano, "Pagan and Christian Historiography in the Fourth Century AD", in *The Conflict between Paganism and Christianity in the Fourth Century*
F. Paschoud, *Cinq Études sur Zosime*, Paris 1976
R.J. Penella, *Greek Philosophers and Sophists in the Fourth Century AD: Studies in Eunapius of Sardis*, Leeds 1990
J. Sirinelli, *Les Vues historiques d'Eusèbe de Césarée durant la Période Prénicéenne*, Paris 1961

Rhetoric

General

P. Brown, *Persuasion and Power in Late Antiquity*, Madison 1992

G. Kennedy, *Greek Rhetoric under Christian Emperors*, Princeton 1983

Julian

P. Athanassiadi-Fowden, *Julian and Hellenism: An Intellectual Biography*, Oxford 1981

G.W. Bowersock, *Julian the Apostate*, Cambridge, Mass. 1978

Libanius

Libanios edited by G. Fatouros, T. Krischer, "Wege der Forschung", Darmstadt 1983

J.H.W.G. Liebschuetz, *Antioch: City and Imperial Administration in the Later Roman Empire*, Oxford 1972

Themistius

G. Dagron, *L'empire Romain d'Orient au IVe siècle et les Traditions Politiques de l'Hellénisme: le Témoignage de Themistius*, Paris 1968

Himerius

T.D. Barnes, "Himerius and the Fourth Century", *Classical Philology* 82, 1987

Synesius

J. Bregman, *Synesius of Cyrene, Philosopher-Bishop*, Berkeley 1982

A.Cameron, J. Long, *Barbarians and Politics at the Court of Arcadius*, Berkeley 1992

Neo-Platonism

J. Coulter, *The Literary Microcosm: Theories of Interpretation of the Later Neoplatonism*, Leiden 1976

Die Philosophie des Neuplatonismus edited by C. Zintzen, "Wege der Forschung" 436, Darmstadt 1977

Proclus, Lecteur et Interprète des Anciens edited by J. Pépin, H.D. Saffrey, Paris 1987

Le Néoplatonisme: Actes du Colloque de Royaumont 9–13 Juin 1969

Simplicius, sa Vie, son Oeuvre edited by I. Hadot, Berlin 1987

The Conversion of Hellenism

A. Cameron, *Christianity and the Rhetoric of Empire: the Development of Christian Discourse*, Berkeley 1991

G. Dorival, "L'originalité de la Patristique Grecque" in *Congresso Internacional as Humanidades Greco-latinas ea Civilizaç o do Universal*, Coimbra 1988

W. Jaeger, *Early Christianity and Greek Paideia*, Cambridge, Mass. 1961

I. Sevcenko, "A Shadow Outline of Virtue: The Classical Heritage of Greek Christian Literature (Second to Seventh Century) "in *Age of Spirituality: a Symposium* edited by K. Weitzmann, New York 1980

INDEX OF PROPER NAMES

Main references are distinguished by figures in bold types.